On Common Ground

Crossing a bare common, in snow puddles, at twilight, under a clouded sky, without having in my thoughts any occurrence of special good fortune, I have enjoyed a perfect exhilaration.

—Ralph Waldo Emerson

On
Common Ground

Caring for Shared Land
from Town Common
to Urban Park

*Ronald Lee Fleming
and Lauri A. Halderman*

*with edited contributions by
John R. Stilgoe, Ph.D.
and Thomas M. Paine, A.S.L.A.*

Preface by John Updike

THE HARVARD COMMON PRESS

HARVARD, MASSACHUSETTS

THE TOWNSCAPE INSTITUTE

CAMBRIDGE, MASSACHUSETTS

Photographs on the front cover (top row to bottom, left to right; credit follows in parentheses):

Middlebury, Vermont (Elizabeth Tegen)
Cambridge, Massachusetts (P. McClennan)
Lexington, Massachusetts (Renata von Tscharner)
Cambridge, Massachusetts (Ronald Lee Fleming)
New Haven, Connecticut (David A. Riemer)
Columbia, Maryland (Howard Research & Development Corp.)
Greenfield, New Hampshire (Renata von Tscharner)
Craftsbury Common, Vermont (Anne D. Prescott)
Salem, Massachusetts (Lauri A. Halderman)
Cohasset, Massachusetts (David A. Riemer)
New Haven, Connecticut (David A. Riemer)
Greenacre Park, New York City (Sasaki Associates)

"Common Land," by John Updike, is reprinted from
New England: The Four Seasons, by Arthur Griffin, by
permission of Houghton Mifflin Company.

Co-published by The Townscape Institute, Inc. with
The Harvard Common Press
The Common, Harvard, Massachusetts 01451

Printed in the United States of America

Library of Congress Cataloging in Publication Data

Fleming, Ronald Lee.
    On common ground.

    Bibliography: p.
    Includes index.
    Contents: Introduction / by Lauri A. Halderman—
The evolution of New England village greens and town
commons / by John R. Stilgoe—Guidelines for greens /
by Thomas M. Paine—[etc.]
    1. Commons—United States—Addresses, essays, lec-
tures. I. Halderman, Lauri A. II. Title.
HD1289.U6L57   333.78'3'0973   81-20215
ISBN 0-916782-24-7   AACR2
ISBN 0-916782-25-5 (pbk.)

Cover design by Peter Good
Special thanks to William I. Koch, Dover, Massachusetts

10 9 8 7 6 5 4 3 2 1

*In Memoriam
Ree Overton Fleming
1908–1982*

Contents

Common Land

by John Updike

We seek, Americans, to inhale freedom, and the air is here, in these communities of houses built one by one, along roads whose curves were derived from the lay of the land. Predating the merciless grid that seized Manhattan and possessed the vast Midwest, New England towns have each at their center an irregular heart of open grass, vestige of the Puritan common, holding, perhaps, a village pump, a weathered monument, a surviving elm. In Rowley, a vacant triangle beside Route 1A that as December narrows becomes suddenly alive with whirling dervishes of Christmas lights. Ipswich has two hearts—the teardrop-shaped Meetinghouse Green at the old center, now overburdened by its sprawling modern meetinghouse, and the elongate, gracious South Green, since the 1830s made Arcadian by the backdrop of a Doric-columned church that in one cold recent night burned to its granite foundation. Away from the sea, the old greens merge with the wider lawns and what fields remain of New England's agriculture. The white house here was once a farmhouse. Once there would have been determined paths beaten to the pump through the cold blue purity of snow.

In New Hampshire, the sheds of the houses reach backward to the barns, to afford the busy occupants roofed passage, and one feels the intensity of winter in such actively sheltering shapes. Here, in regions becoming suburban to Boston, the land is allowed to sleep, and the clapboard saltboxes remember summer as they accept the weak sun on their sides. Wires trace a secret traffic in heat and light, and no doubt feed that cool new hearthfire, the television set. The houses seem to enjoy no very intrinsic relation to the greens in their midst; they send out only an occasional band of children to inherit with casual play the spaces originally set aside for pasturage and militia drills. But the idea, of land held in common, as—more than park or playground—part of a manifest, workaday covenant with the Bestower of a new continent, has permanently imprinted the maps of these towns, and lengthens the perspectives of those who live within them.

Acknowledgments

Although greens are a highly visible feature of the New England landscape, and, we argue herein, memorable in the landscape of the mind, their existence has not been comprehensively documented. Consequently, we have depended less upon the written word than on the testimonies of people with good memories and a willingness to talk, people who have told us the stories of greens both past and present that we never would have discovered otherwise. As the focus of the book expanded to include new common spaces from New York City to California, so did the scope of our research. We are grateful to a legion of people, many of whom we have never been able to thank face to face. Some answered our questions; some tracked down photographs, reviewed our vignettes and case studies, and sent us information above and beyond the call of duty. The roll of contributors is so extensive that we have been able only to list them here. We hope they realize how great their contribution was and accept our thanks.

We do want to pay additional tribute to those who have given us special counsel or support. First, we are grateful to Renata von Tscharner-Fleming, my wife, whose keen eye was valuable on many a green safari. Her photographs invariably turned out better than my own, her observations drawing upon her European architectural training were always helpful, and her nurturing spirit was essential in helping us to prevail over the usual adversities of book production. Grant R. Jones, F.A.I.A., has been a strong comrade whose visual perceptions and poetic imagination have influenced my thinking; and my experience working with him on the planning and research panel of the 1981 American Society of Landscape Architects annual awards helped to define some standards of landscape evaluation that influenced the guidelines chapter of this book. We are grateful additionally to the members of the board of directors of the Townscape Institute, who have shown an enduring interest in our work. They include Philip H. Behr, Philadelphia; Edmond Kellogg of South Royalton, Vermont, who with his wife Celina graciously hosted us on common expeditions; and Roger Webb, Boston. Our board of advisors has also been a source of support; it includes Lester Glenn Fant III, Esq., Washington, D.C.; Professor Edvard Sekler, Harvard University, Cambridge, Massachusetts; and Dr. Charles G.K. Warner, also of Cambridge, whose insights, both cultural and social, have been of particular value in charting the course of the Townscape Institute.

This book and the related activities of the Townscape Institute, a nonprofit public interest organization, have depended upon the financial assistance of individuals and foundations. David Bird of Cambridge has been particularly generous in this regard. He was among the first to step forward with financial assistance through the Charles Sumner Bird Foundation, has watched the process with an erudite eye, and together with Joseph C. K. Breiteneicher provided additional funding through the Bird Companies Charitable foundation. Samuel S. Rogers, a trustee of the Abbot and Dorothy H. Stevens Foundation, was also instrumental in securing a grant for this project, and the Carolyn Foundation of St. Paul, Minnesota supplied funding for which we are grateful. William Koch, Dover, Massachusetts; Henry J. Heinz II; Ann Roberts, New York; and Robert Sincerbaux, Woodstock, Vermont were helpful either in securing funds from the foundations with which they are affiliated or in providing direct support which strengthened our general capacity to operate The Townscape Institute. Their confidence in us over the years has been reassuring. It has been matched by the endurance and general support of my own parents, Elizabeth Ebner Fleming and the late Ree Overton Fleming, who witnessed a decade of tightly budgeted public interest projects without faltering, and whose core support, both emotional and financial, has been a significant factor in our capacity to prevail. I am grateful, in addition, to my friend the young architectural scholar J.A. Chewning, who has helped us with literary references and comments on the manuscript.

In securing some of the foundation backing for this publication, it was important to have early letters of endorsement and support from people and organizations concerned with the issues that we address in *On Common Ground*. Consequently, we wish to pay tribute here at the beginning to those who, without seeing the evidence of a manuscript, endorsed both the concept and our capacity to achieve it. Some are old friends; others have been allies on problems of environmental concern such as billboard control, downtown revitalization, historic preservation, park conservation, and tree planting. We are grateful that they took the time to fashion thoughtful and often eloquent letters, which aided and abetted the search for funds. They included Nancy W. Anderson, president of the Massachusetts Association of Conservation Commissions; Thomas B. Bracken, chairman of the Cambridge Conservation Commission; Anne Farnam, curator at Essex Institute; Barbara Fegan, president of the League of Women Voters of Massachusetts; Nan Heminway, president of the Litchfield Garden Club; Richard S. Jackson, Jr., of the Pittsfield Historical Commission; Thomas W. Leavitt, chairman of the Historical Commission in North Andover; Henry Lee, president of the Friends of the Public Garden; Gregor I. McGregor, chairman of the Massachusetts Conservation Council; William K. Reilly, president of the Conservation Foundation; and Kennedy Shaw, executive director of the Massachusetts Municipal Association.

Other members of the Townscape staff and interns have been helpful during the long course of this project. Ronald T. Reed executed the precise bird's-eye drawings for the case studies and the illustrations of furnishings for the guidelines. Abby Goodman, Jane C. Levin, and Barbara Barros assisted with research, and Randal A. Baron and Rebecca B. Hayden helped compile the inventory of New England greens. Anne D. Prescott contributed picture research and photography, as did David A. Riemer, who also initiated field research of the vignettes. Elizabeth Tegen investigated some greens and commons outside of New England.

We are of course grateful to the chapter contributors whose names appear with their respective pieces. Dr. John R. Stilgoe enlightened us with the evolution of common land; Thomas M. Paine, A.S.L.A., lent his landscape expertise to the guidelines. Robert M. Hodgman is to be credited with considerable research and writing for the chapter on modern-day common spaces.

Dr. Melanie Simo of Harvard University and Duncan Mackay of the Commons, Open Spaces, and Footpaths Preservation Society of England provided us with some perspectives on commons in that country. The late Sidney Shurcliffe of Boston was kind enough to review an early draft of the guidelines, and he made a number of helpful suggestions. Frank H. Spink, Jr. director of publications at the Urban Land Institute in Washington D.C., reviewed our proposals and suggested that we expand the focus to embrace new development; we are grateful for his insight, which gave *On Common Ground* a broader scope and, we believe, made it relevant to neighborhoods, corporations, and developers across the country.

We would like to thank Kathleen Cushman, Bruce Shaw, and the staff of the Harvard Common Press for their interest and work in making *On Common Ground* a reality.

Finally, I wish to acknowledge the special dedication of my colleague and co-author, Lauri Halderman, who has worked doggedly on the manuscript over the past year and a half. She shares my vision of the need for communal efforts manifested upon the face of the land, which remind us of our better selves and of our very necessary link to community and humanity. For both us us, the words of Thomas Boylston Adams's delightful book of essays, *A New Nation*, ring true:

> Every man carries in his heart the image of a city. . . . Each citizen, however vast his imagination or how petty, however generous his understanding or how mean, fixes his personality on the place of his being.

Greens and commons help to fix our communal personality on the land. We hope this book sustains that feeling in certain New England towns and helps it to occur more often everywhere in America.

RONALD LEE FLEMING
Cambridge, Massachusetts
January 1982

An archetypal common in Woodstock, Vermont.

Foreword:
Looking at Common Ground

by Ronald Lee Fleming

Away from these United States and contemplating a different land-scape, the inundated plains of Southeast Asia, I had ample occasion to bring to mind the imagery of my homeland. When I thought of what I valued as defensible, it was not the image of purple mountains or fruited plains that recurred so frequently in my mind's eye. Neither was it the thrusting skylines of cities or the familiar storefronts of Main Street America. Instead, the image that floated like a mirage beyond the barrel of my gun, illusive and yet compelling, was a simple, tree-lined space: the town common.

It was not the common of my hometown, for I had grown up surrounded by the dusty brown hillsides of southern California. Rather my common was a sort of idealized place, a mental landscape of both aesthetic and moral dimension. I envisioned great trees, elms and maples, framing a field that was green and sylvan. Upright houses lined its edges like parishioners waiting for the sermon from the church spire, sage partner to the grange hall cupola. It was more, though, than trees and houses; the green was encircled by a community. The image of the common was powerful not merely because of its coherence of form but because I dimly perceived that it symbolized a sort of compact between people and place, a compact rare in any time.

Band concerts and church suppers, festivals and Fourth of July oratory were all part of that image. But the distinctive characteristic of the common was that the townspeople were its proprietors—they collectively benefited from the land and also served as its caretakers. In early New England the "Proprietors" named in local records were usually the town's first settlers. They sometimes owned the entire town, including this common land which the community used for impounding cattle, grazing horses during long church services, and performing military drill. Townspeople took an active interest in the land. They regulated, in town meetings, how it was to be used and by whom; they cleared it of rocks and trees; and they erected and mended fences around it. Later, as village centers became more commercial than agricultural, communities beautified these formerly utilitarian spaces. Townspeople do-nated trees, monuments, and bandstands, and met there for evening concerts or informal conversation. In appearance and function, the green was the com-munity focal point. It was this image of a space sheltered and steepled, where form and feeling were united, that stayed with me as I looked into the catastrophe of a broken landscape, cratered in places like the surface of the moon.

The ideal image of the green that survived a war with me could not long endure the peace that followed. For upon returning to the United States and then to New England, I discovered that the space floating in my mind's eye was not always a reality. I was working as a design advocate and preservation planner, trying to popularize the notion of a townscape—that the character of these towns was composed of a whole that was more than the sum of its parts. I had ample opportunity to explore old towns, as I sought to encourage more compatible streetscapes and building facades; and I grew appreciative of how greens provided the aesthetic anchor for many town centers.

What I found was that the forces that had preserved these spaces for generations were often in disarray. In some towns there was simply no one keeping watch; villages that had once been residential were now given over to gas stations and commercial strips. In other places the traditional protectors, historical societies and betterment groups, were now small voices in large towns. These proprietors still cared for the green, but they no longer had the social or political power to make themselves heard. More discouraging still were the towns in which the sensibility of proprietorship had changed; the road widenings, the encircling parking meters, the chain-link-fenced basketball courts, and the harsh streetlights were accepted, even sought after, in the name of progress.

These conditions appeared in even the most picturesque towns like Litchfield, Connecticut and Woodstock, Vermont, where local historic districts enabling design control are still not established and where National Register surveys slighted the greens. Finally, after years of attending to building facades, the Litchfield Historical Society asked me to develop a green conservation plan. We discovered that the green was neglected, even abused. Its edges were eroded by highway expansions, traffic signs, and parking meters; its center, whose classic lines Frederick Law Olmsted had sought to conserve more than eight years ago, was cluttered by monuments. The green was configured with a variety of shrubs and bushes more reflective of a local nursery's year-end donation than any landscape plan. All of these so-called embellishments did little to reinforce the dignity of what was already there.

Similarly Woodstock has a green where the elegantly bowered central walkway has vanished, its trees replaced by thin plantings of another species that will never attain a similar stature. This town is only now in the throes of approving its first historic district ordinance. There were no design guidelines when the gracious patron who saved an adjacent building from service station blight and buried the electric wires also supplied tall and spindly wooden lighting poles crowned by diminutive pseudocolonial lights, aborting the pedestrian scale of the common. Both Woodstock and Litchfield have suffered

Two views of the green in Woodstock, Vermont: 1981 and a century before. Once a space with integrity, the green today is bereft of trees and beset by traffic signs.

the intrusion of visitor information booths. Standing behind the welter of road signs that obscures the apex of the green, the one in Woodstock is a compromise between playhouse and toolshed, its only virtue seeming to be the ease with which it could be removed.

It was the appearance of greens and commons like these that moved us to write this book. We began with the idea of examining the changing character of these spaces, and we commissioned John Stilgoe, professor of visual and environmental studies at Harvard University, to give us a perspective on their origins and development. At the same time we wanted to address the design of greens today; we commissioned landscape architect Tom Paine, who had served as project director of our earlier Litchfield study, to think about guidelines—what to plant, where to embellish, how to deal with specific design and maintenance problems. What should one do, for example, if the grass dies along the edges of a path? The parks department in Boston responded by widening the paths, but the problem was not because of trampling but of winter salt runoff; the solution should have been to stop using salt.

The guidelines are brought to life by the inclusion of vignettes that focus on issues in particular towns. These were written by Townscape Institute staff member Lauri Halderman, who analyzes the impact of a sprawling new church on Ipswich's North Green and retells the struggle to save a house from becoming a McDonald's parking lot in Norwich, Connecticut. Longer case studies examine three rehabilitation schemes, revealing how Cambridge's ambitious bicentennial work on the common has been partially undermined by inadequate maintenance, and why even the best of maintenance could not salvage the project at Waltham.

As the book progressed we became increasingly aware of this issue of modern-day proprietorship—who feels responsible for the green, and who in turn often determines how the space is designed and used. We resisted the nostalgic conclusion that, in this admittedly self-centered age, Americans have altogether lost their capacity to care about such spaces, lost their energy for community. Perhaps some towns have lost their "hearts of green," but the interest in historic architecture and townscape is much greater today than it was ten years go, and it is still growing. What is needed is a reawakening of that proprietary spirit that can not only conserve traditional greens but can also create new spaces suited to modern circumstances. And looking beyond the traditional greens, beyond New England, we found places where the spirit was alive and well.

We discovered a number of spaces that visually bore little resemblance to the church-spired, elm-surrounded greens but that were functionally analogous to the old public-private mix of rights and responsibilities. In New York City we found Paley and Greenacre Parks, privately owned spaces that are open for public use, and the city-owned Madison Square and Bryant Parks, which are receiving substantial support from private corporations. We looked at some planned unit developments—those at Columbia, Maryland and Baldwin Hills, California—where open spaces are owned in common and to some extent managed by the residents. Other proprietors range from the residents of Hoyt Street in Brooklyn, who created a community flower garden, to the employees of Kaiser Aluminum and Chemical Corporation, who volunteered to help construct a children's play area and baseball grandstand at Roberts Regional Recreation Area in Oakland, California. In each of these case studies, we identified the management techniques, design characteristics, and

New proprietors, new places. In Oakland, California, employees of Kaiser Aluminum and Chemical Company construct a terraced hill grandstand behind the baseball diamond in Roberts Recreational Area, a hundred-acre tract of open space and recreational facilities that Kaiser has voluntarily "adopted."

Greenacre Park in Manhattan, a privately funded "vest-pocket park" created for the public.

economic and social benefits in order to encourage the proprietary spirit in other new developments.

We entitled the last chapter "Beyond the Village Green," but we confess that in going beyond the green we hope to bring a larger segment of America back to it. Our intention is not literal—though perhaps the inventory of greens and commons at the end of the book will serve as a tour guide for some inveterate travelers—but rather seeks to restore some sense of responsibility for community spaces. The proprietary spirit is needed to sustain traditional greens in New England and Ohio, courthouse squares in the Midwest and South, and new parks and open spaces from New York to California; and these last examples demonstrate that spirit is still possible today.

Certainly that spirit, embodied in the New England common, asserted itself as a metaphor for America as I witnessed the dispiriting landscape in Vietnam. Now, in times of peace but with a world at peril, it is imperative to expand this concept of a defensible space, of a common ground—a space where form and content merge. If this book can advance just a few steps our understanding of how to care for commons both old and new, it will be well worth the labor of its production.

A Tale of Two Commons

WENTWORTH AND WARREN, NEW HAMPSHIRE ARE SMALL UNPRETENTIOUS towns, where maple trees outnumber the townspeople and the selectmen do not keep regular office hours. With their sturdy wooden houses and central plots of common land, these towns could just as easily be located in western Massachusetts or upstate Vermont, but as it happens they are firmly yet comfortably seated at the foothills of the White Mountains in New Hampshire, adjoined for more than two centuries by "the publick Road" that is today Route 25. It is this region that carload upon carload of fall foliage pilgrims visit each October, and that millions of other Americans know only through tourism brochures and idyllic calendar photographs. When people in New York and Texas and Utah—and Vietnam—conjure up an image of the "real" New England, they are envisioning towns like Wentworth and Warren.

Despite a clannish sort of bickering and claims of superiority by natives on both sides of the town line, the two communities have always been much alike. Both were founded in the latter half of the eighteenth century as agricultural settlements, and both remained relatively unchanged as mills and factories sprang up elsewhere in the century that followed. Even Main Street development made few inroads; the two central villages clung to their clapboard houses, their one or two churches fronting on patches of grass, while shops and businesses passed them by. When writers from the Works Progress Administration compiled a guide to New Hampshire in the 1930s, there was little in their descriptions that indicated the passage of time or distinguished one town from the other. Wentworth, they recorded, was "a compact village of small white houses around a triangular Common," and Warren "an attractive little group of houses clustering around its white-spired church and well-kept Common." Houses, churches, and commons: the mainstays of these and many other small New England towns.

A view of Warren in about 1870, with the common occupying a central position in front of the church. The trees that surrounded the space were probably omitted by the artist in order to show the buildings more fully.

Today a cursory glance around Wentworth and Warren reveals that the last fifty years have left a similarly slight impression—with one exception. How is it that today the Wentworth Common is as attractive as it was in the 1930s, while the Warren Common is ill-used and neglected? How is it that while one boasts lush green grass, sheltering maples, and fine old homes, the other is defined by a chain-link-fenced tennis court and a towering Army missile?

The Warren Common appears neglected because, indeed, it is. No garden club attends to its planting, no annual parade culminates here; the town pays a boy to mow the lawn and has little to do with the space otherwise. In Wentworth, though, the president of the historical society can recite the entire history of the common off the top of his head, and the society holds its annual Market Day there. Profits from the most recent Market Day will perhaps be used by the group to furnish the common with a replica of the bandstand that formerly embellished the space. Why, then, does the Wentworth Common appear so well kept? Because there is a group of townspeople—modern day proprietors of the common land, if you will—who believe that the common is still at the heart of the community and want to see that it survives.

An investigation into the history of the two towns reveals that such a constituency has always been essential to the well-being of these spaces. Townspeople wanted to see the commons improved, and townspeople saw to it that the work was done, transforming each from a muddy lot into the showpiece of the town. Although the circumstances under which this was accomplished were somewhat different in Wentworth and Warren, the process and the results were, for many years, the same.

The commons in Wentworth and Warren, New Hampshire: tranquility versus the tennis court. The adjacent Army missile adds insult to injury.

The town of Wentworth was chartered in 1766 and incorporated ten years later. The original charter, which was identical to that of many New Hampshire towns of that era, made no mention of common land, and chances are that, other than some unclaimed wilderness, there was none. Under the regulations of the charter, each grantee was required to plant and cultivate five acres of his own land for every fifty acres of his share in the township within five years. Today, of course, such a task could be accomplished within a week or two; but in a hostile land of floods, blizzards, and hurricanes—a land with no roads, no means of transportation, a few hand tools, and dense forestation—such a requirement commanded all of one's abilities, leaving little time to clear pastures or to plant ground for communal use as well.

In fact, it was difficult to find people willing to take on such a challenge. The majority of grantees had no personal interest in the town other than as a financial investment; their primary interest was to attract settlers to the town, not necessarily to live there themselves. The early records of Wentworth portray a life that was anything but easy; in 1770, worms destroyed all crops except potatoes, pumpkins, and peas. Bridges built laboriously by the settlers were repeatedly washed out, and livestock consisted of little more than a horse lent by the proprietors "on account of distance to the gristmill" and a similarly borrowed cow. In 1768 the proprietors offered a bounty of fifty acres and five pounds sterling to anyone who would settle within a year and fulfill the terms of the charter; in 1769 they increased the offer to fifty acres and six pounds, or one hundred acres. Still, in 1771 the charter was in danger of revocation by the governor because of the lack of improvements made in the town. Slowly, the settlers made progress. By 1790 they numbered about forty families, and by 1795 there were more than one hundred cows amongst them as well as an average of one horse per household. Wentworth had taken hold.

In the face of such trying conditions, it is impressive that the townspeople saw to an act of community as soon as they did. In 1790 they decided to erect a meetinghouse, which was constructed within a year. The structure was located on a central one-acre lot given to the town in 1787 by a settler named Philip White for use as a "Common Burying Ground," and townspeople apparently thought it an appropriate location for an additional common use. Gradually, as some settlers turned from agriculture to trades, they began to build houses convenient to the meetinghouse and the road that led to it. A village began to form, and, increasingly, residents found that a graveyard was an unsightly thing to have in their midst.

At that same time, Wentworth settlers had a grand scheme for the development of the town. Each county of the state boasted a single courthouse, and the shire town, with its considerable traffic, was certain to be prosperous. Wentworth residents decided to petition the General Court for this privilege and accordingly voted at town meeting to convert the meetinghouse to a courthouse. Once again the question was raised: what about the shabby burial ground?

The answer was clear: the graveyard must be removed. In 1812 a group of townspeople, probably the villagers living in the central area, petitioned the town to do so, and a committee was appointed to look into the matter. Within two years a new lot was purchased with town money, the "moldering tenants" were moved out of the village center, and the now-unoccupied common was cleared of stumps and plowed. Wentworth was unsuccessful in its bid to be shire town, but the impetus behind that bid left its mark on the common and environs. Between 1815 and 1820 several houses were erected around the common; and it took on, according to a local historian of that century, such a settled appearance that it was "usually spoke of throughout the town as 'the City,' 'going to the City,' 'What is the news of the City,' etc." There are no descriptions of the common from this period, but it is likely that it was covered with grass and planted with hardwood trees, some of which survive to this day.

The transformation in Warren was even more dramatic. Settlement conditions in the town were similar to those in Wentworth; but the meetinghouse was a bit longer in coming, as residents several times discussed building one and voted against it until 1818. The site chosen for the meetinghouse was a piece of land donated by Joshua Copp and intended to serve also as a burial ground and training field. When the frame for the structure was finally raised on the fourth of July, 1818, it was an event worthy of some unorthodox celebrations:

> Then True Stevens exhibited a mighty feat of jumping ten feet at a leap on the plates and cross-timbers, thirty feet above the ground, the whole length of the frame, and Samuel Knight stood on his head upon the ridge-pole and made flourishes with his feet up into the clear sky, much to the delight of the assembled multitude who held their breath at the sight.

The next twenty years in Warren saw further construction around and on the common: a new chapel located only a short distance from the meetinghouse, a school house and an accompanying privy, a row of chapel sheds that stretched more than halfway "through the very centre of the old common." By the 1830s some townspeople viewed the completed array with a sense of disappointment. The 1818 meetinghouse was out of repair, and the paint was already worn off the new chapel. The space seemed cluttered with tree stumps and ill-matched sheds. "In short," pronounced William Little in his history of Warren, "the whole village looked bad and was an object of remark in the neighboring towns."

The task of regaining control over the common was complex. The Universalists and Methodists vied for control of the church buildings, the town agreed to buy the chapel to convert into a town house, and there was finally an agreement that all of the buildings should be moved and the common cleared. Land was donated or purchased with money raised by public subscription, and the area of the common was increased as well. After the buildings were removed, reports Little:

> [W]hat an amount of work was done on the common! The stumps of the dark old pines . . . were dug out; hundreds of tons of stones were removed, and ploughs and harrows were used day after day. One spring, Henry W. Weeks, Charles Leonard, and others, planted elms and maples all around it, and the good citizens have now in part the village green that Gov. Wentworth wished they should when he so kindly gave the town charter in 1763. It is the pleasantest place in town. The wide spreading trees cast a refreshing shade there . . . May the common be forever preserved.

For more than a century thereafter residents in each town made strides in fulfilling Little's wish, although village life was still far from placid. Wentworth struggled to define the common as an ornamental rather than functional space, not always with success; in 1817, townspeople voted that cattle and horses should not be allowed to run at large within a hundred yards of the meeting-house—and immediately afterward repealed the decision. In fact the village

The Warren Common and its environs today, plagued by a variety of problems: an ill-suited bandstand, an Army mis- *sile that rivals the church steeple for attention, telephone poles and wires, cement-block architecture.*

was periodically overrun with livestock until about 1850, as herds of cattle and sheep were driven through the town on their way to market and paused to graze in Wentworth overnight. On these days "the Village Common would present quite a lively spectacle all covered over with little squads of sheep as they continually arrived," probably much to the dismay of the fastidious villagers. Eventually, though, railroad freight replaced cattle droving, and the village shed its agricultural tone. By 1906 a Wentworth resident boasted "See our new bandstand" in a postcard message, and the transformation of the common from pasture to park was complete.

There is less information about this same period of development in Warren, but it seems that the early clearing and planting efforts of the townspeople were fruitful. William Little, in his 1870 history, makes mention of the pleasant condition of the common as well as of the occasional "caravans with elephants, lions, and tigers—and circuses" that pitched their tents there. With perhaps no other major efforts, the town was able to sustain its common at least through 1938, when the usually reliable WPA writers described it as "well-kept." It is within the past fifty years, then, that the common has slid into its present condition, which is characterized by sparse turf, few trees, cracked sidewalks, eroded edges, and tennis-court blight.

Several factors have combined to plague Warren's large common. It is adjacent to a school which has no proper playground, so the common receives considerable use—not necessarily a bad thing, but a condition that requires constant maintenance. Warren has been derelict in this regard. The town has neither a parks department nor a comprehensive maintenance scheme, and the neglect is apparent: the turf has been reduced to dirt in patches, and most of the nineteenth-century trees have died and been insufficiently replaced. Furnishings are in some cases inappropriate in function—a bicycle rack and tennis court, for example—and in other cases ill designed: the bandstand is well intentioned but more reminiscent of California redwood construction than New England gazebo design. The army missile on an adjacent plot of land makes no pretense of being compatible with the common; presumably it was too large for the backyard of the selectman to whom it belongs. Overused and undermaintained, subjected to inappropriate uses and burdened by unattractive features, the Warren Common is no better off now than it was when covered with stumps and privies.

The answer to the problem of a shabby common is the same today as it was one hundred fifty years ago: attention. Townspeople in the 1830s rallied to the cause with plows and trees, and what is now needed is a modern day rescue team to pick up where their forebears left off. Warren residents then came forward not because they were paid or coerced but because they cared—because the common was a space for which they felt a sense of proprietary interest and responsibility. Is it a concept that has gone the way of crinoline skirts and the horse and buggy?

One need look only as far as Wentworth to realize that a sense of proprietorship is still viable. During the 1960s it was, admittedly, hardly an overwhelming movement but rather one resident who maintained the spirit. Ray Humiston lived in the 1815 Whipple House, the handsome five-bay edifice that fronts on the common, and he felt about the common the way some people feel about their front lawns. Seeing that there were gaps where the older trees had died, Humiston single-handedly planted several maples around the common's periphery, and he did so without asking the town either for money or permission. His presumptuousness irked some townspeople, but his judgment was good; now, although Humiston moved away some years ago, the maples promise to someday rival those planted by the proprietors of the previous century.

Today the Wentworth Historical Society takes an active interest in the common. Upon discovering that the town charter provides for an annual market day so long as the town has more than fifty families, the historical society decided five years ago to revive the tradition. Three of the last five Market Days have been held on the common, bringing both exhibitors and buyers of homemade and flea-market type items from the surrounding region, and the event has proved both enjoyable and profitable. The money raised by this year's Market Day may provide the town with a bandstand, the design of which would be based on photographs of the former 1906 gazebo. In any case the event has drawn attention to the common and created a group that watches over it.

Historical Society President Francis Muzzey admits that not much happens on the common and that no one derives much direct benefit from it. It is not, then, a sense of personal gain that motivates society members to sponsor the Market Day and investigate bandstands. Perhaps it is that townspeople have discovered, as did their forebears, that there is simply something good about working together and taking pride in a space that is the visual and metaphorical heart of the community. And perhaps, if the spirit spreads just five miles down the road, the Warren Common will be revived by a new generation of proprietors.

The 1815 Thomas Whipple House, one of the original village center homes facing the Common. Whipple was active in the early movement to secure Wentworth as the seat of the county court, and he was probably instrumental in the

concurrent transformation of this "front yard" patch of land from graveyard to ornamental space. Twentieth-century occupant Ray Humiston also took a proprietary interest in the common, and planted young trees in the hope that they would attain the stature of those planted in Whipple's time.

Town Common and Village Green in New England: 1620 to 1981

John R. Stilgoe, Ph.D.

"Common" is an old word, rich in meanings acquired over centuries. Yet it is not easily defined. The word denotes something that is readily accessible and openly shared, something that has a general, nonprivate nature. But "common" can also connote slightly unpleasant qualities. It can mean ordinary, undistinguished, almost vulgar. How, therefore, does one define "common land"?

New Englanders have a peculiar interest in the definition, because more than three hundred towns and cities in the New England region claim a grassy piece of ground called "the common" or "the green." Such "common" areas are found wherever New Englanders settled in large numbers; across Ohio, in Illinois, as far west as Wisconsin, people refer to "greens." Clearly the space has cultural significance. It is more than a simple public park.

Understanding the significance of any green involves careful retrospective scrutiny, however, for the origins of the space are hidden by centuries, and its uses have varied through time. A simple chronological analysis produces little insight, because at any one moment a green has served several, widely different purposes; and those are often remarkably different from the purposes served by greens in neighboring towns. Only when the uses are catalogued and arranged in a   historical progression does the meaning of the New England green become explicable.

English Origins

Hidden in the ancient laws of English kings are clues to the present-day uses of New England town greens. Some Anglo-Saxon kings—King Ine, for example—are remembered today largely because they codified traditional uses of particular pieces of ground. The eighth- and ninth-century legal codes form part of what English barristers call the "common law",—the law of common people, not nobles. Much of English common law focused on land-use rights, and sovereigns like King Ine merely confirmed the regulations created and long accepted by peasants.

Englishmen knew two sorts of land. One sort belonged to particular owners. A field might be owned by a knight, a houselot by a wealthy peasant called a "householder,"and a vegetable garden by an impoverished widow. The other sort, far more vast in extent, belonged in actuality to the king, who in theory exercised "eminent domain" over every square inch of English soil. Of course the king used only a very small portion of the land owned by no one else; some acreage he used for hunting parks, some forests he reserved for producing the royal firewood. But most of the land served the general public; in every village the local noble and a group of respected older peasants determined how the "unowned" land would serve the community. Variations in usage occurred everywhere in England, and customs changed through the centuries. The general pattern of use is clear to anyone willing to examine the records of many villages, however, and was well known to such typical Englishmen as those who emigrated to the New World in the early seventeenth century.

English common law recognized the "common of pasture" (the right to graze livestock on a piece of "common" land), the "common of estovers" (the right to cut wood for building or fuel for the cutter's own use, but not for sale), the "common of turbary" (the right to dig peat for fuel), the "common in the soil" (the right to take sand or stone for use on the digger's own land), and finally the rare "common of piscary" (the right to fish in a freshwater pond). The law recognized dozens of other "rights in common," many of which contemporary Americans take "for granted" today. No local or state government "grants" the privilege of fishing in the sea from an ocean beach, for example. Such fishing is seen by all Americans as a right of such age that most Americans never think of its origin. But most states issue freshwater fishing licenses, and therefore continue the long tradition of regulating the public use of bodies of fresh water. The "common of pasture" and other rights in common are consequently difficult to define precisely because traditional usage changes constantly. English courts still try countless cases each year involving half-forgotten "rights" to a particular piece of land; and they must frequently adjudicate the cases according to that well-known British quality of "common sense."

Not every Englishman could avail himself of rights in common. Essentially the rights pertained only to those Englishmen who owned a piece of ground for their private use. Such men included all nobles and a vast number of peasants who owned a small "houselot" of one or two acres along with a house, but did not include the landless poor, the serfs or "cottagers" who inhabited temporary dwellings called "cottages" erected on land owned by someone else. This division in English society is remembered still in American English. In the United States a house is expected to be surrounded by a yard, a piece of land that can be fenced and used as the householder wants; a cottage is typically a seashore dwelling, far less solidly built than a house and usually lacking much land. Cottages are often built more closely together than houses, and often sand and surf wash around or under them. The contemporary American equivalent of the medieval cottage is perhaps better defined as the trailer or mobile home, which is not attached to a yard and is often scorned by residents of houses. Owning a house and yard delivered enormous status to a medieval English family because houses, not families, owned the rights in common. Cottages owned nothing.

Americans have difficulty understanding the way in which a house owned rights in common. The entire concept seems alien to the New World, but in reality much of present-day American law involves the Old World tradition. In a typical English village of 1550, a particular house and houselot owned clearly defined rights to use the common forest, the common pasture, and other pieces of common land. Whoever owned the house could partake of the rights, including the gathering of a certain number of loads of firewood in the common forest and the pasturing of a certain number of cows, horses, and geese in the common pasture. Of course owning a house brought with it many responsibilities, such as devoting one day each month to herding all of the livestock on the common pasture. The entire complex of rights and responsibilities gave rise to the term "householder," which means essentially one who holds the rights and duties pertaining to a particular house. The cottagers in a village had none of the rights of the householders: they could not use the common lands, could not vote, and could not otherwise engage in civil affairs, except to pay taxes to the local noble. Being a householder meant being able to use public resources for private gain; being a cottager meant being trapped in poverty.

The division of peasant society into two classes, householders and cottagers, seemed to peasants as natural as the division of society into peasants and nobles. The divisions originated in forgotten, quasi-barbaric times, and proved self-perpetuating; for a cottager to amass wealth enough to acquire a house, houselot, and rights in common was nearly impossible, except by chance (finding treasure) or by marriage to the householder's only child. For centuries the system worked, keeping society hierarchical, and keeping the householders busy regulating the use of common land. Year after year the village elders determined the maximum number of cattle that could graze the common pasture without destroying the turf, and determined how many loads of firewood each householder could retrieve from the forest. Productive agriculture without the use of the common lands was simply impossible. Only a few householders owned enough land to graze their livestock, provide firewood and building timber, and supply other needs. Until the end of the sixteenth century, the age-old system worked wonderfully.

At the heart of the system lay a great weakness, however, that caused it to fragment under economic pressure. The actual ownership of the common lands lay in the king's hands, of course, although village householders usually thought of the land as theirs. Rising prices and population throughout the sixteenth century burdened the lesser nobility; no longer was it easy for a local lord to live in simple splendor. The nobility began to petition the king for permission to use the hitherto common land for particular uses, usually for sheep raising, since the woolen industry paid great profits. Despite the opposition of the householders, the king began to alter the ancient system of common-land agriculture by reassigning the land. So long and intricate a legal proceeding—Queen Victoria's government was embroiled in it as late as the 1880s—cannot be addressed here. But the result was striking. Many householders saw themselves reduced to the status of cottagers, deprived of their hitherto stable way of life. Their discontent led many to revolt against the king in the 1640s, but for many others a solution presented itself several decades earlier. They left England for the New World, determined to replicate the system of village government and common-land agriculture that was so rapidly crumbling around them.

<table>
<tr><td>The Common
Transplanted</td><td>

New England common land takes its character from the cultural baggage of the Englishmen who arrived in the early seventeenth century. Certainly memory played an important part in their creation of agricultural systems based on carefully regulated common land. Most of the immigrants had been householders, and they wanted to recreate the way of life threatened by reassignment of common land. The remaining immigrants were former cottagers, who aspired to the new social position of householder, and who hoped to attain it in the forests of New England. Forces other than memory reinforced the urge to have common lands, however. Chief among them was Puritanism, which emphasized the community-based nature of religion. The first settlers of New England accepted the Puritan belief that Christian charity ought to be practiced in daily life and that the community should care for its poor. Again, traces of this thinking survive in American English; the full name of one New England state is "The Commonwealth of Massachusetts." Ecclesiastical pragmatism guided the founders, too; a common land system meant that every member of the community would be guided by the will of the community elders, who could enforce religious conformity by threatening to withdraw

</td></tr>
</table>

rights to use common land. Such pragmatism worked, at least in the first decades of settlement. Town elders carefully interviewed families asking to settle, and "cast out," often to Rhode Island or the West Indies, families unwilling to abide by town regulations. Its founders intended New England to be a social, religious, and agricultural Utopia.

To create an agricultural Utopia in the midst of a forest wilderness required extraordinary planning and effort. Englishmen unused to clearing forest and equipped with poor quality axes and pikes made slow progress against the massive trees. Consequently they valued natural grassland because it provided immediately accessible pasture; and they often located towns

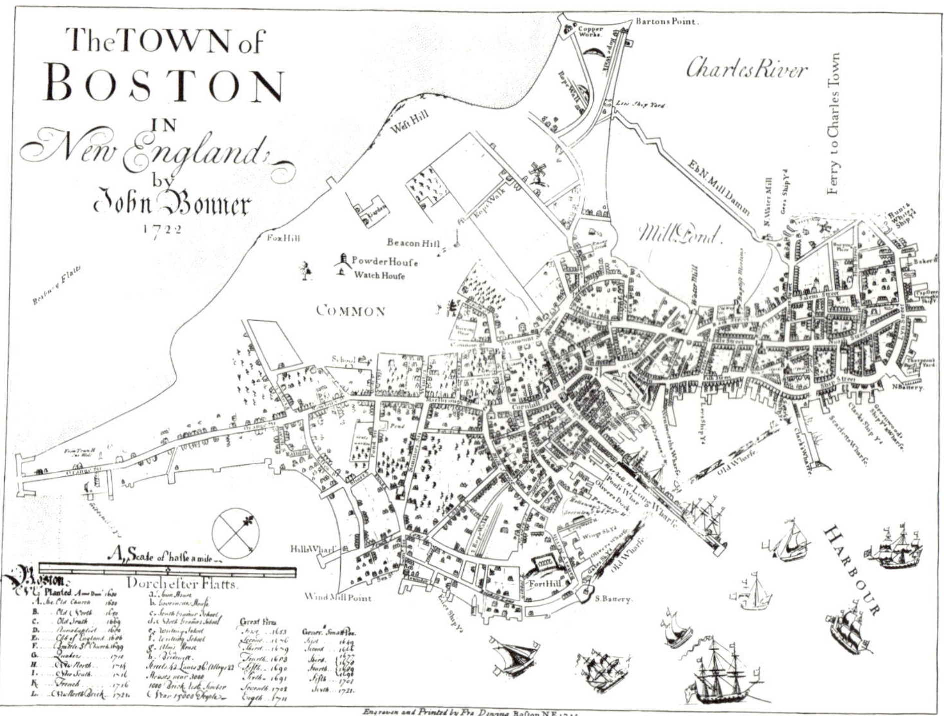

The Boston Common was one of New England's earliest; here is how it appeared in 1722. Note the central powder and watch houses, indicating a military use of the land; and the burying ground to the northeast.

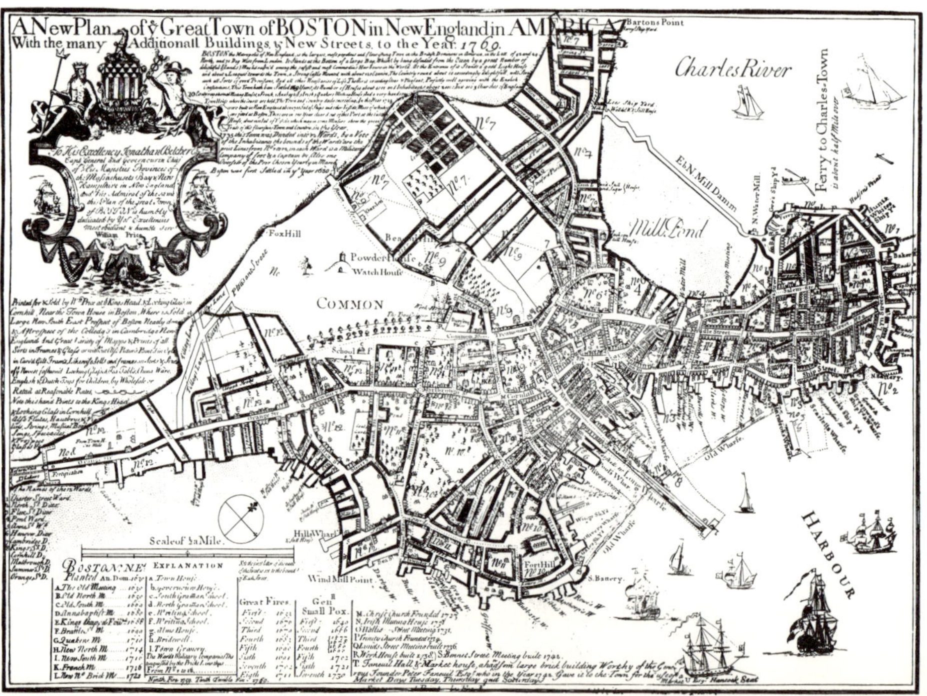

By 1769 much of the Boston Common's land had passed into private hands.

10

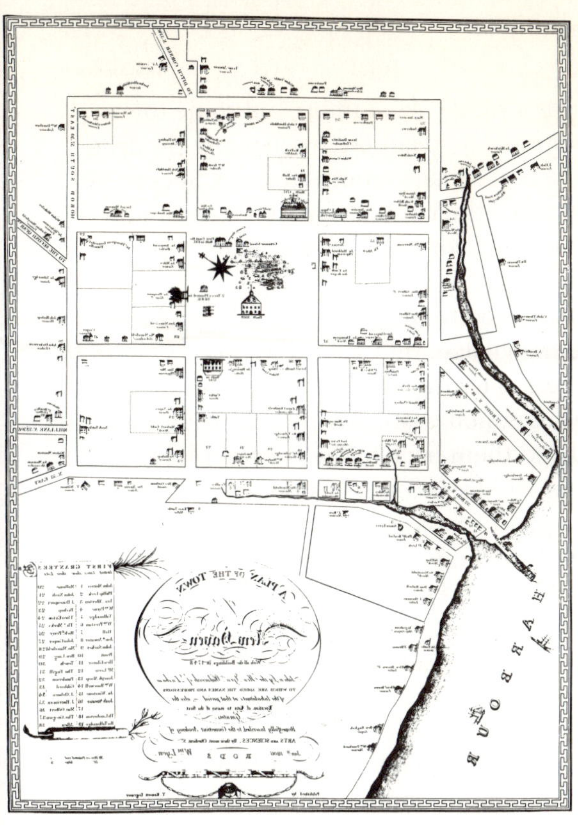

The New Haven Green was laid out as part of the original nine-square town plan. This 1748 rendering shows it as the site of several institutions including a meetinghouse, jail, grammar school, county house, and courthouse; it also served as a graveyard and marketplace. Today the green is bisected by a major city street but otherwise retains its early dimensions. The graveyard and original buildings are long gone, but three nineteenth-century churches provide a focus.

adjacent to salt marshes, freshwater meadows, or upland grassland. Nearby they assigned each family a houselot; and they began clearing trees to make several large communal planting fields. In the first years of settlement, most crops—and all grain—grew in the common planting fields; only when the town was established were the planting fields divided among the families. Community growing of rye, wheat, and other grains was common in many parts of England, but it worked poorly in New England. In the old country, tradition and experience dictated what crops the community planted, and usually the crops succeeded. In a new location beset by a different climate and markedly different soil, most farmers had very individual ideas about the best crops to plant; they distrusted planting a crop according to majority vote. A single vast field planted only to wheat seemed a great liability to the farmer convinced that rye would grow better; it took only several large-scale crop failures to convince New Englanders that diversity made far better sense. Thus the common planting fields soon displayed fences; where single crops had once been planted, a variety of crops, it was discovered, provided more safety. The termination of common planting within one or two decades of settlement proves that the immigrants were willing to experiment, just as the longevity of the other common-land uses shows their reluctance to alter a system of proven value.

Seventeenth-century New Englanders had more freedom to manage their common lands than their English forebears because no nobles inhabited New England. Each town created its common-land system with a free hand, determining what grassland would become the common pasture, what part of the forest would remain common forever, and so on. Each town regulated the maximum number of horses and other stock that could graze on the common pasture, and divided that number by the number of families. New England town society was hierarchical. Families that arrived with more wealth were usually assigned larger houselots and larger rights in common; but some towns assigned houselots of equal size, and some assigned families with many children larger rights simply because large families have many mouths to feed. Secure in the belief that no noble could ever acquire the land designated as common, the first generation of settlers began to use the common lands in very traditional ways.

In the early morning, as the men prepared to walk from their houselots to their plowing fields located just beyond the village, they turned their cows into an open area near the center of the cluster of houses. From there a herdsman led the cattle and any other stock to the common pasture a mile or so away, watched over them all day, and at dusk led them back to the central place. In English terminology, the central place existed as a "close," a place for "enclosing" animals. It was not a pasture, but a paddock. New Englanders now confuse the town close with the town pasture, and residents wonder how such a small plot pastured several score animals. It did not. It only enclosed them temporarily at the beginning and end of every day. Livestock grazed on common pastures, like the several-hundred-acre salt marsh in Scituate.(Unless otherwise noted, all towns mentioned in this chapter are in Massachusetts.) The Scituate marsh was reached by what is still called in that town the "Driftway," the road made by "driven" or "drifted" cattle moving between village and common pasture.

The practice of grazing livestock on common pasture endured for centuries in New England. It lasted longest where it first began, in the coastal towns, because the great salt marshes and grass-covered dunes made perfect, easily accessible pastures. Many coastal New England towns still have small islands called "Ram Island" or "Hog Island," where livestock grazed for entire summers. Sometimes a small island would be devoted to pasturing only one species of livestock; and sometimes a very small one would be devoted to pasturing only males, in order to prevent indiscriminate breeding. Islands made perfect common pastures for bulls, hogs, and sheep; the water kept the animals on the island and kept wolves away from them. Such islands were used as common pasture into the twentieth century.

As settlers moved west across New England they continued the practice

Greens and commons served as military training grounds and encampments from the seventeenth century through World War I. George Ropes painted this elaborate scene called "Salem Common on Training Day" in 1808; the newly planted popla trees, probably larger in the artist's eye than in reality, were part of an embellishment plan to make the common an ornamental as well as utilitarian space. (Courtesy Essex Institute, Salem, Mass.)

of common pasturing, especially in the first years of settlement. Often the pastures endured as common land; mountainsides remained common in New Hampshire for generations. But towns settled after the 1660s often lacked permanent common pastures because the houselots had dramatically expanded in size, many reaching forty acres or more. On such lots, actually farms, families grazed their own livestock. The practice of individual grazing affected coastal towns too; farmers consolidated their holdings, sometimes buying adjacent planting fields as well, and began to graze their livestock on their own land. Other farmers abandoned cattle-raising and consequently abandoned the common pasture.

Land-assignment committees, groups of three to five farmers elected at town meeting to apportion the wilderness among the settlers, eventually were ordered to divide the common pastures among the "first-comers" and their descendants, or else to sell them and apply the money to building a school, a bridge, or a powder house. Some land remained common because no one family wanted to buy it. Beaches and rocky areas attracted little interest because of their infertile soil. Swamps likewise often remained "common wilderness," unless covered with white cedar, in which case farmers bought them and converted the cedar trees into shingles. All New Englanders accepted the frittering away of common land, which typically began several decades after the founding of a town. Changing farming techniques seemed ill suited to the old system, and most towns were content to sell or otherwise dispose of the common land.

One reason for abandoning the common-pasture system, and to a lesser extent the common-forest system, involved political tension. New Englanders thought of householding in the traditional way: to own a particular house and houselot meant having a right in common. But experience altered their thinking. Large families had larger rights in common, perhaps, although all families might own houselots of identical size. If that family moved to another town and the house and lot were purchased by another, smaller family, did the larger rights still pertain? Town after town debated such questions, creating new precedents and tradition.

The issue that proved fatal to the common-pasture system began with the

More recent military uses of greens have sometimes encountered hostility from town officials. When the Vietnam Veterans Against the War bivouacked on the Lexington Battle Green in 1971, more than four hundred were arrested. "We are assembling at Lexington Green much like minute men, but unarmed, bonded in our brotherhood of affecting revolutionary change in this country," read their statement, but town selectmen insisted on enforcing the law that forbade groups to assemble on the green after curfew. In this 1980 photograph, members of the Lexington Alliance Against the Draft engage in a protest.

Revivalist preacher George Whitfield preached to the masses on the Boston Common in 1740, and so did Pope John Paul II more than two hundred years later.

problem of newcomers to a particular town. The first settlers, called "first-comers" in the record books, had rights to use what were often quite limited common pastures. Did a family building a new house automatically acquire a right to pasture livestock on the common pasture? Most towns said no. Ipswich, for example, determined in 1702 that no one could build a cottage on any common land; a fisherman had to buy land from a private party before erecting a house for his family, and thereafter had no right to common land. A few towns, like Salem, which voted in 1702 "that everyone who has a dwelling house and land of his own proper estate in fee simple shall have a right to commonage," allowed any newcomer who bought or built a house to use all of the town's common resources, but most did not. Inheritance perplexed town meetings too. What rights in common did the descendants of first-comers enjoy? Were rights apportioned equally between sons and daughters?

Such questions revolved around a crucial issue. Only first-comers, and in some towns their descendants, enjoyed rights in common. Later arrivals envied such rights, because the rights helped make small-scale farming profitable. If the newcomers were numerous enough to complain powerfully at town meeting, the town usually terminated much of the common-land system—simply because the original common pastures and forests were rarely large enough to support populations much greater than the original one. Innovative planting, farm consolidation, and population growth, therefore, all worked against the old-country system, swaying public opinion against common-land agriculture.

Town meetings devoted much attention to protecting common lands against use by people from outside the town, as well as by townspeople not entitled to use them. "This town's commons are for the grazing and feeding of cattle and for the necessary supply of building and fencing timber and for firewood for household use and not otherwise," declared the Scituate town meeting in 1650, "and from which land after the last day of November next, there shall be no oak timber made use of to be sawn into planks for ship timber." This Scituate act exemplifies seventeenth-century New England common-land regulation; it emphasizes that the common lands are for domestic use, not business purposes. Most town meeting regulations are stark but clear reflections of what amounts to American common law, like one recorded by the town clerk of Ipswich on April 16, 1663: "Ordered that no man shall cut any grass on Plum Island before the tenth of July, nor any family use above two scythes at a time." The Ipswich town meeting scrutinized the condition of the Plum Island common meadows; other town meetings regulated woodlots, specified how clay was to be removed from "clay pits," and ruled how herring and other fish were to be "taken." Plymouth, for example, repeatedly refined the "common of piscary," ordering in 1668 that fish entrails not be thrown into the "fishing grounds," and in 1684 banning the netting and seining of mackerel. As Plymouth grew in population, managing the town's herring brooks and other common fishing grounds occupied more and more attention. Finally, the town began to sell the rights to take fish in certain locations on the estuaries. Selling the rights to the highest bidders proved an easier way of regulating fisheries than specifying how many barrels of fish could be caught by each family. Coastal towns still continue the custom of selling such rights, sometimes because the bidding is a legal requirement binding the town meeting. Norwell, for example, concludes its annual meeting by selling the rights to net herring entering freshwater brooks from the sea.

Common agricultural land, and common land used for firewood, clay, and sand needs, still endures across New England. Since 1620, when the settlers of Plymouth instituted the system, it has been a part of New England culture and land-use law. Today the system is fragmented, and much of the land has been either long since sold to private individuals or else ignored. Norwell, for

In English towns such as King's Lynn, the marketplace was often in a central open space in the shadow of a church. New Englanders sometimes continued this practice on an open patch of common land.

By the beginning of the twentieth century, most New England towns had removed any vestige of graveyards from their greens, preferring to designate new cemeteries away from the town centers. Not so in Little Compton, Rhode Island, where the church and gravestones still dominate the common at the heart of the village.

example, owns clam flats in the marshes of adjacent Scituate, but few citizens care to row out to them and dig.

The system passed through two distinct stages. The first was usually associated with the decades immediately following the settling of a town, whether the town was settled in 1634 or 1734, or even later. This stage involved vigorous use and regulation, and the exclusion of all but first-comers. The second stage began in most towns when the first-comers surrendered their exclusive use to all householders. Salem first-comers gave up their rights in 1714, voting that "all the highways, burying places, and common land lying within Town Bridge and the block houses shall be for common use." With that decision, "common land" meant land owned by the town of Salem and open for use by all citizens. Of course Salem and almost every other town retained the exclusion against citizens from other towns. After such votes, the word "common" began to vanish from town-meeting vocabularies, and the term "town" replaced it. Vestiges of the old common land remain in almost every town, but the vestiges are called the "town beach," the "town meadow," or the "town forest," if they are recognized and called by any name at all.

Meetinghouses, Militia, and Markets

Even as the traditional system of agricultural use of common land withered, however, a parallel system of common-land use increased in importance. Unraveling the connections is important, because what New Englanders today call "the town common" or "the town green" is a space that originated in both systems. The Puritans who settled New England had in mind an ideal town plan, in which houses clustered around a meetinghouse, and fields in turn surrounded the cluster of structures. Puritans deliberately avoided the word "church" when speaking of the building in which they worshiped; for them, "church," "congregation," and "town" were synonymous for the close-knit, smoothly functioning community they hoped to create. According to the ideal town described in "The Ordering of Towns," a pre-1638 town-planning essay written by an anonymous New Englander, the meetinghouse ought to stand at the spatial center of the town. In reality, the meetinghouse often stood where the town's first settlers located; as the town attracted more families (who of course had to accept land further from the meetinghouse), the meetinghouse came to be perceived as in a "corner" of the town. Contemporary New Englanders often fail to realize the original geographical extent of their towns;

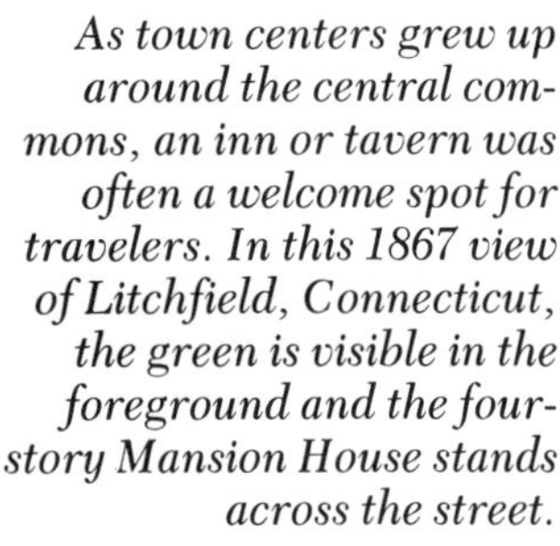

As town centers grew up around the central commons, an inn or tavern was often a welcome spot for travelers. In this 1867 view of Litchfield, Connecticut, the green is visible in the foreground and the four-story Mansion House stands across the street.

The common in Pittsfield, Massachusetts was isolated by wide roads from the start, as seen in this mid-nineteenth century engraving; the famous Great Elm is also apparent. When the roads were transversed only by horses, the width was not too great a deterrent—if we can believe this illustration from later in the century, complete with strolling couples and hoop-rolling children. Today, though, the oval park has taken on the appearance of a traffic island, and few pedestrians brave the three lanes of speeding cars.

most towns split at least once, and some as many as five times. Each time, the newly organized town built a meetinghouse near its approximate center. Understanding meetinghouse architecture explains much about the towns' images of themselves, but deciphering the significance of the "meetinghouse lot" explains more about the day-to-day functioning of town society.

Every New England meetinghouse occupied a special piece of ground called the meetinghouse lot, which was used for several purposes. Often the lot contained the "close" in which livestock was penned before and after grazing on the common pasture. Usually it contained a patch of ground called the graveyard or, more frequently, the "burying ground." In some instances, the meetinghouse lot was made large enough for the men and boys of the community to practice basic military exercises, and to fire their muskets at targets. As towns expanded in population, the meetinghouse lots acquired additional uses. Puritans worshipped twice on Sundays—once for several hours in the morning, and again in the afternoon. Families who lived so far from the meetinghouse that the trip back and forth at noon was burdensome used the lot to tether their horses, as well as for Sabbath-day picnics. In cold weather, however, outdoor eating proved irksome, and the families began to ask that the town build them so-called "warming houses," "nooning houses," or "Sabbath-Day houses." Newton erected two warming houses around 1730, Sturbridge erected several in 1791, and at one point in the eighteenth century the Stonington, Connecticut lot was dotted with thirty warming houses. The simple structures, each fitted with a small fireplace, usually vanished from the meetinghouse lot when the town split into two "convenient" pieces; the newer town immediately erected its own meetinghouse, making the long walk to services and the intermediate picnic unnecessary. Dedham, for example, was laid out in 1637 as one town with one meetinghouse. But portions of it eventually became the towns of Wellesley, Natick, Needham, Dover, Westwood, Norwood, Medfield, Walpole, Norfolk, Franklin, Wrentham, and Bellingham—each of which attempted to erect a centrally located house of worship, with a small space (often part open field, part burying ground) next to it. Even Wellesley, laid out more than two centuries after the founding of Dedham, insisted on having some sort of public open space near its center. The meetinghouse lot consequently served many purposes, some agricultural, some ecclesiastical, and some distinctly secular.

In every town the lot was known as "the" lot. Puritans insisted that everyone worship in one building. They forbade other denominations to settle in New England; and when groups like the Quakers attempted to preach a different theology, the Puritan leaders exiled them or hanged them. Thus almost every town focused on one meetinghouse and one meetinghouse lot, and did so until the middle of the eighteenth century, when other denominations established themselves in the New England colonies. Sometimes a town chose to build a new, larger meetinghouse nearer to its population center, and consequently used a piece of common land—or purchased a likely piece of privately held property—for a new meetinghouse lot. Many towns had two or three such different lots during their first century; the first lot served as a close, perhaps, and the latter served chiefly as a militia training ground, since it was

---

Branford

New Canaan

put into use after common-pasture agriculture had been abandoned. Finding "the" meetinghouse lot in a typical New England town usually means locating the Congregational church building, which housed the worshipers descended most directly from Puritanism, and locating the adjacent field, usually called "the town green." Churches of other denominations often sit on pleasantly kept lots, but only one lot represents the former close union between church and town government.

Until the 1830s, every Massachusetts resident paid taxes to the Congregational church. Town taxes paid for road repairs, bridge building, and for the maintenance of the "town clergy"—that is, the Congregational minister. The complex relationship of church and town cannot be analyzed here; all that need be said is that town meeting was almost invariably held in the meetinghouse, often after prayer, and that Puritan doctrine informed every government decision. A child growing up in seventeenth-century New England learned that the meetinghouse represented the hub of all civil and ecclesiastical authority, and thought nothing of the mixed use of the meetinghouse lot. Part of the lot might be given over to such sacred use as a burying ground, and part of it might be used for military exercises.

As early as 1685, Salem emphasized that its lot "is appointed as the place where persons may shoot at a mark," and in 1713 the town reiterated that the lot "be forever a training field for the use of Salem." Every town insisted that its men drill once every three months at least, on "muster day"; and it provided that its lot be used as a parade ground, where all men and boys of military age

Woodstock

Norwich

Thompson

Stratford

19

lined up for weapons inspection, close order drill, and lessons in advanced tactics by experienced officers. In wartime, which came frequently throughout the seventeenth and eighteenth centuries, muster days occurred often, as did target practice.

Boston possessed the most famous training field in New England, because town regiments assembled at it occasionally for *en masse* exercises. Judge Samuel Sewall understood the necessity for the "trainings," but in 1677 the musketry so frightened his horse that he later noted in his *Journal*, "I could no way govern him, but was fain to let him go full speed, and hold my hat under my arm." The training ground is now called Boston Common; it is essentially a fragment of a once-large livestock close. A century after Sewall's unfortunate ride the ground was still in military use; by 1772 the British regulars were camping often on it and had begun using it as an artillery range. More regular troops arrived as war neared; during the seige of Boston the green hosted whole regiments, some of whose men ripped down the few trees and nearby fences to feed campfires. The soldiers dug fortifications that endured into the nineteenth century as shallow mounds and ditches.

Long after the militia system faded into inactive obscurity, the meeting-house lot in every town retained military echoes. When the Civil War began, town clerks accepted enlistments while standing on town greens. After the war, many towns erected monuments honoring war dead, often siting them on the exact spot on which the men had enlisted in the Grand Army of the Republic. The military use of commons lingered into the present century; some Spanish-American War units tented for a night or two on town greens, and Boston Common still possesses two small obelisks given by sailors of the Royal Navy in recognition of the friendship shown to them by Bostonians during World War II. And on numbers of town greens, vestiges of military use remain. Cannon of every type, from Revolutionary War nine-pounders to Great War howitzers to Second World War anti-aircraft guns, sit silently watching the civilians who carelessly pass their muzzles.

Eighteenth-century New Englanders accomplished the shift from using the meetinghouse lot at least sometimes for agricultural purposes to using it chiefly for public gatherings. Cambridge used its green—which was very large because its original settlers embraced the English common-herding techni-que—not only as a militia training field, but also for Middlesex County elections and for such public debates as that concerning the antinomianism of Anne Hutchinson. The 1637 debate attracted a vast crowd, and one clergyman lectured while standing in an old oak tree. Lexington erected a meetinghouse on its lot in 1713, but two years later built a schoolhouse beside it, which it replaced with another in 1761. Eventually, the town dug a well "for town people on Sabbath days to drink at," and probably to quench the thirst of the young scholars too.

Throughout the eighteenth century, townspeople began to use the meet-inghouse lot for more and more different purposes. During and after this period it is properly called "the green," since its identity came increasingly from nonecclesiastical affairs and purposes. In 1770, for example, the town of Salem built a workhouse on its central green in order that its poor might find useful employment; and Newburyport in 1782 ordered its constables to transport all smallpox victims "to the pest house in the common pasture," an order it repeated six years later, and again in 1803. Newburyport realized that its green was big enough to forestall contagion; and in 1822 the town deter-

By the late nineteenth century in Litchfield, Connecticut, townspeople had transformed their common into an ornamental green complete with surfaced pathways, a Civil War monument, a cannon and cannonballs, and a stone watering trough.

Other towns lagged behind, though, and in Norwalk, Connecticut, cows still grazed on this relatively unimproved field.

mined that it might be big enough to lessen the impact of accidental explosion. It voted that year to erect a powder house "near the common pasture." The Newburyport lot served other civil purposes, too. The town sited its hay scales there in 1785, keeping them on the site until 1823. Other towns willing to purchase a cannon for their defense often erected a "gun house" on their greens, and sometimes saved money by storing the town hearse alongside the field piece. Towns without artillery built smaller "hearse houses."

By the late eighteenth century, the Congregational church's hold on town government was slipping. Military exercises, and civic gatherings like the 1768 tarring and feathering of a British informer in Salem and the burning of a British custom collector's pleasure boat in Boston in the same year, destroyed any lingering ecclesiastical significance of the lots. Henceforth new burying grounds were located away from the town greens; and burials in the grounds adjacent to the greens were curtailed, so that gravestones would not encroach on open space useful for military parades and other active enterprises.

Between approximately 1780 and 1830, the Congregational church congregations surrendered their quasi ownership of the greens to town governments. Baptists, Methodists, and people of other denominations no longer considered the green an extension of the "official" or "state" church, but rather saw it as public meeting ground owned by all citizens. In these years town meetings acquired different characters too. Church buildings still hosted the meetings, but no longer was the Congregational church meetinghouse the only one used. Meetings revolved from building to building; townsmen met one year in a Baptist-owned structure, the next in a Unitarian one, and the third in the Congregational building.

Greens came to be used more and more for public assemblies as the eighteenth century wore on. The English revivalist, George Whitfield, visited Boston in 1740 and preached to such a large crowd that the meetinghouse began to creak, causing a panic in which at least five people were killed. Thereafter Whitfield preached on Boston Common, gathering around him crowds ranging from five thousand on the first day to twenty-three thousand on the last. Great crowds likewise attended the executions of such dangerous criminals as Quakers, several of whom were hanged by the Puritans on Boston Common in the seventeenth century. Such speakers and events attracted the curious in vast numbers. So many people walked away from one hanging that part of the bridge to what is now the North End collapsed under their weight.

The collapse of the drawbridge—which several Puritans noted crushed a notoriously "wicked woman"—illustrated the impossibility of building structures sound enough to hold thousands of people. The common provided Bostonians and their neighbors with a safe place of assembly to hear sermons and addresses and witness executions. Its dearth of trees—which made it an ideal training field for the militia and British regulars—ensured everyone a clear view, while providing just enough limbs to allow the magistrates to avoid paying for a gallows.

The Center
of the Town

As the nineteenth century opened, the old agricultural and ecclesiastical uses of greens diminished; but one vestige of Puritanism remained to reshape public use of the open spaces. In almost every New England town the road network converged on the site of the "first" church: the Puritan, and later Congregational, meetinghouse with its adjacent lot. By the middle of the eighteenth century, innkeepers had learned the usefulness of locating their establishments near the focal point of town activity. Sometimes religious congregations asked that a tavern be erected close to or even on the meetinghouse lot, since the structure offered better facilities for "nooning" than the simple warming houses. So close were the meetinghouse and tavern in Jaffrey, New Hampshire that the congregation actually moved the meetinghouse a short distance after the tavernkeeper complained that it blocked access to his business! Such taverns not only sheltered worshipers at noontime on the Sabbath; they housed wintertime court sessions when the judges found the meetinghouses too cold and drafty, and they refreshed and warmed militiamen training in winter. And since most town roads converged at the meetinghouse, the taverns on the greens served as inns for benighted travelers, who learned to assume that beside every meetinghouse spire stood an inn.

Taverns and inns advertised their services by setting up great signs at the edges of the greens. In Pittsfield, Hubbardston, Paxton, Petersham, and Rutland, signs towered over the greens. Perhaps the largest was the extraordinary sign in Barre, which stood, like those in Petersham and Rutland, on two parallel pillars each perhaps thirty-five feet tall, one capped by a windvane and the other by a directional device that pointed out what roads led to what towns. The inn sign dwarfed everything around it except the meetinghouse at the far end of the green, towering over stagecoaches, pedestrians, and newly planted ornamental trees. Not every New England green possessed such wondrous signs. Many, like that in Groton, boasted only small signboards, simple upright posts marked with arrows indicating what towns lay along the roads emanating from the green.

But the inn signs and signboards emphasized the evolving role of the green. No longer did the green serve only as a gathering place for such civil activities as summertime court sessions and occasional militia musters. Many had become traffic intersections, crossed like the green in Cambridge by a maze of dirt roads. The green in Billerica, for example, was crisscrossed by intersecting roads that led directly across the grass to the tall inn sign marking the destination or temporary stopping place of most travelers. By the early nineteenth century, the Billerica green lay chopped into at least five triangular lots separated by frequently traveled roads. Like many other New England greens, especially those in which the meetinghouse had always been separated from the green by a road running at right angles to the meetinghouse front door, the Billerica lot demonstrated the new power of road traffic to shape space. Since many travelers sought the best roads, and since the best roads were usually the ones most traveled, the roads around or through the greens carried more and more traffic. Few travelers were much interested in the meetinghouses, but they watched eagerly for taverns, knowing that they could find a cooling or warming drink, a hot meal, a warm bed, or correct directions. When the traveler saw a green beyond the trees, he knew a tavern or inn had to be close.

Road traffic caused a variety of industries to locate near greens. Sometimes two or more inns competed for travelers' money, but often the lone inn was joined by a blacksmith shop—the necessary resort of many horseback travelers riding rough roads—and eventually by a wheelwright-harnessmaker shop, too. Road traffic and local trade attracted other businesses to the location, until a tiny retail community collected at the edges of the green. By the middle of the nineteenth century, townspeople in many communities referred to the cluster of businesses around the meetinghouse and the green as "the center," a colloquialism that emphasized the centrality not of religion, but of business. A general store, sometimes a newspaper office, an attorney's office, and by the 1830s a bank might gather to acquire some share of the local and road trade. Often such enterprises were situated on small plots of land bought from owners of land that abutted the greens—or sometimes on pieces of the greens themselves.

Encroachment on town greens appeared first in coastal towns like Newburyport, not only because of the increased traffic and business generated by an ocean port, but because rope makers used the lot to establish ropewalks, the long outdoor contrivances on which they twisted rope. (The Newburyport ropewalk of 1771 stretched 608 feet along the east side of the green and terminated at another privately operated structure, a windmill.) Sometimes such businesses paid rent to the town, but often they existed on pieces of the green acquired by purchase from towns convinced that large greens served no useful purpose. So long as the militia mustered every three months according to law, town meetings resisted most encroachment or else compromised with the encroachers. The town of Harvard, for example, learned between 1775 and

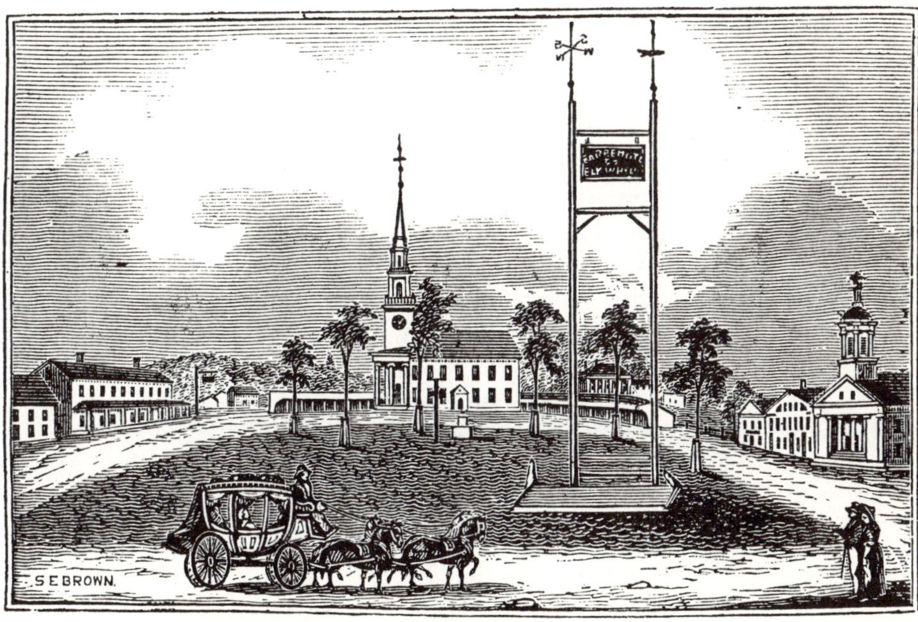

Taverns and inns found it profitable to locate where roads converged, usually adjacent to the meetinghouse and its green. Towering signs, like this one in Barre, were erected to attract customers—but they often detracted from the visual quality of the town.

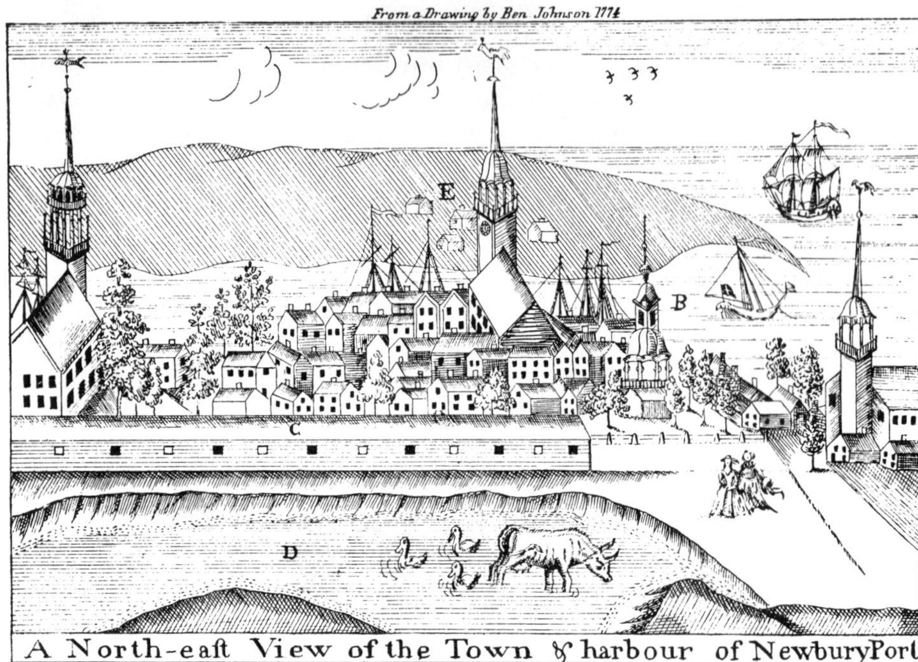

The late eighteenth century witnessed the onset of rope walks, long sheds in which rope was twisted, which were often built on the town's common land. This one in Newburyport stretched 608 feet along the east side of the common.

1782 that its original thirty-acre green had been reduced through sale, gift, and encroachment to sixteen and one-half acres. Some of the trespassers returned acreage they had illegally used, but others kept their encroachments after purchasing the land from the town. After the War of 1812, however, when a standing army and navy began defending the nation, the small triangles of land clipped from the green by intersecting roads disappeared into private hands eager to use the locations as building sites for inns and other businesses.

Despite commercial and industrial encroachment, the greens continued to host public gatherings. In 1809, for example, the agricultural reformer, Elkanah Watson, tied three Merino sheep to the Great Elm on the Pittsfield green and invited his neighbors to examine the superiority of the Spanish-bred creatures. From that tentative beginning developed the American country (or county) fair, designed to educate and stimulate the nation's farmers. New England greens offered the young "agricultural improvement societies" perfect places for their small shows of livestock and produce. In 1851 the townspeople of Amherst assembled to examine the displays of the fifth annual agricultural show; they found 500 cattle, 390 oxen, 123 horses, 600 showings of poultry, and hundreds of visitors trampling the ground into dust. But such shows soon outgrew the greens. The Marshfield Improvement Society acquired its own grounds, as did many other societies; New Englanders learned to visit the "fair grounds" for such events as horse racing and sledge pulling, and of course for the ever larger shows of livestock and farm produce. The acquisition of fair grounds lessened the need for public gatherings on the greens. Fair grounds often provided seating and other facilities the greens lacked, and events like Independence Day assemblies and fireworks displays shifted away from the centers of towns.

The popularity of the agricultural fair and its placement in a space of its own hint at a cultural division in nineteenth-century New England. Towns slowly divided into agriculturists and villagers; the former cherished traditional lifestyles and found themselves subtly belittled by the villagers interested in commerce and—increasingly—in manufacturing. Mill towns developed by nascent industrialists in the 1840s and later decades often lacked any greens at all; and older towns often pared their greens by selling portions of them or by using some acreage for school buildings and other town structures such as firehouses. Villagers began to perceive greens in new ways, and farming people gradually did, too.

The Spirit of Beautification

Low-keyed nostalgia signalled the change in perception. In the spring of 1797 the town meeting of Lexington voted to erect a monument commemorating the opening battle of the War of Independence. Two years later a simple monument stood on a gentle rise on the green, where a schoolhouse had once been. Townspeople did most of the work voluntarily. They graded the site for the stone, and consumed $19.62 worth of food and drink "furnished when fixing the ground for the monument" by the nearby tavernkeeper, who was reimbursed by the town meeting. The dedication on Independence Day required more publicly purchased refreshment and inspired townspeople to mark the battle with subsequent celebrations. In April 1822 they re-created the battle, directed by aged survivors, and two years later welcomed General Lafayette, who received the fourteen remaining survivors on the green under

A variety of popular and spectacular common activities in the late nineteenth and early twentieth centuries: the Smoker's Circle and Firemen's Muster at Boston, a balloon launching at Salem, and a patriotic pageant at Litchfield, Connecticut. (Salem photo courtesy Essex Institute, Salem, Mass)

Following the Civil War, many towns chose to honor veterans with this "everyman" type of statue found in Townsend, Massachusetts.

Nowhere were centennial celebrations more elaborate than in Lexington, Massachusetts, which proudly proclaimed itself the "Birthplace of American Liberty." The widely attended festivities included a speech by President Ulysses S. Grant, who fell through the platform created for the event.

a triumphal arch trimmed with evergreen branches and flowers. In 1835, on the sixtieth anniversary of the battle, the townspeople reinterred the bodies of the militiamen who died in the fight. A large mahogany sarcophagus containing their remains was buried on the green, beneath the monument erected in 1799.

Gradually, the townspeople of Lexington became aware that their green —even though it looked like any other in New England, divided by roads and already encroached upon—existed as a sort of national shrine. In 1820, they voted to erect a fence around it, to stop cross-cutting traffic and preserve it forever. But old attitudes endured, too; the town meeting voted down a proposal to paint the fence as intolerable extravagance. Ostensibly, the town voted to fence the lot in order to rent it as a cow pasture, and it devoted its annual twelve-dollar rental income to the education fund. Perhaps because it was painted in 1822, the wooden fence lasted for twenty years; then the town erected another, composed of stone posts and wood rails and designed to restrain the cattle still grazing on the lot.

But by 1840, nostalgia and a new craving for spatial beauty had begun to reshape greens everywhere. The farmers of any town saw the green perhaps once a week, when they arrived to shop and pick up mail; but the villagers saw it every day, and it was they who led the struggle to "improve" the green. Often nostalgic patriotism motivated the villagers, but sometimes it was disgust that prompted their efforts.

Until the 1840s, most observers who commented on the appearance of town greens reported them as anything but well kept. Occasionally a traveler reported conditions like those noted by a visitor in Litchfield, Connecticut, who lamented that "there are fragments of old fences, boards, woodpiles, heaps of chips, old sleds bottom upward, carts, casks, weeds, and loose stones lying along in wild confusion," all overrun by droves of sheep and hogs. As late as 1853, a traveler in Fairhaven, Vermont, discovered "great stumps . . . standing on the green," and dismissed the place as "an uneven and barren sand waste, lying open to the public, traversed by vehicles in all directions." The rank vegetation, mudholes, and rubbish resulted largely from the division of greens by roads. Once a green was cut up into a number of parcels too small for public use, it frequently became a sort of "no man's land," cared for by no one. Most greens never reached the nadir of the Litchfield and Fairhaven greens; but the ragged grass, half-dead trees, and other unsightly features disturbed enough villagers that a spirit of beautification slowly developed.

As early as 1794, the citizens of Canton planted trees on their green. An awareness of ancient trees as "living witnesses" of patriotic glory prompted some New Englanders to insist that trees under which militiamen had enlisted or gathered be preserved from harm. Cambridge understood the meaning of such trees as the "Whitfield Elm," under which the revivalist preached in 1740, but the most famous tree on the green was another elm under which Washington took command of the American revolutionary army. The tree lived for decades after, honored in poems by Holmes and Lowell, and carefully respected by everyone especially after the last veterans died and it became the only living witness to patriotism. Other towns honored their own so-called "marker trees," because such trees provided living—and therefore inexpensive—monuments to the militiamen who marched away to Lexington, to Concord, and to other battlefields. Other trees, like the Great Elm in Pittsfield to which Watson tied his sheep, lived on because they attracted the attention of beauty-interested individuals like Lucretia Williams, who threw herself in front of the axeman about to fell the tree in order to make space for a new meetinghouse. Her husband donated enough land to locate the new structure back from the tree, and helped spark interest in beautifying the entire green. Salem named its green "Washington Park" in 1802, a year after a militia colonel gave $2500 to level it and fill in its "ponds" to make the green a better training field. Eventually, the townspeople erected a fence with four ornamental gates, the western one surmounted by a carved medallion of Washington. The Lombardy poplars set out by the town in 1802 blew down in the Great Gale of September 23, 1815, and the townspeople replaced them with elms.

Slowly but certainly, the beautification movement reshaped the greens. Much of the driving force, however, originated with the villagers. People like Lucretia Williams and the well-to-do merchant families whose houses abutted the Salem green wanted to overlook pleasant open spaces, not mudholes. Their aesthetic sensibilities derived from the nation's understanding of romanticism and transcendentalism, and from a desire to make beautiful the places hallowed by patriotic sacrifice. Townspeople who lived far from the green often thought the improvements only extravagance, and in some towns—Norwell for example—the stone edging for the green was donated by a public-spirited citizen irritated by the town meeting's refusal to beautify the place. Towns that had large numbers of families living near their greens usually beautified them years, and sometimes decades, before towns in which the green lay far from the village, surrounded by only one or two businesses or houses.

No one knew what name to ascribe to the greatly improved lots. John Barber, an astute and painstakingly accurate observer of the New England landscape in the 1840s and the author of several illustrated books on the subject, used phrases like "open ground, or common," "enclosed green," and "small public green, enclosed by railing" to describe the lots of Ipswich, Framingham, and Leicester. "A small enclosed common, oval in its form, is in the central part of the area, around which the public buildings are situated," he remarked of Westfield. "It is newly set out with shade trees, and will add to the beauty of the place." Not every town had money enough to fence in its "common green." Many chose to avoid the Lexington solution of renting the grazing rights, especially if the green was too small to produce enough income to pay for the fence. In Woburn, for example, the town meeting chose to fence in each tree with protective stakes; and others, like Upton, simply set out saplings with no protection at all from grazing livestock and careless teamsters. Most towns planted elms, not only because such mature specimens as those at Pittsfield and Lancaster set a standard of arboreal beauty, but because long-lived elms seemed a better investment than Lombardy poplars and other species that did poorly in the severe climate.

The tentative beautification movements of the early nineteenth century blossomed in 1853, in Stockbridge. The first aim of the Laurel Hill Association was the improvement of a wooded hill near the center of town, but soon the association began planting trees along streets and improving the cultural activities scheduled in the town. Planting shade trees along well-traveled roads was not a new idea—as early as 1637, the town of Watertown, having in mind travelers on hot summer days, voted "to mark the shade trees by the roadside with a 'W' and fine any person who shall fell one of the trees thus marked eighteen shillings"—but planting trees for shade *and* beauty was new. Agricultural improvement societies had offered prizes for the best-managed woodlots; their efforts helped stimulate interest in high quality trees, as did the opening of such rural cemeteries as Mount Auburn in Cambridge. But village improvement societies—note well the difference in title that distinguishes them from societies devoted to bettering agriculture and farm life—acquired their inspiration partially from romanticism and partially from the simple belief that beautiful surroundings shape the human spirit. The quest for "moral improvement," therefore, produced a spatial improvement phenomenon that attracted many of the nation's intellectuals, including the landscape architect Frederick Law Olmsted, whose great Central Park in New York City origi-nated partly out of a belief that beautiful surroundings would help civilize New Yorkers. Some two hundred village improvement societies were active in the 1870s in New England. By the early part of the twentieth century, magazine writers correctly concluded that the societies had dramatically improved the New England village landscape.

Not every town took up the cause of beautification immediately. If the Laurel Hill Association was the first village improvement society (it seems certain that it was the first to organize itself officially and to publicize its efforts), it may have been because Stockbridge was already becoming a haven for upper-class urban dwellers anxious to busy themselves in the summer months. Poorer towns, especially poor towns with few villagers living near their greens, took longer to form societies. Their reluctance stemmed from a vague awareness that village improvement societies grounded their thinking in European romanticism accessible to the well read only, from an unwilling-ness to "waste" money, and from a smug satisfaction in the landscape of their parents' generation. Amherst formed its Ornamental Tree Association in 1857,

The Washington Elm on the Cambridge, Massachusetts common was much revered as the site at which George Washington took command of the army in 1775. New Englanders were dismayed to learn that elms were susceptible to Dutch Elm disease, and eventually even the Washington Elm was deemed hazardous and was removed.

attempting to improve its muddy green. A year after the association began considering improvements, the newspaper in town condemned the green as "a mere higglety-pigglety swamp, with patches of grass, gravel pits, muddy ponds, old frog holes, and swales," an understatement of some distinction. After rains the land flooded so badly that some Amherst college students painted a horse belonging to the president of their school, and launched the bedaubed creature around the largest pond, having first built a raft for it. Perhaps the largesse of water swayed the association; its first improvement was a fountain that did little to beautify the wasteland. In 1864, however, it set out fifty trees, many of them elms, and began shaping the place into something more attractive than a swamp.

Planting trees for the sake of public beauty was not actually novel. A few upper-class Bostonians had done so in the 1650s. But convincing the typical rural New Englander to spend public funds on ornamental trees proved nearly impossible throughout the nineteenth century. The example of Amherst makes clear the real division in many small towns between farmers and villagers. Quite clearly, the only way the villagers of Amherst could improve the green was by forming a private society and donating the improvements. The town meeting simply refused to waste money. The division is often ignored now, but its reality shaped the name of the entire beautification movement. The societies called themselves "village" improvement societies, not "town" improvement societies, and they typically limited their activities to improving the green and public land immediately adjacent to the "center" of town.

Only the aftermath of the Civil War convinced many town meetings to contribute to the improvement of greens, and even then the improvement was a limited one. Town meeting after town meeting voted to erect monuments to the war dead. Some towns built memorial buildings, usually town halls, but most erected statues acquired from national firms that specialized in producing likenesses of Union soldiers. Larger towns, and smaller ones with generous donors followed the lead of Pittsfield and commissioned a sculpture after viewing drawings submitted by a number of artists. Pittsfield delighted in its statue, a twenty-five-foot-high bronze color-sergeant holding aloft his flag and staring into the distance. Most communities honored enlisted men, not one slain soldier in particular, partly because town meetings wished to honor all veterans equally, and partly because custom-made statues proved too expensive for small-town budgets. Some communities erected obelisks like that specified by the Norwell town meeting, and—as Norwell did—placed them on the exact spot where the veterans had volunteered for service.

Cities erected vastly larger monuments, like that raised by Cambridge and dedicated on July 13, 1870. According to the official proceedings of that day, the committee charged with erecting the monument "endeavored to fix upon a position the most conspicuous that the Common could afford," and so sited the fifty-five-foot-high memorial "in the direct line of vision, as approached from North Avenue, Cambridge Street, Harvard Square, and the Appian Way, on the southeast section of the enclosure." The committee noted explicitly that the monument "has been built with great care," and that it ought to "endure for ages." With eternity in mind, the citizens of Cambridge inserted a time capsule in the cornerstone, and watched a derrick lower another stone onto it. On dedication day, they heard the mayor make clear the linking of revolutionary heroism with the valor that saved the Union. The Cambridge Common, like the greens of so many other towns, had become a monument to yet another war.

Until the first decades of the twentieth century, the New England green basked in the soft light of remembered patriotism, secure from neglect and usually free from further subdivision. Annual Independence Day celebrations linked Minutemen with the Grand Army of the Republic, and the Union veterans insisted that the monuments honoring their fallen comrades be well maintained, as well as their surroundings. Greens received the devoted attention of wealthy individuals, some of whom paid for granite curbings to be installed around them, and some of whom—like Jerome Wheelock of Grafton —provided improvement funds to be used after their deaths.

At least some of the late-nineteenth-century improvement of town greens depended on the generosity of businessmen who recalled with affection their childhoods and sent funds "home" from New York City, Chicago, and other great cities. During "Old Home Week," a festival of the era in which emigrants from small New England towns all returned on the same date to visit parents

The horse-drawn trolley is a picturesque addition to this view of Brattle Street, near the Cambridge Common.

But the tangle of electric wires that soon radiated out of Harvard Square was anything but scenic.

Some Massachusetts towns, such as Montague, remained unchanged by time.

The cows grazing on the Deerfield Common still appeared at home about 1906.

and other family, to gather for clambakes and dancing, and to socialize with each other, the donors examined their improvements and received the good wishes of thankful townspeople. Many towns received gifts of libraries, town halls, and improved greens from men and women grateful for happy, secure childhoods. The town of Norwell was perhaps most fortunate; donors bequeathed funds for a library, town hall, and substantial improvements to the town green. Such benefactors were often motivated by the old village-improvement-society belief that fine surroundings produce fine character. Long after some towns had dissolved their societies, their greens remained handsomely kept because some far-off former townsman had created a fund to hire someone to scythe grass, prune trees, and paint the flagpole every other year.

July 4, 1876 encouraged a spate of improvements, too. The centennial of independence prompted Congress and President Grant to urge all Americans to "publicly assemble" in honor of the occasion. Most New England communities celebrated with parades of Civil War veterans, orations, and with the planting of "centennial elms." Grant perhaps aided the elm-planting fashion, because he himself planted an elm on Lexington Green on April 19, 1875, the anniversary of the battle fought there a century earlier. The townspeople of Lexington took the precaution of preserving the sapling within a network of wire, in order that it might prosper and live as long as the great Washington Elm in Cambridge. But the tree planting may have been prompted, too, by a growing awareness that even elms die. In 1869, for example, the Whitfield Elm was removed from the Cambridge green because it impeded road traffic, and around the same time the Great Elm in Pittsfield, having suffered a lightning bolt strike some years before, was felled. The ancient elms on New England greens threatened to lose half-live limbs during storms, and felling them became a sad but necessary matter of insuring public safety.

As years passed, the centennial trees matured and shaded the annual Memorial and Independence Day convocations. Their presence, like the presence of the Civil War monuments, ensured the careful maintenance of the greens. Henry James, writing about New England town landscapes in 1907 in *The American Scene*, noted simply that "having spoken of them as 'elm-shaded,' you have said so much about them that little else remains." Somehow the towering elms that shaded greens and streets seemed to intensify the silence of depopulation, the abandonment of farming, and the days marked only by the arrival and departure of infrequent trains. So many New Englanders had moved to the West in search of better land, or to manufacturing cities in search of higher paying jobs, that many towns were reverting to forest. In such towns, particularly those in the hill country of New Hampshire and Vermont, the well-kept greens struck visitors as oases of order in a landscape becoming disheveled, almost wild.

Had James looked more closely, however, he might have discerned real threats to the simple greens. As early as 1901, the landscape architect Frederick Law Olmsted, Jr. worried about the susceptibility of elms to insects like the leopard moth and elm-leaf beetle. Almost every green in New England had been planted by amateurs, not professional landscape architects, and in almost every instance, the regional love of elms had dictated a potentially deadly situation. While Olmsted's illustrious father had specified a diversity of tree species for Central Park, the younger landscape architect learned that New England towns insisted on elms despite the likelihood of disease. He recommended elms to the town of Amherst because "there is no other sort of tree which so well gives the effect of a lofty overarching canopy of foliage." Not until seven years later did Amherst citizens detect the first signs of large-scale blight, and then only among chestnut trees; but ten years later scarcely a chestnut lived, even in the forests far from the green. The simply planted greens represented a type of design that owed almost nothing to professional designers; they also represented the insidious potential of mono-culture that professional landscape architects understood and attempted to avoid.

Catastrophe struck between 1870 and 1920, when scores of elms, including famous ones like the Great Elm on Boston Common, became diseased and began to topple during storms. A few towns, like Grafton, congratulated themselves that their eighteenth-century patriots had assembled beneath oaks, not elms, but the widespread blights afflicting elms threatened many greens with total deforestation. The elm-shaded beauty lauded by James and

A rapid development transformed numerous village centers, leading Harvard residents to issue this poster advocating zoning bylaws.

other observers vanished rapidly. No longer did greens exhibit the living witnesses to Revolutionary War events. Some greens had no trees that had witnessed War of 1812 enlistments.

Other changes threatened greens as well. The perfection of the telephone and transmitted electricity ensnared many greens in a complex network of utility lines supported by half-smoothed, often crooked wooden poles. And electricity made possible the trolley car, perhaps the almost-perfect rural transportation vehicle. Interurban trolleys ran nearly everywhere in New England, humming through woods and fields, operating alongside—and sometimes in—roads. The cars required a catenary of electric wires, supported by yet more wooden poles; and the catenaries helped finish off many diseased street trees whose falling branches snapped the fragile copper wire. Rural trolley cars required no stations, but lines frequently joined and divided at major road intersections, and trolley car companies discovered the advantages of building loops around greens. Cambridge Common, a green totally encircled by trolley wires today, was one of the first to become a rotary for electric cars.

Before the popularization of the motor car, most towns used their greens on ceremonial occasions and sometimes on summer afternoons and evenings. Most recreation was passive, finding expression during the 1870s and later decades in bandstands that sheltered brass bands playing the martial music the nation had loved since the Civil War. Now and then, New Englanders used the greens a little more actively. On July 4, 1876 the townspeople of Waltham erected a large tent on their green in which to hear orations, worship ecumenically, and dance in celebration of the centennial of liberty. But most often, New Englanders strolled on their greens, if they used them at all. As early as 1838, the town officials of Newburyport laid out a walk and planted trees on their green, and a year later they exchanged a fragment of the green for private land in order to make a more convenient promenade. Year after year, Newburyport made its green more enjoyable for strolling, adding an enclosing fence, then a granite curb, and later even water lilies in the former frog pond. On Independence Day the citizens assembled to hear music on the green and watch fireworks, but even then the enjoyment was quiet. Even the trolley car companies recognized how little the greens were used. Their guidebooks emphasize the visual beauties of the greens passed by their lines, but never suggest that passengers alight to walk about them.

Automobiles and the new pastime of "motoring" changed the use of greens—and their appearance. No one could enjoy music while automobiles passed around the greens, drowning out the bandstand melodies composed by John Philip Sousa and others. At least the trolleys had slipped by silently and without generating fumes. As motor cars increased in number and speed, many greens suddenly seemed either gigantic obstructions to traffic or else potentially useful traffic islands. Pittsfield rounded the already curved edges of its green in order to speed motor traffic; in many other towns highway engineers broadened curves and intersections at the expense of greens. By the 1920s, many New Englanders recognized that their greens had become almost inaccessible. To reach them meant crossing one or more of the busy lanes of traffic that attracted more and more stores to the streets fronting on the greens. The busiest roads became designated as state highways, carrying ever larger numbers of cars and trucks through the "centers." Often the greens remained visually attractive, but they were too noisy for quiet sitting or strolling. As

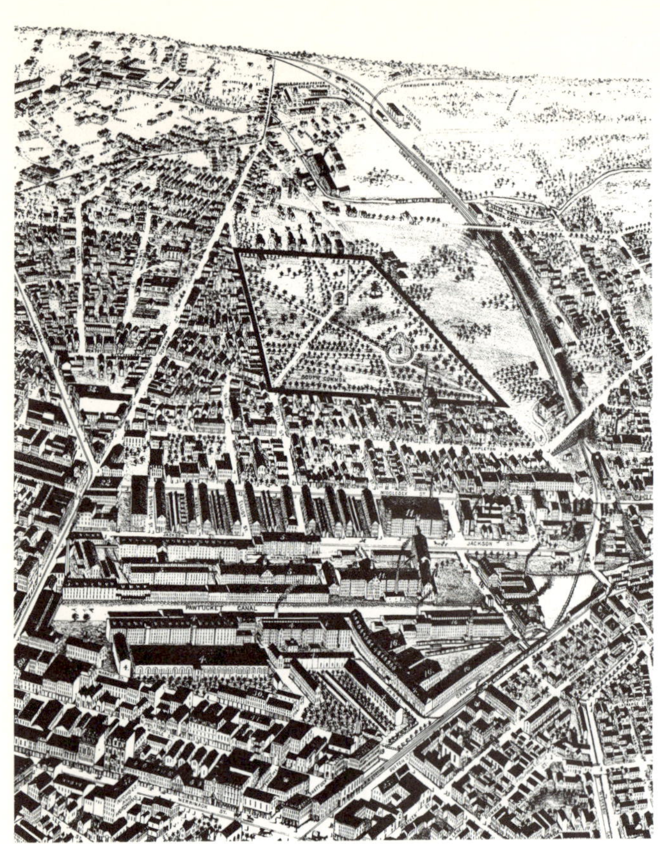

*Today some traditional commons have been altered bey-
ond recognition. The South Common in Lowell,
Massachusetts, a grassy park in the mid-nineteenth century* (outlined in black), *has kept pace with this changing
city and today serves as the site of a housing project,
school, football field, and swimming pool.*

stores spread down the streets that led to the greens, fewer and fewer people
lived near them; on Sundays, when stores were closed and traffic was lighter,
few people arrived to stroll. Of course, retail trade meant that shoppers and
store employees used the greens as lunchtime picnic spots on a spring day or to
wait for a bus, but sustained relaxation soon connoted private backyard recreation. Only in isolated towns like Montague, where no new businesses
arrived to join the bank and general store, did greens retain their simple
loveliness. Along with ramshackle fishing docks, run-down dairy barns, and
stone walls, quiet, "unspoiled" greens like those in many western New
England small towns became part of the calendar-image vision of New
England. Potential tourists saw the calendar photographs and reserved rooms
in the ancient inns that fronted greens still quiet and lovely.

Many greens retained their aging and sometimes slightly dilapidated
beauties until the autumn of 1938, when an awe-inspiring hurricane swept
over New England, blowing salt air as far inland as Montpelier, Vermont, and
toppling disease-weakened elms along with healthy oaks and other trees.
When the storm passed, many town greens lay in ruins. The 120-mile-an-hour
wind destroyed fifteen hundred trees in the town of Amherst alone, as well as
many of the trees on the Amherst green. After the cleanup ended, the real
horror of the deforestation became clear, for only then did New Englanders
notice the ugliness so long hidden by the trees on every green. The unmasked
utility poles seemed impossible to hide with the maple saplings set out on some
greens; and townspeople confronted vistas marred by traffic lights, road signs,
and parking meters. Tree wardens and park departments did what they could
to save damaged trees, but the scars took years to heal. Again, greens in rural,
western New England, where the hurricane was less intense, weathered the

storm far better, their beauty making the ravaged eastern greens look even more ugly by comparison.

Only in a few towns did informally organized groups try to restore something of the nineteenth-century beautiful simplicity. Women's and garden clubs planted flowers and sometimes set out young trees, and businessmen supported their efforts by donating funds and materials. But many greens lost their chief constituencies as religious congregations, schools, and libraries frequently relocated to larger sites away from town centers. Suburbanization shifted the focus of town life from a single center of religious, civil, and educational activity to a number of centers; even Independence Day and Memorial Day celebrations relocated to cemeteries or school fields. Active recreation of the sort popular after the middle 1950s bypassed most greens, except those large enough to accommodate a small playground and perhaps a softball field. Greens became almost invisible—places bypassed by motorists, unvisited by bicyclists and pedestrians, and crossed only by an occasional jogger and by the tender of the flag.

<table>
<tr><td>Greens
Today</td><td>New England lacks the Spanish tradition of the corso, the evening walk about a central plaza, the time of quiet conversation, of flirtation, of showing off new clothes. A stroll in a New England town leads down quiet sidewalks or across open meadows or along a beach, perhaps, but it never takes place in the company of large groups of people. As a casual meeting place, the contemporary New England green is far less popular than beaches, playing fields, and shopping mall concourses.</td></tr>
</table>

Yet townspeople are keeping many greens alive in other ways. The national bicentennial stirred up nostalgia and patriotism, causing some communities to reexamine their greens much as they had done a hundred years before, and provided federal funding for appropriate projects. Townspeople in Keene, New Hampshire elected to construct a traditional style bandstand for

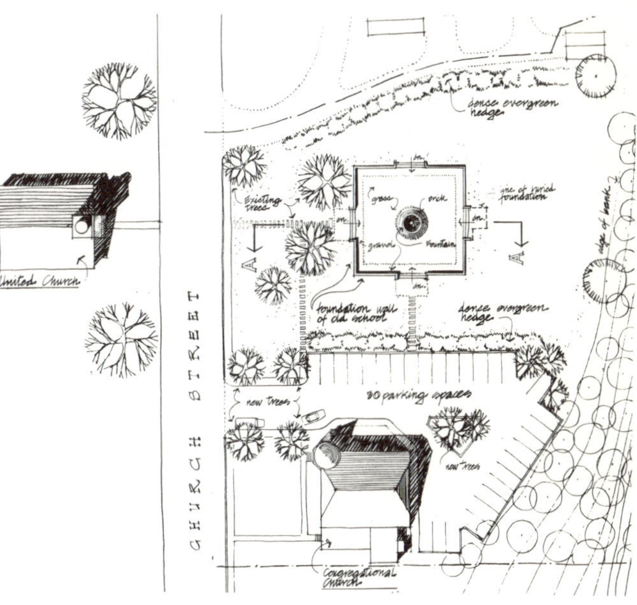

In Bethel, Vermont a schoolhouse fire provided an empty site and the opportunity to create a new town amenity. The town purchased the land, which had been a common until a school was built there more than a century ago. Bethel spent $18,000 on demolition, landscaping, and development; the result was a new common on the site of the old, complete with a relocated fountain and the old school foundations defining the space. Town residents use the space for concerts, puppet shows, and dances.

the common there, and Salem, Massachusetts received money to repair its elaborate cast-iron fence. The city of Cambridge undertook a major rehabilitation of its common that had been in the planning stages for several years but was hastened in order to make the space respectable for the 1976 festivities.

One can still hear summer band concerts in Union, Maine; Petersham, Massachusetts; and Wolcott, Connecticut, to name a few; Union is also one of several towns where one can attend a Christmas carol gathering on the green. There are annual flea markets in Chelsea, Vermont and Barre, Massachusetts; puppet shows on the new common in Bethel, Vermont; and church suppers in Monroe, Connecticut. Spring, summer, and fall fairs are abundant, although the horse and cattle shows of the nineteenth century have largely been supplanted by arts and crafts exhibitions. In Vermont there were fairs in at least ten towns this past year, including the twenty-ninth annual Cracker Barrel Bazaar in Newbury with its popular fiddlers' contest. The town clerk in Wakefield, Massachusetts reports that the green there is used "for everything": art exhibitions, fairs, sport, and passive activities.

The historic districts movement has also thrust some greens into the limelight. As is discussed more fully in the section that follows, many town centers and architecturally significant neighborhoods have been designated as historic districts within the past ten years, and this status both calls attention to the appearance of the area and affords some protection. As communities develop a greater appreciation for the brick row houses and sturdy mill buildings that have been neglected for the past fifty years, they may also rediscover the greens that lie in their midst.

Today some greens merely slumber day after day, but others show new signs of life. There is no single use for commons today, no uniform appearance, any more than there was three centuries ago. But commons remain a part of New England life, still at the heart of many communities, often revealing in their appearance and uses the people's covenant with their shared space.

Guidelines for Greens

by Thomas M. Paine, A.S.L.A.
and Lauri A. Halderman
with vignettes by Lauri A. Halderman

NEW ENGLAND GREENS AND COMMONS ARE A DISTINCTIVE LAND FORM, THE product of a particular set of traditions and values. Whether one of these grassy squares is known as a green *or* a common is today simply a matter of semantics, and for the sake of brevity we shall refer to them collectively as "greens." But semantics aside a green is not a park, nor a garden, nor an athletic field. It should neither look like Central Park nor be subjected to weekly football matches; it is a green, and should be designed and used as such.

Just what should a green look like? What species of trees are traditional? What materials should be used for a bench or a fence? We realized, as we toured New England to look at contemporary greens and dug into local and regional photo archives, that there has never been a single style or appearance to which all greens should conform. The greens in Deerfield, Massachusetts and Temple, New Hampshire are both outstanding—yet they are by no means identical. Based on the historical origins of the space, the nature of the architectural context, and the realities of current use, each community will arrive at a somewhat different solution to the question of how its green should look.

The statue of the Minuteman, by Henry Hudson Kitson, at the Lexington Battle Green. Another Kitson statue presides over Washington Square in Salem.

A large green can sometimes support more than one focal point. In Cohasset, Massachusetts, church and flagpole coexist in harmony.

This is not to say, though, that anything goes. There is a certain vocabulary and sensibility that dictates the parameters of acceptable design, and the greens in many towns reveal that someone there intuitively understands this. Simplicity is the key. A good stand of native deciduous trees, furnishings that are traditional in materials—cast iron, wood, granite—and design, a well-tended carpet of grass: these are the elements that make up a handsome green. If the powers that be in every town shared this sense, there would be no need for these guidelines. As is apparent, though, in Keene, New Hampshire, where an abstract sculptural fountain crowds the traditional bandstand, and in Bristol, Rhode Island, where a basketball court has claimed a substantial corner of the common, some communities may need more explicit direction. We hope they find these guidelines helpful.

Analyzing a green is the first step, as we discuss in each of the ten sections of this chapter. Does the green have a focal point, or does it need one? Too many road signs? Not enough trees? Only after a careful scrutiny of the green, perhaps accompanied by research to discover the space's unique historical identity, can one decide what is appropriate and then propose changes.

Some communities may find, or already know, that no improvements are needed; others will find that a bit of work is in order. Getting a green in shape is not, however, the end of the effort; all will go for naught unless measures are taken to ensure the green *stays* that way. The first necessity is a thorough routine of landscape maintenance, and a sample program, arranged in calendar fashion, is included in this book (see Guidelines Appendix). Year-round attention such as this will attend to the needs of the turf, trees, and other plants, while additional touch-up work may be needed for benches, fences, and other furnishings. This maintenance will protect the green from the ravages of weather and activity-related stress. It will not, however, protect the green from larger dangers—the appropriation of part of it for a parking lot, or the construction of an unsightly information booth—or preserve the surrounding architectural context. An attractive green enclosed by pseudocolonial facades, oversized signs, and a sea of asphalt is like a picture in a garish frame: the entire ensemble suffers. What is needed is a greater magnitude of protection, such as that afforded by the historic district.

Since the first historic district was established in this country, in Charleston, South Carolina in 1931, some greens in each New England state have been encompassed by historic districts—most within the past ten to fifteen years, following the passage of the National Historic Preservation Act in 1966, which provided funds used to conduct statewide surveys of buildings and sites. Basically, a historic district is a designated area of buildings, structures, sites, or objects that have architectural or historic significance. There are two types of historic districts, those listed in the National Register of Historic Places and those designated locally; both afford protection for structures within district boundaries, but the type and degree of protection differs. National Register status prevents demolition of any building as part of a project that uses federal funds and provides tax incentives to owners who choose to rehabilitate their buildings. A review agency, the Advisory Council on Historic Preservation, is authorized to comment upon federally funded projects that will affect National Register buildings or districts—and a negative comment is sometimes enough to alter the project's course. This might have been the case in Middletown, Connecticut, as we discuss in a vignette in this chapter, where a Housing and Urban Development (HUD) project included a proposal to demolish the

Originally located elsewhere in town, this period fountain is an appropriate addition to the common in Bethel, Vermont.

Well-intentioned benefactors in Keene, New Hampshire have overburdened this small common with a contemporary stone fountain, traditional bandstand, Civil War statue, cannon and cannonballs, benches, fences, and barrels. Some of these embellishments should be relocated.

historic Mather-Douglas House. Preservationists took the case to court and won, and part of the judge's ruling was that HUD should have contacted the advisory council since the area in question was part of the South Green Historic District.

The National Register offers only limited safety to a historic district, since, for example, if an owner wishes to demolish a building with his own money the listing has no legal bearing. National Register status does, however, carry prestige, and preservationists often bolster their claims that a building is of merit by citing this official recognition. The numbers alone are impressive: in Massachusetts, there are currently more than 1,000 listings on the National Register, about 800 of which are individual buildings and 200 are areas, for a total of about 15,000 properties. The Massachusetts Historical Commission has recently come to favor the creation of multiple resource areas, in which an entire town or city is surveyed and all those properties deemed eligible for the National Register are nominated simultaneously. When the multiple resource area was approved for the city of Cambridge, more than 800 properties were listed. "Personally," says Patricia Weslowski of the commission, "I feel that looking at a whole community at once makes good sense." She notes that this technique not only saves time and paperwork but also ensures that the criteria used for evaluating buildings throughout the city are the same.

Greater control is offered by the local historic district, enabled by legislation at the state level. Five of the six New England states, Vermont being the exception, currently have local as well as National Register historic districts; and though the specific legislation varies from state to state, the basic premises are the same. In Massachusetts, a historic district can be established by a vote of two-thirds of a city council in a city or two-thirds of a town meeting in a town. Each town has its own historic district commission of three to seven members, usually including nominees submitted by the local historical society, the regional chapter of the American Institute of Architects, and the board of Realtors; and owners of buildings within the district must obtain a "certificate of appropriateness" from the commission in order to make any alterations to exterior architectural features. No buildings may be torn down or new structures erected within the district without a similar certificate. If the commission desires it can issue written guidelines, but many prefer simply to decide each case on an individual basis.

It all sounds rather stringent; it's meant to be so. And, reports Frank Beard of the Maine Historic Preservation Commission, the local historic districts have received a tremendous amount of community support. Since they are established at the local level—not to be taken lightly, given what Beard calls the "Maine personality"—the historic commissions are highly respected. Beard feels the districts succeed not only in providing design quality control but also by promoting awareness of the need for historic preservation. Clark Strickland of the Connecticut Historical Commission agrees the commissions are, on the whole, effective, citing their involvement in lawsuits such as that in Norwich (see vignette in this chapter) and their ability to effect changes in proposed plans. Despite a stricter enabling law in Connecticut, which states that a district can be formed only if seventy-five percent of the property owners in the proposed area vote affirmatively, there are currently sixty-eight districts in forty-five towns; more than a quarter of these districts include a green or small park. "The local historic district has infinitely more influence than the National Register," reports John Anderson of the historic district commission in Concord, Massachusetts. Yet in Concord there is no resentment of that power. "The feeling is that the commission is a tool, not a barrier." The commissions, Anderson says, act in the interest of buildings that are historic and also ones that are simply good housing or interesting. He is coordinating a program of workshops and a newsletter for all the local district commissions in Massachusetts so that members can exchange news and ideas. Finally, Ted Sanderson of the Rhode Island Historical Preservation Commission adds that the full effect of the local historic district cannot be assessed. Many atrocious remodeling and construction plans are

In Litchfield, Connecticut, the green is large enough for several embellishments, but they should not be so scattered as to create the appearance of a cemetery.

Clustering them is more successful, as demonstrated by these ground plaques in Lexington.

undoubtedly never proposed, he says, simply because of the district's existence.

There are communities, however, that have opposed the establishment of historic districts. Some object simply to the increased paperwork and delay that can be caused by the reviewing commissions; but more serious is the resistance to the perceived ability of the commissions to determine to some extent what an owner may or may not do with his private property. Architects have complained that rigid design controls stifle their creativity; building owners assert that historic district status constitutes the taking of private property without due compensation, prohibiting, for example, an owner from demolishing an existing structure and erecting one of greater value. The complaints regarding the guidelines have been justified in some communities, and the answer is to develop design criteria that are flexible enough to accommodate new construction that is compatible yet varied. As to the arguments of the constitutionality of historic districts, it has long been the right of the United States government to regulate private property for the public good. So long as the courts continue to agree that historic districts and architectural preservation do indeed promote the general welfare by preserving environmental amenities, property owners will have to be content with some amount of private sacrifice. In most communities, residents have found that the restrictions are worth the results—which include increased property values as a result of the appearance of the entire district.

A landscape maintenance program and historic district are effective tools for protecting the green, but what is needed most of all is a group of townspeople who will look after the green as if it were their own. In most towns the green is only one of many parks tended by the department of public works, the focus of garden club activities once a year, or the place everyone notices when attending the church fair. But what every town needs is a constituency, a group large or small that keeps an eye on the green throughout the year and can provide occasional assistance. In towns with local historic districts the district commission fills this role to some degree, but its function is only to oversee proposals and projects, not to originate them. Perhaps an existing

organization—historical society, garden club, or civic association—can "adopt"
the green, and perhaps all it needs to do is persistently remind town officials to
repair the fence and speak out against the addition of yet another monument.
In towns with financial troubles, though, this group can help keep the green
alive. Members could, for example, donate some new trees to the green, a
frequent practice in the nineteenth century kept alive in Boston by the Friends
of the Public Garden. This nonprofit citizens group oversees the Boston
Common as well as the adjacent Public Garden and works with the parks
department to attend to the needs of the city's most prominent open spaces.
The Friends, like any nonprofit corporation, are eligible to receive grants and
donations—and to seek them out, which officers actively do. Organized in the
early 1970s, the Friends of the Public Garden now has approximately 2,000
dues-paying members, including between fifty and one hundred out-of-state
well-wishers.

Most towns do not need an organization of this magnitude, but the idea is
a good one. Greens began as spaces that were the responsibility of community
members, and perhaps it is time for a group of proprietors in each town to
stepforward again. In the following pages, we shall address ten major areas in
which citizens can take specific actions to maintain and preserve their greens:
focus, landscape, footpaths, furnishings, interpretation, encroachment, traffic, townscape, use, and maintenance are the categories we have designed.
With each of these sections we have provided one or two vignettes, to illustrate
our points with graphic instances of steps taken by actual communities. These
guidelines and examples will suggest to communities what they might do and
how to do it, but they are inanimate; they need Friends of the Green to put
them into action.

FOCUS

Introduction   The classic village green is dominated by a monument, flagpole, bandstand,
fountain, or adjacent building such as a church. These prominent features,
usually located at the center or head of the green, serve three important
functions. First, the dominant feature serves as a focus for the viewer's
attention, providing a desirable sense of orientation within the space. Second,
the character of the green is often determined by this feature. A Civil War

*Sculpted shrubs in Canton, Connecticut create an overly
formal appearance; natural shaped species are more in
keeping with the character of greens. The "God Bless
America" sign is equally questionable.*

*Shrubs should be confined to the ground and not in-
cluded in raised planters, where they will appear
awkward as they do here in Bridgewater, Massachusetts.*

monument creates a sense of dignity, while a bandstand, for example, is more cheerful. Finally, the dominant feature is frequently the most distinctive element on the green. It is this fountain or statue that is the most clearly remembered and that gives the green a unique identity. In Lexington, Massachusetts, the Minuteman statue on the green is associated not only with the green but also with the entire town.

Today many greens lack this focal point, either because they have no distinctive feature or, as is more often the case, they have too many features vying for attention. The guidelines that follow discuss how to preserve an existing focal point and how to redress certain problems if it is lacking.

FOCUS GUIDELINE 1
Maintain the dominance of an effective focal point.

New furnishings for the green should be compatible with the existing dominant feature and sense of orientation. The height and weight of any features to be introduced should be of a scale that is secondary to the dominant focal object, and the materials should be complementary. It is not necessary that the new material be identical to the old, although this is one option: a new granite-post fence, for example, is likely to be a fine addition to a green with a granite memorial. It is equally acceptable, though, to introduce a fence of wood, provided that it does not overwhelm the monument.

The location of new additions such as monuments must also be carefully considered. If located near the existing dominant feature, these are almost certain to conflict, and it is better to find a more distant site. Too many monuments scattered at equal distance will, however, create the appearance of a cemetery more than a green; unless the green is quite large, it is advisable to find another location altogether. Exceptions include a minor addition such as a ground plaque, which can be located near a large monument and will add to its dominance, and benches that can be grouped effectively around a monument or flagpole.

FOCUS GUIDELINE 2
If the green has no focal point, consider creating one.

Some greens are simply open expanses of grass, with little more than a few trees or shrubs. While it is possible to have an attractive green with no principal feature, such a focal object is often a worthwhile addition. A simple flagpole marks the space as being more than just a patch of grass, while a bandstand can be useful as well as attractive.

If a major new element is to be selected, the highest quality materials and standards of design should be employed. Suitable options are discussed in detail in the "Furnishings" section of this chapter.

Any embellishment should be suited to the green in both appearance and function, and the selection of a new principal feature is a good opportunity to involve members of the community in the green's maintenance. An open meeting for review of proposals or a mail-back flyer can help determine what type of feature is most wanted or needed. Furthermore, involving towns-people in the decision can engender a sense of ownership for the new feature—a good deterrent to neglect and vandalism.

Care should be taken, however, in involving the public in the actual design of the feature. Public service organizations are often eager to donate a statue or amenity to the green, and their generosity should be appreciated; but many greens suffer from well-intentioned embellishments that are inappropriate. Do not add a statue or amenity simply because it is available or because a group is willing to donate a new one of their own design. Instead, enlist the services of a professional designer, and channel the enthusiasm of public service organizations and historical societies into raising funds to hire a designer of top quality.

It is, of course, possible that a suitable fountain already exists or that a local contractor will create an historically accurate bandstand—but these are the exceptions rather than the rule.

FOCUS GUIDELINE 3
If several embellishments compete for dominance, relocate or reorganize them.

The majority of greens have at least one monument or flagpole. In some towns, though, the green plays host to an information booth, Civil War monument, fountain, flagpole, and assorted plaques and markers—all on one or two acres. So many embellishments are bound to create a hodgepodge that does not do justice to any of the individual features.

Clustering several of these embellishments can often solve this problem. Together, two or three markers can define a small space within the context of the larger area, to which benches might be added. If there is not sufficient room on the green for this new configuration, or if it would upset the balance of the dominant embellishment, consider relocating some or all of the features. A small, adjacent traffic island or other parks within the town are sometimes appropriate locations. Not all embellishments look good side by side. Care must be taken to group those of similar or compatible materials and styles.

Markers signifying an exact historic site on a green, such as the location of the first meetinghouse or a famous tree, should not be relocated. If such a marker appears isolated and is not in a location that permits other features to be grouped with it, it can perhaps be set flush with the ground or framed with crushed gravel or stonedust.

The relocating of embellishments should be accomplished without offending any organizations that originally contributed these features. Be sure to consult the Veterans of Foreign Wars, the American Legion, the Daughters of the American Revolution, or any other groups involved.

FOCUS GUIDELINE 4
Provide additional focus by enclosing the green with a fence, rows of trees, or both.

Fences and trees are often unobtrusive, but they perform the valuable functions of framing the space and setting it off from its surroundings. Narrow greens in particular suffer from the visual and aural encroachment of street traffic, and fences and closely spaced trees can act as a buffer. Greens with a great number of embellishments also benefit from such enclosure, since the repetition of posts and rails or tree trunks helps to unify an otherwise disjointed space.

For further discussion of enclosure by fences and trees, see the "Detail" and "Encroachment" sections of this chapter.

The original West Gate on Washington Square, depicted by John Warner Barber in the 1830's.

A Resurrected Arch
Salem, Massachusetts

When Samuel McIntire erected the East and West Gateways on the Salem Common in 1805, the handsome structures did "much to honor his taste," according to a contemporary observer, as well as to embellish the town's central open space. The wooden gateways did not withstand the New England climate, though, and by the 1850s they had deteriorated and were removed. Little more remained than two carved fragments and a daguerreotype—until 1976, when a group of Salem residents and officials decided it was time once again to establish a dominant feature on the common.

The inspiration for the original West Gateway was a visit to Salem's common by none other than George Washington, who was greeted with much fanfare by the townspeople on October 29, 1789. Within the next few years it was proposed to erect some sort of monument in honor of the first president, and Salem residents apparently were pleased with the suggestion of gateways for the common. Contributions were solicited in 1805 and the design of the gateways was undertaken by Samuel McIntire, a Salem builder-architect renowned for his skill in carving architectural ornamentation.

For one face of the West Gateway McIntire carved a relief profile medallion of Washington's head, probably deriving the design from an existing engraving; for the other, he carved the state seal. These were affixed on either side near the apex of the gateway, and a carved, gilded eagle stood astride the peak, as seen in early views. Located opposite Brown Street, the main approach to the common, the commanding West Gateway served as both a culmination of the vista and a formal entrance to the common, recently beautified and renamed Washington Square.

By the 1970s Washington Square had become a shadow of its former self. Many of the mature trees had died, the cast-iron fence was dilapidated, and the walkways and turf showed serious signs of wear. Washington Square mirrored the condition of the city, which was in "a dejected state," according to Robert B. Murray, who was consequently brought in as the director of the "Visible Cities" program in Salem. Designed to provide an economic shot in the arm to several cities throughout Massachusetts, Visible Cities in Salem provided funds to upgrade a number of key structures. Additionally, the state bicentennial commission made some federal money available for appropriate projects. It was in response to this offer that Salem resident Fred Johnson first suggested replicating one of the old McIntire arches.

Bob Murray was enthusiastic about the idea, and

he interested another Salem resident and skilled sculptor, Raymond Parga. They first investigated creating new medallions by casting the originals, which were in the possession of a local museum; but there was some fear of causing damage to the pieces, and the method proved too costly. Parga then set to carving new medallions modeled after the old, and he also fashioned a gilded eagle for the top. Meanwhile, the Army Corps of Engineers provided advice and assistance in erecting the plywood-sheathed steel body of the arch, while others researched historically accurate paint colors.

The arch was dedicated with much ceremony on July 4, 1976. Draped like a statue, it was theatrically unveiled as a town parade finished winding its way to Washington Square. Smaller than the arch of the previous century, and relocated to a corner that is now more prominent than the earlier site, the new McIntire Arch reigns over the square in a somewhat different manner from its predecessor—but, as was clear from its Fourth of July reception, it is equally successful.

In the early stages of the project, Bob Murray worried that the arch might be deemed a white elephant, an embellishment that would receive a cold reception in a town with many pressing needs. But, as he notes with pleasure, the McIntire Arch has done more than just add a bit of color to the historic square. At the time of installation, Murray and other members of Salem's bicentennial commission thought it would be wonderful if the project could provide job opportunities for some of the many townspeople who were then unemployed. The directors therefore secured, through the state bicentennial commission, a special federal grant to hire five unemployed construction tradesmen to carry out the physical labor; the number of housepainters and masons who applied for these few positions indicated the popularity of such a scheme. The arch also inspired an additional project; after it was erected the entire southwest corner of the square was rehabilitated. A new brick pathway with granite edging was laid, an access ramp for the handicapped was cut into the curbing, and new bollards were installed to protect the area from encroaching automobiles.

Murray recognizes, though, that there was a larger underlying reason that the arch project was important. Washington Square is not a secluded preserve but rather a central, viable, open space that was formerly the showpiece of the town. Its degeneration

Salem's new arch.

was indicative of Salem's general state, and he hoped that a bright new corner would have positive implications for the town. "The common is a uniting point in the center of Salem," Murray observed, "and I felt that if we could bring vitality back to the common it would all come together."

While the blue-and-white arch cannot claim all of the credit, it does seem that Salem began to get back on its feet not long after the bicentennial. Today the downtown has a new indoor shopping complex, a pedestrian district, and contemporary construction surrounded by older renovated buildings, in a combination that the redevelopment authority asserts is so successful that it is "easy to forget what Salem looked like just ten years ago." Future plans include an extensive rejuvenation of Washington Square, so that the entire seventeen acres may one day do justice to the dominant yet elegant McIntire Arch.

LANDSCAPE

Introduction

As we discussed in the introduction to this chapter, a green is neither a park nor a garden. This distinction is particularly evident in the type and arrangement of plants and trees.

While a garden may include flowering plants of every hue, a green is traditionally just that—green. It needs no tulips, rhododendrons, or magnolias; instead, the mainstays of the green are deciduous trees, with a carpet of grass and perhaps a few shrubs. These shrubs and trees should be neither elaborately geometric in arrangement, like those at Versailles, nor clustered dramatically in the picturesque English tradition. Most greens are not very large—three or four acres is average—so trees are not used to create or accentuate grand vistas, as they do in Olmsted parks. On a green, trees should simply be planted in more-or-less even rows around the edges to provide definition and enclosure of the space.

Within this general framework there is, however, room for variety. There are distinctions between the landscape of greens small and large, urban and rural, in southern Rhode Island or northern Vermont, and even those in adjacent towns—in accordance with individual character, tradition, and preference. The challenge is to provide plantings of both the proper quality and sufficient quantity. In New England, as a result of the 1938 hurricane, street widening, Dutch elm disease, and the toxic effects of road salt, most greens today are pale comparisons of their former selves. These guidelines may help to reinstate some of the green's lost glory.

**LANDSCAPE
GUIDELINE 1
Maintain
characteristic
planting of the
space.**

Most greens in the past have been planted with native deciduous hardwood trees, such as maples, elms, and oaks. These typical New England trees should continue to grace greens and commons. Not only are such species in keeping with the historic character of these open spaces, but they are tried and true survivors of the region and will grow successfully under most conditions of New England weather and soil.

In order to determine which trees and shrubs are most appropriate to a specific green, prepare a master list of possibilities. Enlist the services of someone who is familiar with local vegetation and create an inventory of species that are locally prolific—and therefore hardy.

From this list, select species that complement each other and the plantings already on the green. Factors influencing your choice should include overall form and foliage, bark characteristics, fall color, winter appearance, fruit, and flowers. For example, just for the sake of variety you probably will not want all flowering species or several types of trees that grow to the same height. A handbook on regional species, such as Donald Wyman's *Trees for American Gardens*, will be helpful with such details. Another good reference is *Trees in Urban Design* by Henry F. Arnold, which includes information on growth rate, salt resistance, and transplanting limitations as well as aesthetic criteria.

Species with certain characteristics should be avoided. Do not select types that are prone to pests and diseases, vulnerable to site constraints such as wind or high water table, difficult to transplant, excessive in littering, or unusually sensitive to road salt. For example, avoid paper birch (bark invites vandalism); swamp white oak and magnolia (transplanting difficulties); beech,

Norway maple, and weeping willow (shade too deep for grass to grow beneath); and silver maple (breaks in high winds).

Exotics—species that do not grow naturally in the area—should be used sparingly if at all, unless they have been on the green for so long that they have become a local tradition. Evergreens, even native ones such as white pine, also look out of place and should be kept to a minimum. A single spruce or Scotch pine serves well as the town Christmas tree, but a cluster of them is no substitute for a row of graceful, arching elms.

A word about elms. In *Trees for American Gardens*, Donald Wyman asserts that the American elm is "without question the most popular shade tree in North America." Long admired for its unique vase-shaped form, the elm was a favorite choice for greens during the nineteenth and early twentieth centuries. Unfortunately, elms in general and the American elm in particular have proven highly susceptible to disease and insect troubles. Dutch elm disease and phloem necrosis, a fatal virus, have claimed so many elms that some greens have completely changed appearance. Robert Nathan Cram, in his 1922 thesis on greens and commons, reported that "the trees about Washington Square—[the Salem Common] are principally elm with some maple. A number of the elms are of such girth that they must have existed some time before the leveling in 1801." Today, of a total of 107 trees that once stood on the Salem Common, only four elms survive.

There is still no certain means of protection against Dutch elm disease, but there are some good preventive methods. Annual treatment with Lignasan, a fungicide, costs $400 per tree (in 1981); but it has a ninety-five percent success rate for healthy trees and is worth the cost for specimen elms. An alternative method is to use an insecticide (Methoxyclor) to kill the beetle that spreads the disease, but the success rate of this method is somewhat lower. For infected trees, there is little hope. Infected branches should be pruned before autumn, when infected fluids return to the tree roots, to save the tree for as long as possible. Dead trees should be removed quickly and disposed of away from others to avoid contamination.

As Dutch elm disease can be spread through the trees' roots, elms should be spaced at a greater distance apart than the thirty feet that is otherwise desirable. If the crowns of mature elms are overlapping, the roots are probably intertwined as well, and they should be severed. If possible, dig a trench between the trees to a depth of three to four feet, and replace the removed soil with sod; repeat this every three years.

Despite the attention that American elms require, they are definitely still worth planting. There are alternatives such as the Zelkova and the Groenveldt elm, and more recently the Dedfree elm, but these are not truly as spectacular as their American relative. Be certain, though, to consult a tree specialist and to observe a rigorous annual maintenance program.

LANDSCAPE GUIDELINE 2
Locate trees according to historical, spatial, and environmental factors.

Before planting any new trees on the green, prepare a plan of preferred locations. This plan should reflect the following considerations:

Historical precedent. Old photographs and post cards of the green can help determine where trees formerly stood. There is no need to re-create slavishly the green's former appearance, but historical continuity is certainly appropriate, and often these earlier locations are still spatially the most favorable. To avoid repeating past mistakes, try to learn why the previous trees died on these sites.

*The location of existing trees, plants, embellishments, and peripheral struc-
tures.* The siting of new trees should respect what is already on or around the
green. Do not obscure statues, other embellishments, or, as a general rule, an
established view such as that of a church facade. Coordinate the location of new
trees with the existing landscape as well, especially with existing rows of trees.
Often the top priority should be sites that fill out an existing planting pattern
rather than creating new ones.

Topography, soil conditions, hydrology, geology. There is little sense in
planting trees where they will not grow. With the help of a landscape architect
or a member of the parks department, analyze the green for advantageous and
unfavorable growing conditions. Be sure to take note of conditions that are not
easily changed, such as height of the water table, location of bedrock, and
problems of soil drainage and erosion.

Established pedestrian routes and areas. Do not locate trees or shrubs where
they will disturb pedestrian traffic, unless you are trying to change existing
patterns of use. Trees can be successfully employed as obstacles, discouraging
the use of softball diamonds and dirt paths, but be sure not to interrupt
appropriate pedestrian areas.

**LANDSCAPE
GUIDELINE 3
Plant trees along the
perimeter to
provide a strong
sense of enclosure.**

The edges of the green are the most important location for trees; they should
be the top priority for planting. This landscape plan is both historically
authentic and practical today. Nineteenth-century beautification efforts, such
as those in Salem, Massachusetts and New Haven, Connecticut, established
the traditional green as a grassy open space enclosed by single or double rows
of trees. It was not a sophisticated plan, but it did serve nicely to define the
shape of the green and to distinguish it from the surrounding village or town.

Today, with the ubiquitous sight and sound of automobiles, a separation of
green and roadway is essential. A fence will help, but trees are still the most
attractive and effective barrier.

Most greens already have some evidence of enclosing rows, but in many
cases the enclosing effect has been diminished because individual trees have
succumbed to disease, storms, automobile accidents, street widening, and old
age. As a first priority, gaps should be filled in, and as a second priority, a new
row of trees should be added if necessary. Plant trees that are fourteen to
sixteen feet high and a minimum of three and one-half inch diameter; trees
smaller than this are susceptible to abuse and sickness and will not have
significant visual impact. Staking or guying the new trees—with compatible
materials—is necessary to protect them.

The rows will be most effective if the individual trees are spaced about
twenty to thirty feet apart. This distance is somewhat less than is usually
recommended but will cause the trees no harm. Avoid perfectly straight,
evenly spaced rows, which create the appearance of a mall or boulevard.
Instead, slightly stagger the members. The variety is rewarding: narrow gaps,
like gateways, are inviting, and the overall pattern is less regimented. This
arrangement also disguises the inevitable damage that occurs over the years
from decay or accidents.

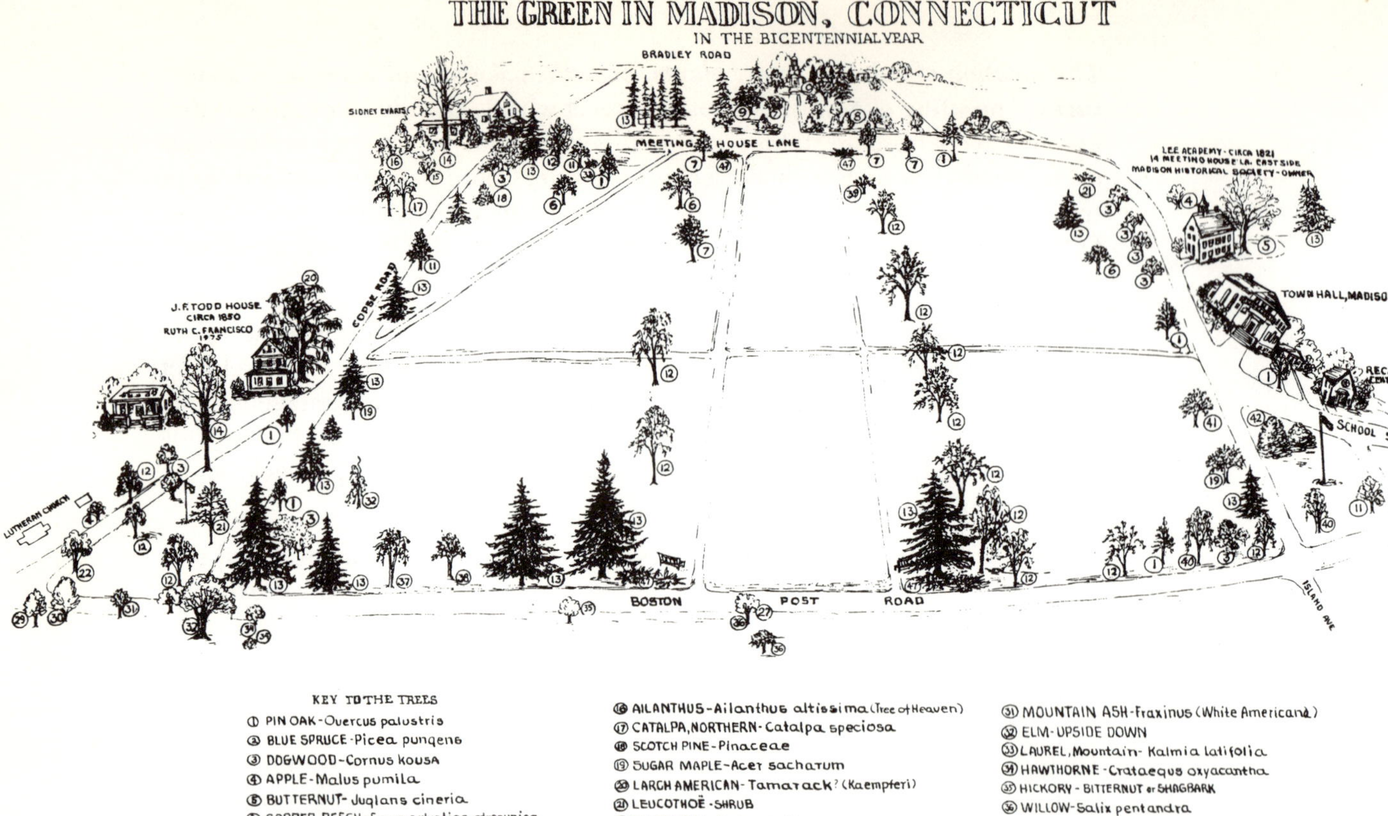

KEY TO THE TREES

1. PIN OAK - Quercus palustris
2. BLUE SPRUCE - Picea pungens
3. DOGWOOD - Cornus kousa
4. APPLE - Malus pumila
5. BUTTERNUT - Juglans cineria
6. COPPER BEECH - Fagus sylvatica atropunica
7. LINDEN - Tilia cordata
8. ARBORVITAE - Thuya
9. RED MAPLE - Schwedlerii
10. NORWAY MAPLE - Acerplataroides
11. NORTHERN RED OAK - Quercus rubra
12. AMERICAN ELM - Ulmus americana
13. NORWAY SPRUCE - Picea abies
14. TULIP TREE - Liriodendron
15. MAGNOLIA, SAUCER - Magnolia soulangeana

16. AILANTHUS - Ailanthus altissima (Tree of Heaven)
17. CATALPA, NORTHERN - Catalpa speciosa
18. SCOTCH PINE - Pinaceae
19. SUGAR MAPLE - Acer sacharum
20. LARCH AMERICAN - Tamarack? (Kaempferi)
21. LEUCOTHOË - SHRUB
22. WHITE OAK - Quercus alba
23. SUMAC - Glabra - (Rhus)
24. CHESTNUT - AMERICAN - Castanea dentata
25. BLACK LOCUST - Robinia pseudoacacia
26. WHITE PINE - EASTERN - Pinus striobus
27. SYCAMORE, AMERICAN — Platanus occidentalis
28. CEDAR, BLUE ATLAS - Cedrus atlantica glauca
29. SEQUOIA - Meta
30. SEQUOIA-GIANT - Gigantea

31. MOUNTAIN ASH - Fraxinus (White Americana)
32. ELM - UPSIDE DOWN
33. LAUREL, Mountain - Kalmia latifolia
34. HAWTHORNE - Crataegus oxyacantha
35. HICKORY - BITTERNUT or SHAGBARK
36. WILLOW - Salix pentandra
37. ENGLISH ELM - Campestris
38. BEECH, AMERICAN - Fagus grandifolia
39. ORIENTAL MAPLE - Acer palmatum
40. WEEPING ELM - Wheatleyi
41. SILVER MAPLE - Acer saccharinum
42. HEMLOCK - EASTERN - Tsuga canadensis
43. LOCUST - Gleditsia triacanthus inermis
44. WHITE BIRCH - Betula papyrifera
45. WEEPING WILLOW - Salix babylonica
46. WEEPING BIRCH - Pendula

Putting the Green Back Together Again
Madison, Connecticut

The hurricane of 1938 wreaked havoc on many greens, and that in Madison, Connecticut was no exception. Within three hours the force of the storm had uprooted thirty-nine trees and strewn them about the green; mostly elms and spruce, some of these were nearly a century old. Yet catastrophic as it was, the hurricane also mobilized the garden club of Madison and gave rise to a proprietary relationship that has continued ever since.

The garden club had been established in Madison in 1924, but for the first decade or so members were not concerned with the town green—nor was there any reason for them to be. After having served as a military training ground and as a pound for the geese of nearby residents, the green was improved in the 1850s by a group of diligent townspeople. Prominent among them were members of the Scranton family, who yoked their oxen and leveled the space at their own expense. Young elm trees were garnered from an outlying wooded area and replanted; and over the next fifty years, the green was encircled by a white rail fence and embellished by a flagpole. There was little more to be done except for routine maintenance, much of which was carried out by T. S. Scranton until he was past his ninetieth year in the 1920s.

The hurricane damage to the green was so extensive, though, that major assistance was needed. The garden club decided to come to the rescue and take up the cause of rehabilitating the historic space, which is the focal point for a cluster of period residences and public buildings. Club members assumed responsibility for the trees on the green, and at that time planted elms down the center of the green's main expanse and also around the edges. Spruce and dogwood trees completed the garden club's first gift to the green.

Today the garden club, in cooperation with the town, which maintains the green, and the Congregational church, oversees all planting on the green, determining both type and quantity. Mrs. Joan Friborg Gram, head of the Civic Beautification Committee, said that the club takes into consideration such factors as year-round beauty, color, and heartiness when choosing new species. The club occasionally refuses to plant trees offered as gifts, as it is desirable to keep the green sufficiently open for activities such as summer fairs. At one time, noted Mrs. Gram, the practice of planting memorial trees was so popular that a moratorium was declared to prevent the green from becoming a forest.

The garden club keeps meticulous records of its work, maintaining a list of every tree planted on town property. The type of each tree and the date it was planted are entered into a log which helps the club make future planting decisions.

The town of Madison has benefited not only from the garden club's close attention to the green but also from its financial assistance, since the trees are purchased with the club funds. The club also enlists the services of a private firm to prune, spray, and feed the trees on the green as needed. Finally, the club has provided a certain amount of assurance for the future of the green. The garden club maintains an account of several thousand dollars to be spent only if lightning—or, in this case, a hurricane—should strike twice.

LANDSCAPE GUIDELINE 4
Plant trees and shrubs sparingly in other locations, for special design purposes.

Resist the temptation to overplant. Historically, most greens were relatively austere in character, and there is no reason to clutter them today. Too many groves of trees rob the green of sunlight, while shrubs seem better suited to a garden.

Legitimate reasons to plant within the edges of the green include defining subspaces, if the green is large enough to accommodate them, and landscaping of embellishments. The latter presents the best opportunity to employ shrubs, which can help a monument or bandstand fit better into its context of grass and trees and can also screen obtrusive objects. Avoid the lone shrub at the head of the green and the awkward clusters that simply break up an expanse of grass.

Choose species of shrubs whose natural shape does not require extensive pruning. Such species not only require less maintenance but also are more in character with the rest of the green; shaped shrubbery is not appropriate. Consider the year-round appearance of the shrubs and decide whether evergreens or deciduous varieties are more suitable; some possibilities are yews, euonymus, mountain laurel, and the deciduous honeysuckle and viburnum. Ground covers such as English ivy or periwinkle may be combined with shrubs, but they should by no means compete with the standard ground cover of turf. Other small plants might also be used; for example, on the common in Deerfield, Massachusetts ferns have been used in a small fenced enclosure surrounding a monument.

LANDSCAPE GUIDELINE 5
Restrict flowers to planters or other suitable containers.

Townspeople should be judicious in deciding whether they want any flowers on the green. Flowers are short lived, susceptible to vandalism and accidental trampling, and tend to make the green resemble a formal garden if they are extensively planted at ground level. If flowers are desired, they are best kept in one or two attractive planters. Sometimes an old trough or fountain is available, but new granite curbs are equally appropriate if set in the ground to create a square or rectangular planting area.

Flowers can appear isolated if one small planter is located in a broad expanse of grass. Consider clustering them near benches or around monuments with other plants such as shrubs.

**LANDSCAPE
GUIDELINE 6
Preserve the
existing topography
of the green.**

A few greens, such as those in Newbury and Middlebury, Vermont and Harvard, Massachusetts, retain dramatic hills and inclines; but many others have a long history of regrading, including the removal of stones, the smoothing of ground for military drills, and the filling of wetlands. Most of this work, completed in the nineteenth century, was carefully done by hand. One of the charms of these greens is that, despite the leveling efforts, they are often not completely flat but slightly irregular, and this topography is an important aspect of the landscape. Rough grading by machine should be avoided, as it will obliterate these subtle modulations.

The only reason to alter topography is if surface water is collecting along paths or at the base of structures where it is inconvenient and can cause damage. Usually minor regrading of flat areas to a pitch of one-quarter inch to the foot will correct this situation without recourse to a storm drainage system, which can be both expensive and harmful to the supply of water available to plants and turf.

FOOTPATHS

Introduction

Destruction of the turf from overuse is an indication not of vandalism but of popularity. Dusty paths and large areas of bare dirt are, however, unattractive, and the solution is to pave areas that receive the heaviest use.

The key is to provide a sufficient but not excessive number of paved footpaths and activity areas suited to the size and use of the green. Too many footpaths make the green overly urban in character, more like a plaza than a green space, and they are an unnecessary expense. In fact, greens in rural areas, or greens that are small and purely ornamental, sometimes require no paths at all.

If well designed and maintained, footpaths can be an attractive asset to the green. The following guidelines provide assistance in creating and choosing materials for paths that are appropriate in scale and arrangement.

There are two categories of footpaths: those that provide access from one side of the green to another and those that lead to an embellishment or furnishing within the green. The need for one or both types of paths depends upon the size and the use of the green.

Large urban greens, such as those in Boston and New Haven, are crisscrossed daily by office workers, shoppers, and visitors. Accordingly, these greens boast extensive webs of paths that link opposite sides and corners, enabling pedestrians to walk through the green instead of around it. The equally large green in Hadley, Massachusetts, though, is hardly used at all. It has no paths, nor does it require any. Most greens fall somewhere between these two extremes.

Certain frequently used features, such as benches, almost always require access paths, even on greens of only one or two acres. Other embellishments may or may not require access routes. A seasonal bandstand probably does not need a paved path, nor does a flagpole that will not be closely examined. The need for additional paths is often plainly evident, as the bare dirt lines worn into the turf indicate that pedestrians have found routes that are more desirable or more natural than those provided by the designers. In most cases it is advisable to pave these de facto paths, unless the green is already too cluttered with paving.

If there are already a number of paved paths, yet pedestrians continue to create new paths in the turf, the problem may be that the existing paths are arranged impractically. Some existing paths may receive almost no use, and these could be removed. It will be necessary to observe the green over a period of time and to keep a record of pedestrian activity in order to determine which paths are popular and which are little used. One easy way to observe path usage is to visit the green soon after a light snowfall; the tracks in the snow are a good indicator of the most popular routes.

Traditionally, village greens have not been elaborate in design, and it is desirable to maintain that classic simplicity. Paths should be laid out in a manner that is straightforward and practical rather than overly intricate; often two or three paths that intersect in the middle of the green are all that is needed. Larger greens or those with an urban rather than rural character can successfully support a more formal geometric arrangement, but again, the less elaborate the better.

On greens of all sizes, one way to reduce clutter is to depress paths slightly beneath the adjacent grade. Viewed obliquely from a distance, paths are thereby hidden.

Paths should be straight, in the manner of natural paths that pedestrians wear into the grass, rather than curved. Curvilinear paths impart instead a picturesque, garden quality typical of late-nineteenth-century Olmstedian park design. Such a style is inappropriate to village green paths, which were usually laid out by local townspeople with an eye more toward convenience than toward landscape design theory.

Narrow paths are less intrusive than massive areas of pavement, and they are rarely an inconvenience. A width of four to five feet is usually sufficient, even on greens that are traveled by bicyclists and baby carriages as well as pedestrians.

Except in urban areas, where particularly heavy pedestrian use of parts of the green may call for some differentiation routes, all paths on one green should be of the same width. Such uniformity helps to keep these paths inconspicuous.

**FOOTPATHS GUIDELINE 4
Provide access for the handicapped to the major path.**

If federal funding is involved in the rehabilitation of a green, the town must follow strict Housing and Urban Development requirements applying to access for handicapped persons. Even if the funding source does not dictate such amenities, access in the form of curb cuts and ramps should be provided.

As a general rule, ramps should be less than one-in-twelve gradient, at least three-feet wide, and less than thirty feet between landings for long slopes. Curb cuts should be located to one side of the path centerline, for the sake of the blind who may rely on the cue of the curb in their path.

Handicapped-access facilities should be sufficient to provide enjoyment of the green for all, but they need not dominate every feature. Curb cuts to the main path are essential, while a concrete ramp encircling a tiny wooden bandstand is not. Provide access in ways that are inconspicuous and justified by the level of anticipated use.

**FOOTPATHS GUIDELINE 5
Pave off-path areas if necessary.**

If well watered and drained, and given regular periods to recuperate, turf can withstand intensive use—but not too much of it. A yearly flea market poses no threat, nor should a weekly band concert, but daily games of frisbee may. Restricting or relocating the activity is one solution, but if you agree to allow such activity the area should be paved.

Such treatment is acceptable if the paving is of materials and scale compatible with the character of the green. The area in question may be small or large. A flagpole, for example, usually does not need a footpath but may require a paved circle of three to five feet in diameter for the daily raising and lowering of the flag. Benches that do not front directly on a footpath may also benefit from a two- or three-foot-wide paved strip that extends the full length

Polite reminders, including one to frequent the paths rather than the grass, at the Boston Common.

of the bench. This paving should also run underneath the bench itself, as the shade will prohibit growth of good turf.

Monuments that are frequently inspected at close range may require a circular or rectangular area surrounding them; occasionally the area involved can be substantial. The Civil War monument on the Cambridge Common has been an established gathering place for many years, and as part of the bicentennial rehabilitation a large circle was reinforced with granite cobblestones and brick pavers.

FOOTPATHS GUIDELINE 6
Choose footpath and paved area materials that are attractive, compatible, and durable.

A number of paving materials are suitable for pathways and paved areas. Brick is the time-tested favorite. Hard-burned pavement brick is best for paving purposes, as softer brick tends to break up in frost. Avoid bright reds and yellows; a good waterstruck or sand-molded brick is earthy red or red grey.

If brick is prohibitively expensive, consider bituminous concrete top-dressed with peastone to simulate an old-fashioned gravel path. Another possibility is stone dust on a gravel base, with brick edging to prevent the stone dust from scattering into the surrounding grass.

Neither bituminous concrete nor ordinary reinforced concrete is of sufficient quality or attractiveness to be recommended for use by itself. On wide expanses or gathering places, these materials would be visually disastrous. Nor should bluestone be used, except sparingly, as it is not salt resistant.

Cobblestone and granite block wear well in heavily trodden areas, but many users object to cobbled paths because they are particularly hard on wheelchairs, bicycles, and baby carriages. Closely laid brick, though, provides a surface almost as smooth as concrete.

Do not use more than two different paving materials; and if different materials are to be used side by side, be sure they are compatible with each other and with their surroundings. Avoid contrasts of color or texture that are either weak or overly harsh. For example, grey granite curbing used with concrete is too weak, and a white kiosk surrounded by red brick paving is too strong, but a white embellishment such as a flagpole or bandstand surrounded by granite or bluestone is satisfactory. Good paving combinations include brick and cobblestone, cobblestone and bluestone, and stonedust- and peastone-dressed bituminous concrete.

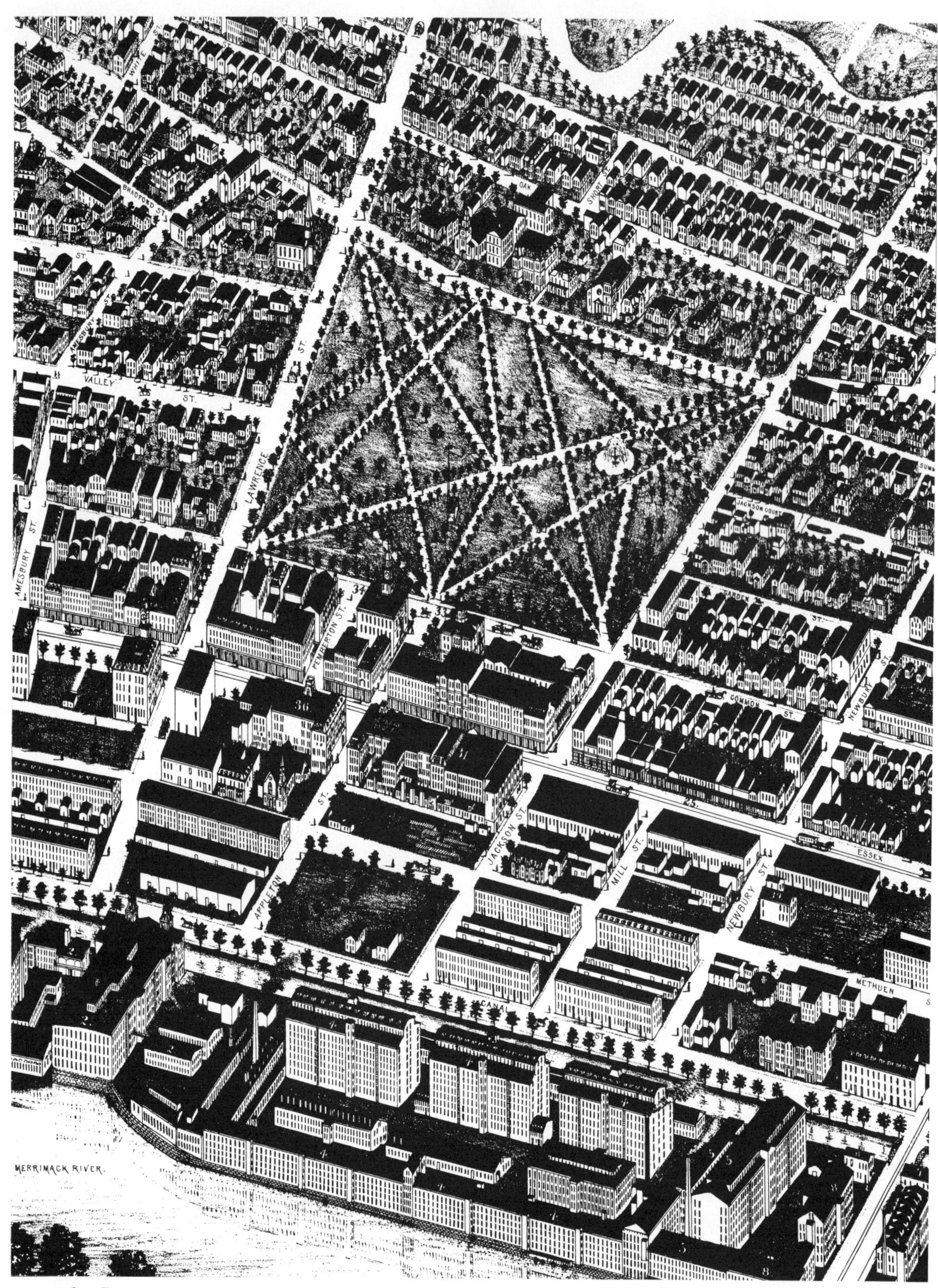

A bird's-eye view of the Lawrence North Common, published in 1876. Mill buildings are visible in the foreground.

Commemorating Camella
Lawrence, Massachusetts

Camella Teoli Way.

Camella Teoli was fourteen years old when, in 1912, she testified at a congressional hearing on the "Bread and Roses" textile mill strike that had occurred earlier that year in Lawrence, Massachusetts. Camella was merely one of hundreds of children who had worked long hours in the mills for wretchedly low pay, and one of many injured in the course of the job; she required seven months of hospitalization after a machine for twisting cotton pulled off her scalp. Her vivid testimony helped bring about legislation that improved conditions for children and adults alike. Yet when she returned to work in the Lawrence mills she received little recognition during the period of antiactivist sentiment that followed, and over the course of the next half century her contribution was largely unknown.

By 1980 Lawrence had discovered a new pride in its past, and Mayor Lawrence LeFebre decided to hold a celebration to honor the city's labor and ethnic history. The event was held on the North Common, where meetings and speeches during the course of the strike had also occurred; and it included banners proclaiming "Bread and Roses Too"—the strikers' demand for both better wages and humane conditions—in the forty-five languages then used by the workers as well as the singing of the Industrial Workers of the World theme song. The highlight for Teoli and her family, though, was when the mayor officially designated a long and broad path through the common as "Camella Teoli Way." It was an unusual gesture in an unusual celebration, and it was reported by several newspapers and magazines that covered the event.

Unfortunately the designation seems to have cap-

tured the imagination of the national media more than that of the local parks department, since in 1981 there is nary a sign to indicate Teoli Way, and city officials had difficulty recalling which path it is. Perhaps, as Ronald Lee Fleming has suggested, the naming of a walkway should be only a beginning. Fleming thinks that in order to memorialize more effectively Camella Teoli's contribution to the city's heritage the site might also be marked by a view of the mill in which she worked, fragments of spindles, or her testimony embedded in the pavement.

In fairness, the overseers of Lawrence's North Common have had more basic problems than commemorative paths on their minds. Nearly eighteen acres in size, the common has been a formidable area to maintain, and there has been no defined policy on how the space should be used. A popular baseball diamond and basketball court have damaged the turf; some areas of the common are devoid of trees, while others are overly dense; and cars occasionally drive along the excessively wide pathways. Vandalism has been a problem that parks officials attempted to combat a few years ago by surrounding some monuments with incongruous chain-link fencing.

More recently, though, the city has experienced something of a renaissance. Extensive rehabilitation promises to restore life to the downtown, and the common has been designated as one component of the Heritage State Park in Lawrence. Using state and federal money thus allocated to this centrally located space, the city is soon to begin implementing plans that include planting trees along the common's perimeter, relocating athletic areas and restoring turf, removing superfluous pathways, erecting explanatory historical markers, and taking down the chain-link fences. A "tot lot," concert and sitting area, and new lights and benches throughout promise to make the square attractive to a wide variety of users. The 1848 common will take on an appearance that this generation of Lawrence residents has never known—and yes, there will be a sign to point out Camella Teoli Way.

Eyesore fencing to be removed as part of the common rehabilitation project.

Off-path areas should be selectively paved if warranted by use or unusual stress on the turf; the area around this fountain in Norwich, Vermont, is one example. (The fountain, incidentally, was a gift from the Women's Christian Temperance Union, presumably to supply water instead of some other liquid refreshment on the Common.) Extensive paving is not recommended but is sometimes needed on urban commons. When the monument in Cambridge became a popular gathering place, a wide radius of cobblestones and bricks was the practical solution.

FURNISHINGS

Introduction

A green is not simply a patch of grass and a few trees. Today the typical green is embellished with a variety of elements both functional and ornamental, including fences, benches, lights, bandstands, monuments, markers, flag-poles, drinking fountains, signs, trash receptacles, bicycle racks, and bus shelters. These features can be an asset to the green, but because of their overwhelming number and poor appearance they are too often a liability.

It seems self-evident that furnishings should be of the highest quality design and materials, and that they be kept in good repair. On more greens than not, though, the benches are missing slats and the trash receptacles are merely rusty oil drums. Part of the problem is that towns often lack enough money to devote to greens; but it is also true that available funds are not always well spent.

Quality, not quantity, should guide selection of furnishings, and all purchases should be part of a long-range furnishings plan. It is better to buy one high-quality bench than five inferior ones, for if you buy one quality bench a year you will have ten at the end of a decade; if you buy inferior ones now, within ten years you may have none. This long-range strategy will also result in lower maintenance costs, since higher-quality items need less attention. Equally important, though, is a regular maintenance schedule that provides for a coat of paint *before* the fence has cracked and rotted; such a schedule is proposed in the "Maintenance" section below.

The design and materials of the furnishings should be compatible with the historical character of the green. Traditional materials and design are usually the most appropriate, but in some cases contemporary selections are equally good. The guidelines that follow provide more specific recommendations for choosing individual pieces, as well as advice about coordinating these pieces into a unified system.

FURNISHINGS GUIDELINE 1
Restrict the number of furnishings so that they do not overwhelm the green.

If one trash receptacle is good, then ten must be better—or so goes the prevailing logic that oversees many greens. Benches, lights, and other facilities are indeed necessary to encourage use of the green, but too many are simply unattractive. Their arrangement on the green must similarly strike a balance between what is functional and what is visually acceptable.

Assess the existing quantity and spatial arrangement of furniture. If particular benches and bicycle racks are rarely used, you may be able to eliminate or relocate them. If, however, the furniture supply and demand are evenly matched but the green appears cluttered, consider grouping some elements. Planners often strive to create spaces for privacy, but, as the work of William Whyte on urban open spaces documents, many people prefer to be in the midst of activity. Benches can be clustered in groups, sometimes together with a monument or drinking fountain or around a tree. Such an arrangement simplifies the green without depriving users of any facilities.

A second solution to the problem of clutter on the green is also possible if the demand for facilities exceeds the current supply. Rather than adding new features to the green itself, locate them in the surrounding area. Benches and trash receptacles can be placed on the sidewalk across the street, affording sitters a view of the green, and a bicycle rack might adjoin a public building such as a library or town hall. This solution relieves the green of an additional burden and also helps the green and townscape to appear coherent.

FURNISHINGS GUIDELINE 2
Select new furnishings to coordinate with the existing style, or replace the entire system.

In order to maintain a desirable sense of simplicity on the green, there should not be a random assortment of furniture styles, colors, and materials within a small space. Instead, each category of furniture—benches, lights, etc.— should be of a single design. The only exception is the large urban green, where two contrasting styles may coexist without excessive confusion.

If the existing furnishings are attractive and practical, there is no reason to change styles; maintain a sense of continuity and simply add new ones to match as necessary. If you decide upon a change of styles, though, try to make the switch all at once rather than in phases. Economically this may be difficult, but visually it is more successful to change from one system to another than to employ two that were not chosen for compatibility.

Choose the style of each category of furnishings with an eye toward overall coherence. If, for example, the green has a wooden fence and flagpole, then a wooden bandstand would be more appropriate than one of stone or brick. A green fence complements benches painted in the same color, while a fence of cast iron would be better accompanied by benches of the same material and finish. Not every furnishing needs to be made of the same material in order to be compatible, but the use of like materials is the most direct way to achieve a sense of coherence. Another means is to furnish the green with elements in the manner of a particular period, such as the late-nineteenth century.

On greens of more than five acres, there may be room to accommodate two styles of benches or lights. In this case, choose two designs that are sufficiently different to contrast rather than appear almost—but not quite—the same. A good example is the Cambridge Common with its two types of benches, one of traditional design in wood and the other of low, backless, granite blocks in the areas that receive greater use.

Before purchasing new furnishings in quantity, you might obtain one sample for a trial period. Those benches that look so attractive in the manufacturer's catalogue actually may be somewhat uncomfortable. Before installing twenty of them on the green, purchase one with an option to return it after thirty days. Place it prominently on the green, let townspeople try it, and solicit their response. You can also employ this technique for litter receptacles, lighting fixtures, and street signs.

It is possible that you will not want to light the green at all. If it is in a residential area, or in a small town, the green may not receive enough night use to warrant the expense of fixtures and electricity. Lighting does, however, deter vandalism, encourage more extensive use of the green, and lend a certain status to the green at dusk and night.

Choose lighting of a relatively low wattage and lampposts that are scaled to pedestrian height. Locate the lights within the green near facilities such as benches and embellishments of visual interest, perhaps clustering several lights together in one or two areas. You may want to spotlight a feature such as a flagpole or a monument; if so, be careful to keep the lighting soft to avoid seeming garish.

At the edges of the green, existing street lighting may be sufficient. If it is not, use the same fixtures as are within the green. The use of relatively short posts and low-intensity light may require a greater number of fixtures than are normally used, but if the lights are regularly spaced they will reinforce the rhythm of the repeated fenceposts and trees, and will not appear overwhelming.

Along the street itself, the posts must be taller to provide sufficient light for motorists. If the green is along a state highway, the state department of public works will have to approve your proposals.

Let There Be Lights
Little Compton, Rhode Island

Purchasing and installing new furnishings can be an expensive proposition, as Carlton C. Brownell was well aware. Consequently, when Mr. Brownell, who is director of the Little Compton Historical Society, hit upon the idea of erecting traditional lighting fixtures on the Commons, he knew that the cost would be substantial—excessive, in fact, in terms of what the town budget could afford.

Nevertheless, Brownell thought there were several good reasons to pursue the idea. The lamps would be in keeping with the character of the Commons, a well-kept grassy triangle largely taken up by a stone-walled burying ground and dominated by a nineteenth-century Congregational church. In fact, the Commons had formerly been lit by kerosene lamps of the style he envisioned, but none now remained. Furthermore, it seemed a propitious time for such a project: the year was 1976, the nation's bicentennial and Little Compton's tricentennial. After receiving cost estimates of about $17,000 for the project, Brownell decided to explore alternative means of funding.

Working through the nonprofit historical society, Brownell first obtained a $1,000 grant from the Bird Companies Foundation as part of a bicentennial funding program. This was a start, but still a long way from the total. Brownell then turned from the private to the public sector, and in particular to a constituency that was sure to benefit from the project: the townspeople.

As Samuel Chamberlain noted in his *Six New England Villages*, "Little Compton's winter population has changed but little during these past centuries." It is a stable town, home to families that have remained for generations and whose surnames today correspond to those in the old burying ground on the Commons. Would it not be appropriate, Brownell reasoned, for a few townspeople to honor their ancestors by donating a memorial in the form of a lamp?

The idea was well received, and the cost within reason. For $500 one could "purchase" a single lamp, with a brass plaque inscribed with the ancestor's name and dates. There was even room for an additional word or phrase, if one desired; hence the plaque for I. Richmond Elwell also bears his title, "Town Lamplighter." A number of people made smaller donations, which helped to cover the cost of nondedicated lamps as well as installation and wiring. Business firms also contributed, a local contractor lent his men and a backhoe for several days to erect posts and bury wires, a local electrician did the electrical work for the cost of materials, and volunteers replaced the sod after installation and painted the posts. Town funds were not involved at all.

More than a dozen lamps were installed in 1976, and some townspeople liked the project enough to revive it a few years later. Increased costs, a decrease in the number of eager volunteers, and the absence of bicentennial funding dampened the response, though; and by the third time the idea was brought up the price of nearly $1000 per lamp had become prohibitive. Part of the reason for the price inflation was simply the increased cost of the lamps, but the policies of the electric company also played a role. The company insisted that the lights be run on meters as an individual item rather than as part of the town's yearly electric bill, because only the company's own standard fixtures were eligible for the reduced rate.

Wiring posed an additional problem. Carlton Brownell wanted to bury all of the wires that encircle the Commons but was told by the electric company that this would be "simply impossible." The poles and wires are particularly noticeable on the western end of the Commons, where a lack of trees makes the gaunt forms all too visible.

Despite this minor eyesore, the Commons in Little Compton is the heart of a very attractive village center. The drywall stone fence that encircles the burying ground is unusual for a common, but appropriate in this region where many surrounding farms have identical fences defining fields and roads. The landscaping of the common is as meticulously maintained as the grounds of the library, grange, church, and other local institutions that enclose it. And the black nineteenth-century style lamps, with their shiny brass plaques attesting to the devotion of Little Compton residents, are the perfect finishing touch to this handsome setting.

The greatest funding resource that any green has is the people to whom it belongs. What is needed are some creative means of tapping this resource, and the Little Compton project is one example of how this has been done. People like to get a little credit for their assistance, or to dedicate their gift to a friend or relative. Most people would also rather give something tangible—a lamp, a bench, or a tree—than simply a sum of money, and such embellishments become the focus of community pride. Other than one incident in which a single rock was thrown at a lamp, Little Compton's project has experienced no vandalism. Other communities would do well to take note of this community's success and develop similar programs of "Gifts to the Green."

One of Little Compton's classic lamps, and a brass plaque detail.

The first step in selecting furnishings is to become familiar with what is available. This book will acquaint you with the wide variety of furnishings currently in use on greens and commons throughout New England, while manufacturers' catalogues and guides such as *Streetscape Equipment Sourcebook 2* provide additional examples and information on ordering them.1 If you are interested in reproducing a piece that is no longer available or in designing your own, write to the manufacturer of a similar item; many firms are willing to do custom work.

Choose furnishings made of traditional materials such as wood, stone, and metal, and avoid the more contemporary materials such as concrete (except for footings and other concealed elements), stone aggregate, and plastic. Specifically, we recommend the following:

Wood. Southern yellow pine and western cedar are durable woods suited to the New England climate. These should be pressure-treated with preservative to prevent rot, and paint can be used as an additional protector. Wood can be used alone or in combination with other materials for benches, flagpoles, fences, light posts, litter receptacles, and signs.

Stone. The best all-purpose stone for this climate is granite; others lack its durability. The common gray-colored variety can be supplemented by red or yellow granite obtained from special quarries. Other suitable stones include marble, limestone, and slate. Marble and limestone can be used for monuments and ornamental fountains, but should not be used for markers, since weathering will soon make any inscriptions difficult to read. Granite can be used for these same furnishings and also for drinking fountains, benches, and fenceposts.

Metal. Wrought iron, galvanized steel, cast aluminum, and anodized aluminum are all strong and resistant to vandalism. Use them for light posts, litter receptacles, bicycle racks, and fenceposts; in conjunction with stone for fountains; and with wood for benches.

All of the above materials can be used in their natural state, but wood and metal can also be painted with handsome results. Avoid bright, primary colors and choose instead white, gray, black, and muted shades of green and brown.

The following recommendations are for specific furnishings:

Bandstands. The traditional round or polygonal bandstands that first ornamented greens in the nineteenth century are still the most appropriate today. A few large urban bandstands, such as those in Boston and Salem, are of stone but almost all the rest are of wood. Often they are quite intricately painted in contrasting dark and light tones for a handsome effect. The rectilinear shape of brick does not lend itself well to the light and airy qualities that a bandstand should have.

Benches. There are basically two types of benches: those with backs and those without. If you choose backless, platform-type benches, they should be at least twenty inches deep to allow people to sit on one side and thirty-six inches to permit back-to-back seating. Benches should be designed, however, to accommodate users of all ages, and seating with back support is more comfortable for the elderly. Armrests give added support in sitting and standing; they constitute an additional expense but may be worthwhile.

The back of the bench should join the seat at a slightly obtuse angle; a

The bandstands in Middlebury, Ashby, Grafton, and Townsend are each unique but equally appropriate in their traditional design and materials, primarily painted wood. The Canton bandstand is somewhat less graceful; the brick structure in Bristol is much too rectilinear and heavy.

63

Waltham, Massachusetts

Westford, Massachusetts

New Orleans, Louisiana

Cambridge, Massachusetts

Burlington, Massachusetts

Woodstock, Vermont

Salem, Massachusetts (19th Century)

Easthampton, Massachusetts

In Waltham, the nineteenth-century style cast-iron and wood benches are well-suited to most greens and commons, although some users have complained that the seats are too small for comfort. Those formerly found in Salem, which are being replicated elsewhere, and those in Coliseum Square in New Orleans are somewhat less usual and should be sought out. The Cambridge model is chunkier and less traditional but it wears well on an urban common, the wood should be treated to prevent cracking. Those in Burlington and Easthampton are more susceptible to vandalism and disrepair, and the Burlington style concrete base should be avoided. The curvilinear granite bench can be used sparingly, as it is in Westford where two are used for focus around the flagpole. An unusual and delightful six-sided arrangement is found in Woodstock.

ninety-degree angle is uncomfortably rigid. Benches in which the back slopes or curves into the seat tend to impair "settling," and users find themselves continually sliding off.

The ideal dimensions for a bench are a back height of about seventeen inches (minimum thirteen to fifteen inches), a seat depth of fourteen to sixteen inches, and a length of eight to ten feet for greens in villages and towns—although in cities benches may be longer. The attractive Victorian-style benches that are gaining in popularity are, regrettably, only four feet long (unless joined in units of two, for a total of eight feet, and divided by a single armrest, like those at Boston's Quincy Market). However, a park official in one town remarked that he had chosen this short length specifically to prevent local derelicts from sleeping on the common!

Fasten the benches onto the pathway or other paved area to prevent theft and also to provide stability for the elderly and semiambulant.

Bicycle racks: There is probably no need for a bicycle rack on a small village green, but one may be appropriate in a city. With the increased popularity of bicycle riding, there is now a variety of racks available other than the traditional waist-high—and invariably rusty—style. Choose one that is low to the ground and preferably of metal painted in black or a similarly unobtrusive color. You will need to pave the area beneath and immediately around the rack.

Bus shelters and information booths. These structures properly do not belong on the green, but in a few cases there is no other location for them. Keep them small, and use wood and glass as the building materials to create a square or rectangular facility with a roof. Do not use concrete block or metal frame and plastic construction. Paint any structures inside and out as often as necessary to keep them clean of graffiti.

Drinking fountains. A public drinking fountain is a much-appreciated amenity. Be sure that it is relatively low in height so as to be accessible to children and the handicapped. Locate a fountain directly to the side of a pathway, where its use will not obstruct pedestrian traffic, pave the area beneath it, and provide an access route. The fountain should be of a design that enables all water to be drained from it in the winter.

Fences. There are many attractive fences of wood, metal, stone, stone and chain, and various other combinations. Metal or metal and stone tend to be better suited to urban greens, while wood is more frequently used in towns and villages. Select a fence that is sturdy, especially if the green is in an area prone to wayward automobiles or vandals. The fence should have an opening at each pathway, and there should be a sufficient number of openings to accommodate use. The lovely green in Falmouth, Massachusetts, for example, is unfortunately almost entirely encircled by a white rail fence that discourages strollers from entering.

Lampposts and lighting. There are many traditional gaslamp-style fixtures available, and these are usually the most compatible with other green furnishings. Contemporary round or rectilinear luminaires, executed in aluminum, painted black, and mounted on posts of the same material, are appropriate for urban greens. Avoid the standard "cobra head" street fixtures, which are ill suited to the green in design and height.

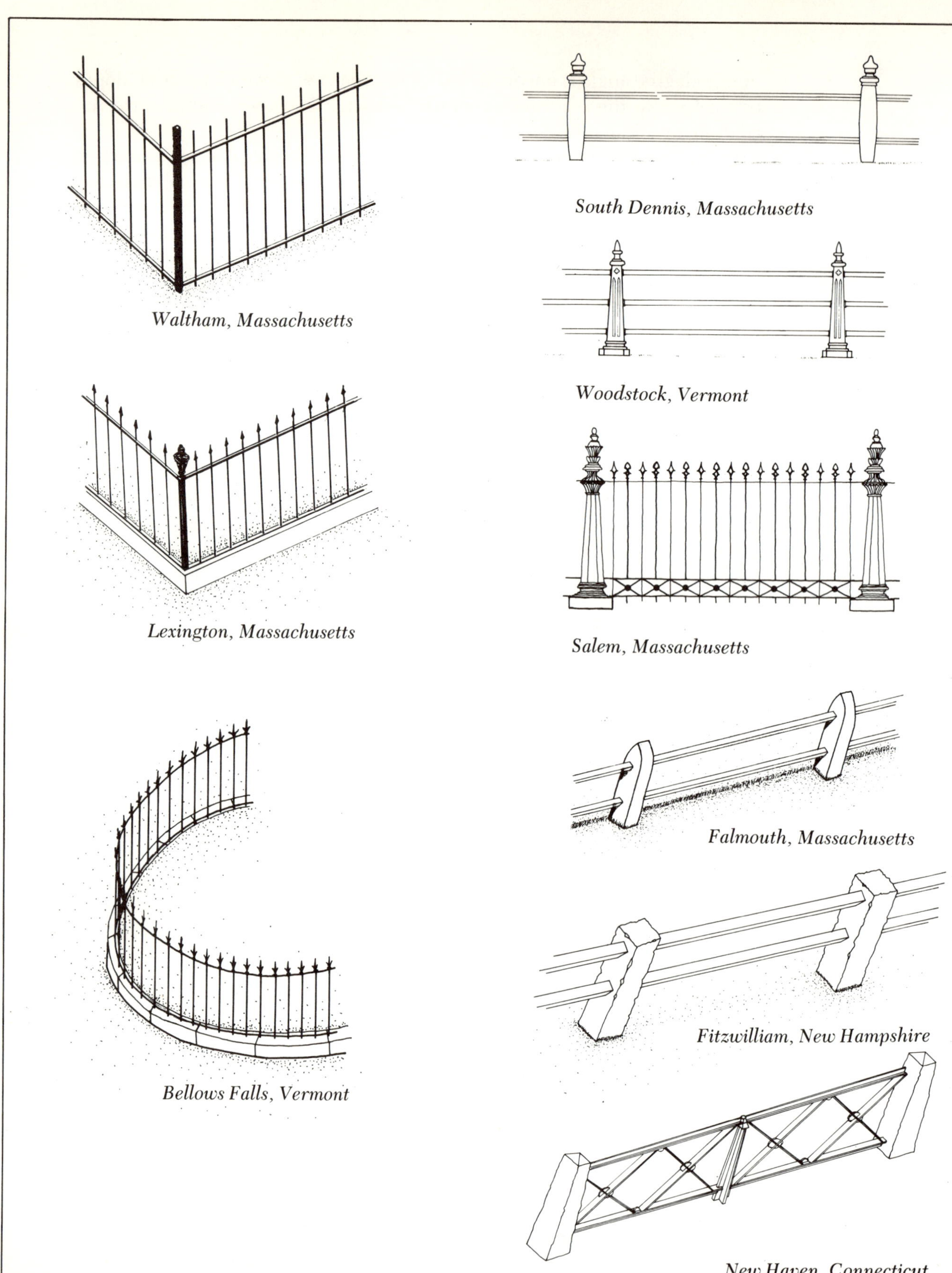

A variety of materials is used in these fences with equal success: wood at Falmouth and South Dennis; woodand granite at Fitzwilliam; granite and iron at New Haven; cast iron at Woodstock and Salem. Of the lighter weight fences used to enclose monuments, those at Lexington and Bellows Falls are more suitable than the stark style at Waltham.

Height is the critical dimension for lighting. The green is a pedestrian area and, accordingly, the lampposts should be about twelve feet high; in contrast, most street and athletic field posts are at least thirty feet high. Avoid overly bright light by choosing a 150 or 175 wattage, and use incandescent light instead of the harsher mercury vapor, metal halide, or high-pressure sodium; these candescent lights cast a blue or yellowish pallor. Along the streets surrounding the green, provide a similarly reduced level of light, although the posts should be taller (about thirty feet) to accommodate automobile traffic.

The Perils of Patriotism
Dedham, Massachusetts

The Dedham Common fence, once again restored to white.

The incident began innocently enough when, in 1975, Dedham Commissioner of Public Works Paul Sullivan noted that the fence around the town common was in need of a new coat of paint. In a burst of bicentennial enthusiasm, Sullivan thought that instead of the usual white he would employ a patriotic scheme of red, white, and blue. His decision was all that was needed to enact the plan, since although the town had recently voted into existence a historic district commission and a district that encompassed the common, the state had yet to respond with its official approval. Without discussion or fanfare Sullivan simply dispatched public works employees armed with gallons of red, white, and blue, and soon the fence was considerably more colorful.

Not everyone in Dedham wanted a tricolor display in their midst, however. The painting was only about two-thirds complete when the telephone of Robert Hanson, then the chairman of the historic districts commission, began to ring. Those concerned included not only the historic district commissioners and nearby residents but also a good number of people who had happened to be driving by and thought the fence looked garish. Some noted that it was also hazardous. Because the fence had only two horizontal wooden rails between each post, the tricolor scheme involved painting each section a single color, and it was discovered that the particular shade of blue employed was not visible at night. This gave the appearance of an open lane between the granite posts, and it seemed only a matter of time before a late-night driver might unwittingly crash through.

The selectmen were persuaded to hold a special meeting to consider the citizens' complaints; but they were not convinced to order any change in the work begun by the public works department. "We are in the bicentennial year," they commented, and voted to finish painting the fence red, white, and blue.

The job was completed but townspeople continued to voice their disapproval. As Robert Hanson recalls, "we got a lot of interesting mail," ranging from aesthetic critiques to carnival applications. At least one resident decided to take action and ventured out into the night to splash white paint onto a number of the red and blue sections. The town's only response was to station a police guard on the common.

The issue came up again at the next meeting of the selectmen. About ninety persons attended, most of whom opposed the recent painting, and they presented a petition signed by more than two hundred residents. Selectmen and historic district commissioners disagreed as to whether the new paint scheme had any historic basis—one selectman claimed it was an old Dedham tradition, but no written or photographic evidence supported his claim—and townspeople rejected a compromise plan that called for making the fence primarily but not entirely white.

The final vote was ambiguous, with the selectmen taking the stance that they would not object if the fence were repainted white. Townspeople then had the authority necessary to do as they pleased. Led by historic district commission chairman Hanson, who applied most of the primer coat himself, a group composed largely of members of the Dedham First Company Militia wielded brushes and undid the well-intentioned but unpopular damage. The fence today is white—and the historic district commission is empowered to see that it stays that way.

Looking at a Gift Horse
Easthampton, Massachusetts

Purple, orange, and purple: hardly a traditional color scheme.

They may look like purple and orange to the uninitiated, but as any Lions Club member can tell you, the trash barrels in Easthampton, Massachusetts, are actually purple and gold, the official Lions Club colors (and the school colors of Williston Academy, a private secondary school in the town).

The one hundred or so barrels that are located on the Easthampton Common and throughout the remainder of the town are a gift from the local chapter of the Lions Club, which has provided such amenities for a number of years. In fact, no one can remember the last time the town had to purchase trash receptacles, so no one really knows how much money the town is saving by this gesture. Lions Club members obtained the metal barrels free of charge from various sources, but paint alone cost about three hundred dollars. And then, it is no small job to paint alternating purple and orange bands on one hundred barrels, not to mention applying one hundred Lions Club decals.

We cannot fault the club for its intentions, but we wonder about the appropriateness of the barrels' color scheme. On a common that boasts green grass, green trees, and even green benches, purple and gold are exceedingly visible. As one looks down the length of the common, the barrels have undeniably become the center of attention, overpowering even the geraniums and marigolds. In the rest of the town, too, the presence of purple and gold barrels is not a subtle one.

Easthampton residents seem unperturbed about the variegated barrels. A parks department official was grateful for the club's generosity, and commented that "if they want to put out purple and gold barrels, we won't stop them." Gene Flaherty, president of the Easthampton Chamber of Commerce, could not recall that anyone had ever commented unfavorably on the barrels. "As long as it's clean and painted, it's appropriate for a trash barrel, isn't it?" he said.

Easthampton is clearly a town that takes pride in its common. The trees and grass are well maintained by the parks department, and the flowers are donated by the chamber of commerce, which also tends to any gardening needs. We hope that the Lions Club will continue its auspicious relationship with the town, but we wish that at some future time the barrels that furnish the common might be an inconspicuous shade of green.

Litter receptacles. If your budget allows, select receptacles that are more attractive and durable than the ubiquitous fifty-five-gallon oil drums. Possibilities include those made of wrought iron, wood, or galvanized steel. The receptacles will complement the benches if they are similar in material and are the same height as the top of the bench backs; alternatively, they might be made of wrought iron to relate to the design of other street furniture elements such as tree guards. If you must use oil drums, paint them frequently—preferably dark green—and replace them as they become dented. Be sure receptacles are securely fastened to avoid theft and removable to allow emptying.

Ornamental fountains. Although a visual pleasure, these are also expensive and troublesome to maintain. If you decide a fountain is worth the effort, design one that is in scale with the green. Consider its appearance both with and without running water, because you will not be able to operate it in winter; and avoid those that resemble contemporary abstract sculpture. A nineteenth-century-style form, such as that in Bethel, Vermont, is much more appropriate.

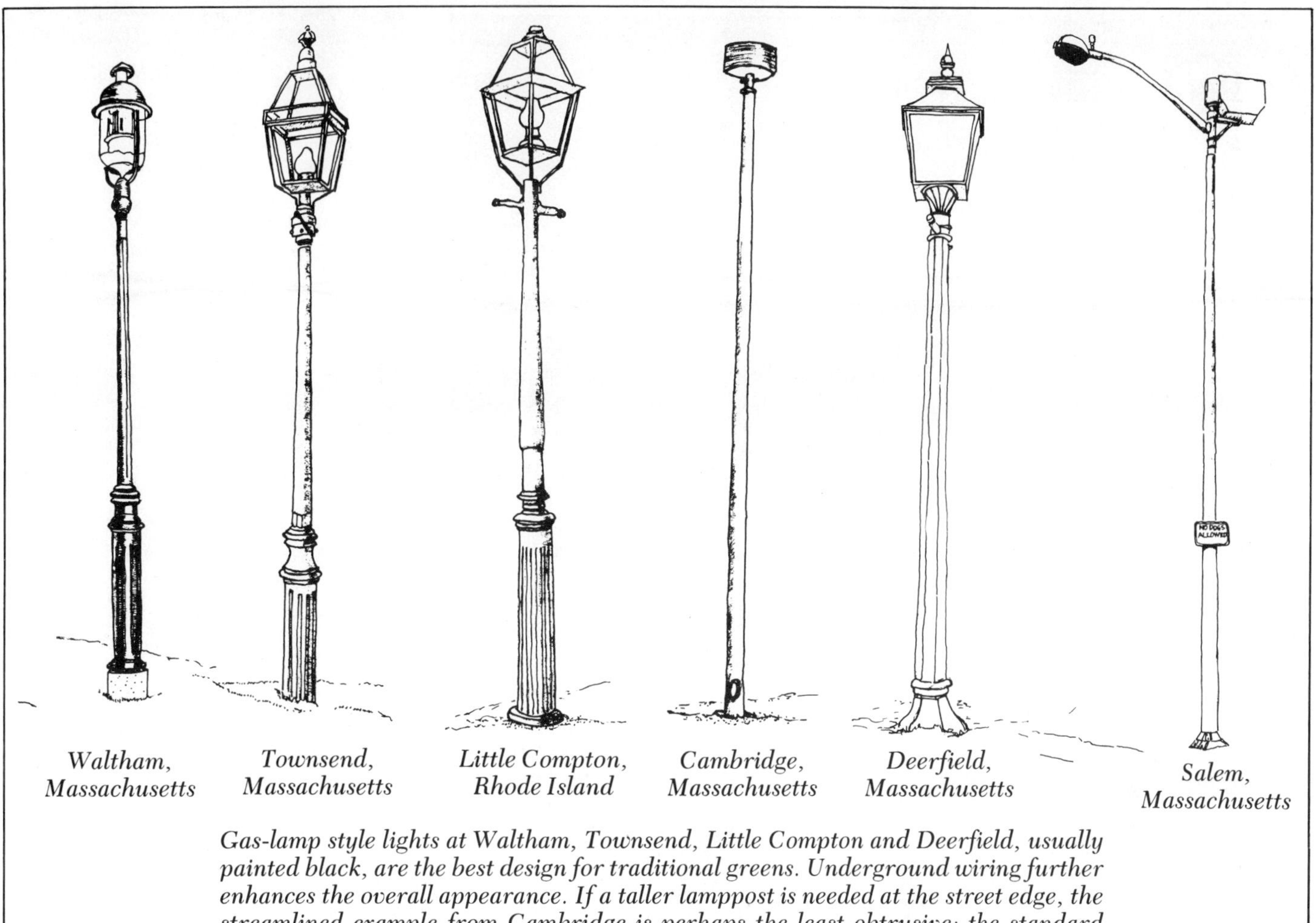

Gas-lamp style lights at Waltham, Townsend, Little Compton and Deerfield, usually painted black, are the best design for traditional greens. Underground wiring further enhances the overall appearance. If a taller lamppost is needed at the street edge, the streamlined example from Cambridge is perhaps the least obtrusive; the standard electric company model at Salem is undesirable.

Markers. Permanent markers should usually be made of granite, which accepts a clean line for incised text and is relatively resistant to weathering. The stone can be polished or smooth-faced on the text side, and smooth or rough-cut on remaining surfaces. Keep the marker as small as will accommodate the text and a reasonable border; it should be of a height that is accessible to children as well as adults. Bronze markers are harder to read, and attractive to thieves because of their value. Anodized aluminum is comparatively inexpensive, accepts both text and illustration, and can be anchored to a granite base (see "Interpretation" section for further discussion).

Signs. Signs announcing a country fair, local charitable event, or the name of the town and green can all be assets if attractively designed. Wood is the preferred material, and metal second; plastic is never acceptable. All that is needed for a temporary sign is a neatly painted flat surface, while a permanent one may merit a more elaborate design incised into a durable piece of wood. Classic serif typefaces should be used, and one or two colors is sufficient.

If there is no location other than the green for traffic and street signs, try to persuade local and state authorities to consider using these styles rather than the standard public works variety. In all cases, signs should be relatively small; eight to twelve square feet is sufficient for most signs announcing special events. Permanent signs can be set in a concrete footing, while signs for events can usually just be driven into the ground.

More expensive than oil drums, but certainly more attractive, are these cast iron receptacles in Chelsea, Massachusetts. These are coordinated in style with the bus shelter and tree guards, and all correspond with the late nineteenth-century architecture of downtown Chelsea.

If oil drums are to be used as trash receptacles, painting them is recommended—but not with cartoon figures.

An unusually accommodating fence surrounding the Village Green in Falmouth, Massachusetts.

New replica bandstand in Medina, Ohio.

An attempt at traditional lighting is marred by the use of inferior materials and by the height of these 14-foot posts at Woodstock, Vermont.

INTERPRETATION

A green is intrinsically useful as a recreational and aesthetic resource, but the addition of interpretive material can help people appreciate it more fully. An explanation of the life of this historic space—how it originated and how it has changed over time—can enrich the perception of visitors and townspeople alike. Furthermore, an understanding of the green's past roles and functions will give the community a better perspective on how the green should be used today.

Most people have a geneaological interest in their past, and this inquisitiveness can be broadened to include the "lineage" of the green and town. Involve the community by soliciting information about the green from longtime residents and by initiating a search for old postcards, maps, and photographs. Check your local library for histories and accounts that mention the green and its environs, and investigate the registry of deeds and the records of the department of public works. You might also investigate state institutions, such as the state historical society, and regional organizations like the Society for the Preservation of New England Antiquities in Boston.

Your audience on the green will be broad—children, adults, one-time visitors, and daily strollers. The information you convey must therefore be widely intelligible yet not lacking in depth. Seek out historical authorities to help you with the final text of any material you develop; and employ a graphic designer, preferably one with exhibit experience, to assist in presenting this material in a lively and engaging format.

INTERPRETATION GUIDELINE 1
Use interpretive material to convey historical and contemporary information.

The most common form of interpretive material is a monument or plaque that marks the location of a historic event or structure: "Here Washington took command of the troops" or "Here stood the first meetinghouse." What is usually lacking is a lengthier text that provides a link between the past and the present, informing the reader *why* the meetinghouse stood there and what happened to it. There are many stories to be told about greens that have less to do with specific events than with daily life. What did this green look like in the eighteenth and nineteenth centuries? How was it used then as compared to now? How does this green compare to those in other towns? An understanding of this general type of information gives the individual events and buildings greater meaning.

The green is also a good place to provide some environmental education. With markers or a printed flyer, designate different species or plants and animals found on or about the green. This information might be as limited as a description of the two or three dominant species of trees and the handful of birds that frequent the site—or it could be as comprehensive as the system on the Boston Common that identifies each tree by its Latin and common name. It is also possible to trace the evolution of the landscape through time, from wetlands to agricultural land to recreational open space.

INTERPRETATION GUIDELINE 2
Consider a variety of media.

Immobile markers, usually of granite, are a traditional green furnishing, and they are quite handsome when well executed. However, they convey only a limited amount of information, and they have a tendency to make the green appear cluttered. With the help of a professional designer, consider alternatives such as photographic panels, flyers, artifact displays, and spoken presentations to supplement or replace existing markers.

Old postcards, such as this one of the Village Green in Falmouth, can be valuable sources of information about how a space formerly looked. Sometimes a marker can incorporate such an illustration, perhaps even standing at the same viewpoint.

Tree markers: an easy means of providing environmental education.

People like pictures, and old photographs, maps, and drawings can help bring the green to life. These should be accompanied by text whenever possible. Although it is difficult to present such artwork in stone, contemporary materials such as porcelain enamel and photo-silkscreened, bronze-finished aluminum accommodate linework or photographic illustration. The flat panels can either be displayed on the exterior walls of nearby buildings or mounted to create freestanding markers.

Another material to consider is cast bronze. This can be used to create bas-relief displays or to reproduce artifacts. When embedded in pavement, bronze becomes quite shiny from the scuffing of shoes across it, and it is attractive and extremely durable.

Visual material can also be combined with text in pocket-size flyers or leaflets, which have several advantages. They are mobile, do not leave a

Guides on the Green
Lexington, Massachusetts

If you see someone on the Lexington Battle Green wearing breeches and a tricorner hat, it could be a Revolutionary War apparition—but it's more likely a costumed member of the local historic guide program.

The guides are rarely at a loss for words on the subject of the green. The site of the 1775 Battle of Lexington, which signified the beginning of the American Revolution, this green is perhaps the most famous in New England. Schoolchildren learn in history classes of Paul Revere's midnight ride and the colonial skirmish with the British, while regional travel books and even ordinary road maps inevitably single out the location. Consequently, the Lexington Green is also one of the region's most visited.

Bringing history to life on the Battle Green.

Some tourists come simply to see a prototypical New England village green, dominated by the white Congregational church and enclosed by equally handsome houses and former taverns. More often, though, visitors are interested in the unique history of the site. The several markers located along the perimeter of the green are helpful; but they provide only limited historical information to already travel-weary readers. Furthermore, many visitors come uncertain of what to expect of this famed shrine; anticipating a development like Colonial Williamsburg and finding only a grassy triangle, they wonder if it is actually the right place.

They usually are not in doubt for long, though. In 1981 twenty-seven volunteers took turns assuring visitors this was the place and providing a thorough yet easily digestible account of Revolutionary War events. The guides are well versed in Lexington's past, gleaning information from study sheets issued by the program director and spending additional time with reference books on reserve at the town library. Prospective guides must pass an oral examination before gaining certification from the town, and experienced guides usually meet with the new group to pass along advice and tips. "Tourists love anecdotes," trainees learn, and they are encouraged to enliven their spiels with stories and even jokes about colonial life. Each guide eventually develops his own style, though, and the information conveyed and tone of delivery vary according to individual preference.

Typically the guides are of high-school age, although some senior citizens have also been involved in the program. They enter it in order to learn more about Lexington as well as to inform visitors. Serving as a tour guide can also be a reasonably lucrative pastime; although the guides are unpaid they are allowed to receive donations. The guides do not attempt to give a full history of the Battle Green; rather they discuss only the revolutionary period for which is is famed. Most guides have found, however, that tourists appreciate additional information, such as Lexington's other points of interest, restaurant advice, and road directions.

If the weather is good, there are usually three guides to be found on the green from 9:00 a.m. until 6:00 p.m. The program operates daily from April 19th—the date of the 1775 battle, which is reenacted each year—through mid-September, and on weekends until the end of the fall foliage. Most towns could not support so extensive a program, since few greens are as popular tourist meccas as Lexington's, but a limited guide program is viable even in small towns. Although the green itself may not have a distinguished past, it can serve as a starting point for discussions about the history of the town. Nor does the tour need to be exclusively historical in nature; the green can be a good place to learn to identify trees and discuss local flora and fauna.

The Lexington guides enjoy their work, and it seems that the tourists are grateful for their service. A tour that starts with only four or six people often ends with as many as eighteen, indicating that the information provided is a popular addition to the visitors' otherwise silent and self-directed experience.

Supplementing the guide program are explanatory markers on the green and directional signs located around the town. The markers are of anodized aluminum, a material which will accept both text and line art. Created under the direction of Ronald Lee Fleming, each marker contains a map that pinpoints the viewer's location and directs him to other markers in the system.

Three types of interpretive material at the Cambridge Common: enamel panels, which can incorporate text, line art, and photographs, a bronze relief panel, and bronze horseshoes embedded in the pavement (showing the route of William Dawes, who alerted the Minutemen to the advancing British). Bronze is an attractive material but expensive and susceptible to theft; porcelain enamel or anodized aluminum is thus preferred for panels.

permanent mark on the green, and can be kept for reading thoroughly at a later time. Flyers can be distributed at local information centers or through an inconspicuous box situated on the green; pick-up and return slots will help to avoid litter.

The volunteer guide is the most extravagant interpretive tool available to a town. Guides are only appropriate in municipalities that receive a large number of visitors to the green, such as Lexington, Massachusetts, but they can add a color and dynamism not otherwise possible. For most towns, it is more realistic to consider staging occasional dramatic performances that recount the history of the green and its environs. School groups could develop such a play as a project that combines history and art, perhaps with the aid of the local historical society.

INTERPRETATION GUIDELINE 3
Integrate interpretive markers with other green furnishings.

Markers with general information should be located along the most frequently visited edge of the green; they should also be sited in careful relation to the paths, paved areas, benches, and lighting. If several markers are to be erected, arrange them in a cluster rather than a row to avoid creating a wall that would disturb the view of the green.

Occasionally, a marker can act as a focal point for a certain area of the green, but in general it should not dominate the space.

A marker that bears a reproduction of an old view of the green should be located as close as possible to the original vantage point, even if that area is not the most frequently visited. If it is not possible to use that location, consider, for comparison's sake, placing a second marker next to it with a contemporary view from the same point.

ENCROACHMENT

During the course of the past one hundred years, the majority of greens have decreased in size as portions of their land have been expropriated for other purposes. Communities widened older roads and built new ones in the centers of their increasingly commercial towns, frequently at the expense of the green. Even towns that took pride in their greens were not able to resist the temptation of taking a bit of open space for development; as early as 1891, one author lamented that the size of the historic Battle Green in Lexington "has been considerably reduced by cutting Bedford Street through the eastern side."

Greens have lost ground to roads, right-hand-turn lanes, parking lots, public buildings, basketball courts, and even cemeteries. Although this trend has abated somewhat it continues today. It is imperative that communities act to protect what little green space remains and, if at all possible, to reclaim what has been lost.

ENCROACHMENT GUIDELINE 1
Defend the green against state highway encroachment.

The widening of state highways has sometimes been accomplished by appropriating land from the edge or edges of the green, resulting in roads that are exceedingly wide and greens that are correspondingly small. Fortunately, as a result of federal legislation in 1966, this problem is less prevalent today than it was in the earlier part of this century. Section 4F of the Department of Transportation Act of 1966 and Section 138 of the Federal-Aid Highway Act both address the issue of taking park and recreation land for highway use, with this paragraph:

> [S]pecial effort should be made to preserve the natural beauty of the countryside and public park and recreation lands, wildlife and waterfowl refuges, and historic sites . . . . [T]he Secretary [of Transportation] shall not approve any program or project which requires the use of any publicly owned land from a public park, recreation area, or wildlife and waterfowl refuge of national, State, or local significance as so determined by such officials *unless (1) there is no feasible and prudent alternative to the use of such land, and (2) such program includes all possible planning to minimize harm to such park, recreational area, wildlife and waterfowl refuge, or historic site resulting from such use.* [emphasis added]

Two aspects of this statement merit further discussion. The first is that in order to be protected, the green must be recognized as a park or historic site; such recognition is provided by designating the green as part of a local historic district or listing it in the National Register of Historic Places. The second is that the legislation discourages such appropriation, but does not prohibit it. Friends of the Green groups should be informed about any highway proposals and, if necessary, quickly and vocally come to the green's defense.

ENCROACHMENT GUIDELINE 2
Defend the green against local expropriation for traffic, recreation, and other purposes.

Although there may be no legal recourse to stop expropriation of the green, a vocal group of citizens can make a difference. Keep abreast of any plans for parking lot expansion, right-hand-turn lanes, sports fields, or other projects that would whittle away at the edges of the green or steal some open space from the interior. Take immediate action against any such plans.

First, notify your state historic commission. The state historic preservation officer may have experience with similar cases and can offer suggestions for effective action. Try to publicize the project plans, and your protests, as much as possible: write editorials for the local newspaper, send press releases

The town of South Royalton enclosing the green in the 1870s.

Curbed Enthusiasm
South Royalton, Vermont

Sometime about 1910 the Village Improvement Association in South Royalton, Vermont, died out, "apparently," wrote the author of a 1911 town history, "from lack of something to do." The association had been active for more than ten years in improving the village, devoting attention chiefly to the centrally located green. Having created "one of the best-kept parks in the small villages of the state," members simply retired from active service and sat back to admire their handiwork.

Had the organization survived until 1977, members would have found that this sort of work is rarely ended. The issue facing the South Royalton Green in 1977 was not so much qualitative as quantitative. Over the years the boundaries of the green had become vague as streets were developed and the area of the square they surrounded was sometimes increased, sometimes diminished. The central village area had become commercialized, and as downtown parking demands increased, cars occasionally parked along the edges of the grassy square or even in the middle of it. With no protective fence or curbs, the green was vulnerable to erosion and damage from the heavy vehicles. A clear definition of where the street left off and the green began was needed.

This problem was brought to the attention of the Vermont Division for Historic Preservation, which determined an appropriate course of action. The town of Royalton surveyed the green, then applied to the division for financial assistance to install curbs around the green's edges. The state agency agreed to fund the project in accordance with the submitted survey lines.

All was well until the United church, which faces the green on the Windsor Street side, realized that the new curbing would slightly decrease the available on-street parking for parishioners. Church leaders quickly went to the Royalton selectmen to protest the plan, requesting that the street be enlarged—and the green accordingly diminished—in order to allow angled instead of parallel parking at the green's edge. With no further discussion, the selectmen agreed.

The state historic preservation office was not pleased with the town's decision and withdrew the promised Economic Development Administration grant. A few South Royalton residents who live in the immediate vicinity of the green were also unhappy because they feared that the widened street would allow higher-speed traffic. These residents circulated a petition and brought the issue to a town meeting, but the church was adamant and had the support of the selectmen.

Despite the loss of outside funding, the town went ahead with the project. The green's National Register status offered no protection once the work no longer involved federal dollars. A swath of the green eighteen feet wide on the Windsor Street side was paved, leaving embellishments such as the Handy Memorial Arch perched precariously at the green's edge; trees that were similarly stranded have since died. Only after this reduction in the size of the green was curbing installed—and probably to keep the grass from encroaching on the parking lot.

The case of South Royalton exemplifies townspeople's changing attitudes toward these central open spaces. Scarcely a hundred years earlier, South Royalton had been devastated by a fire in the central village area. Before the ruins had finished smoking—as they reportedly did for ten days—the business leaders had already decided to erect a large commercial building on one side of Chelsea Street and petition the town to buy the lots on the other side. These lots on the south side of the street adjoined the green, and the businessmen persuaded the town to devote the lots both to widening the street and enlarging the parklike square.

A few years later the Village Improvement Associ-ation was formed, and in 1900 the group assumed responsibility for the green. This new group was accorded that task by the Park Association, a group of forty-one public-spirited citizens who had joined together in 1881 and purchased the green on behalf of the town. The Park Association depended upon annual payments from its members to maintain the green, but the later Village Improvement Association instead sponsored events and outings to raise money. Their imagination knew no bounds; two association members mobilized the "idle talent" in the village and in 1900 presented two recitals of the "grand opera, Queen Esther" which netted ninety-seven dollars for the construction of new gravel sidewalks. Other picnics, concerts, and plays provided money for setting out trees along the town railroad line, laying out additional walkways, preparing promotional brochures to attract visitors to Royalton, and maintaining the fountain and fence on the South Royalton Green.

It is clear from these early accounts that the village center—its green in particular—was the pride of the town. Village Improvement Association members would undoubtedly be surprised to learn that today's townspeople view a civic improvement project as an opportunity to substitute asphalt for green space.

Today cars crowd around the base of the Handy Memorial Arch and encroach upon statuary, obstructing views of the otherwise still attractive green.

to the regional papers, and investigate the possibilities of television time through local news or interview shows. Organize supporters to attend town meetings, deliver flyers, and put up posters. Collecting signatures on a petition to "Save the Green" can be a good indicator of the size and influence of your supporting constituency.

Often there is a legitimate need for more downtown parking or a soccer field, but the green is not the place for these. Form a two- or three-person committee that can work with local officials to recommend alternative locations.

As a last resort you can take your case to court. Such proceedings are, however, lengthy and costly, and it is best to arrive at some solution locally.

Wooden bollards on the common in Wentworth, New Hampshire are too far from the edge of the turf to protect it completely.

Traffic signs in Littleton, Massachusetts create an unattractive approach to the common.

ENCROACHMENT GUIDELINE 3
Define the edges of the green.

Where the grass of the green meets directly with the road, there is rarely a definitive edge. Instead, pedestrians and careless motorists wear down a three- to five-foot-wide strip of grass, turning it into dirt. Cars park on this dusty shoulder, street sweepers further grind it down, and winter road salt kills any trace of grass that remains. The next time the road is paved, the green, townspeople are chagrined to discover, is five feet narrower on each side.

The solution is to provide a clear demarcation of where the road ends and the green begins. Curbing the perimeter of the green is the most straightforward means of doing so, preferably with granite. Sidewalks can help, although they too can usurp areas of grass; and fences and trees are additional reinforcers.

All of these methods prevent gradual erosion of the green's edges and also the sudden, intentional claiming of five- or ten-foot strips for road widening or additional parking space. Town officials are reluctant to appropriate land from the green for other purposes, if they have just invested money in curbing, fences, and trees.

ENCROACHMENT GUIDELINE 4
If possible, enlarge the green by reducing or eliminating roads and reclaiming adjacent land.

In many towns an earlier configuration of the green is still apparent. The one or two small islands of grass near the green, today encircled by roads, were formerly part of the green itself. Particularly if the main green is small—narrower than 150 feet or less than one acre in area—reclaiming these isolated pieces can markedly enhance the appearance of the green and its environs.

Town officials are more eager to enlarge existing roads and construct new ones than they are to eliminate roadways. If, however, you can demonstrate that a road is underused, you may be able to make a convincing case for its elimination. Traffic studies documenting the number of cars that use each road or turn lane would be necessary. It is also possible that you could convince officials to make a road narrower, and hence the green larger, if there have been a number of traffic accidents owing to conflict or confusion among several lanes.

Approval for modifying the roadway must usually be obtained from both local and state highway authorities. Use of state or federal funds at the local level for such an alteration is unlikely, except as part of a larger downtown renewal project; but funds can sometimes be obtained through state highway departments.

Fighting the Highwaymen
Middletown, Connecticut

If an urban renewal project includes plans to construct a highway though your village green and demolish a historic house, and the local redevelopment authority refuses to listen to your protests, what can you do? In Middletown, Connecticut, determined preservationists had a simple but powerful answer: take the case to court.

The Metro South Urban Renewal Project, like scores of projects of the 1960s, sought to revitalize a downtown area through demolition and new construction. The plan was first drafted by the Middletown Redevelopment Agency in 1964; in order to establish eligibility for federal dollars, it was submitted to the Department of Housing and Urban Development (HUD) for review. HUD approved the application in October, 1969, and executed the loan and grant contract the following September, after which time HUD officials served as overseers of the locally directed project.

As plans continued, the details of the Metro South Project became more widely known. Its purpose, redevelopment officials said, was "to create a direct alignment of streets for improved traffic flow and safety and to achieve the objective of creating as much taxable land as possible in the project area." In physical terms, this meant cutting through Middletown's South Green and paving 17,000 square feet of it in order to join some streets—Broad with South Main and Church with Union. The change would reduce the number of intersections in the area from five to three and traffic lights from three to two, thus "easing traffic flow." To compensate for the area to be paved, the redevelopment agency proposed annexing 23,000 square feet of land onto one of the green's other sides, an offer officials deemed fair since the green would actually gain more area than it would lose. Part of the plan also called for the demoliton of the Mather-Douglas house, an early nineteenth-century Federal structure which stood in the way of the proposed road.

It was not until 1973 that representatives of the Greater Middletown Preservation Trust (G.M.P.T.) met with officials of the redevelopment agency to express disapproval—a bit late, some said, but preservationists countered that the impact of the project had not been publicized earlier. Agency officials proved reluctant to consider alternative plans, so the G.M.P.T. took its first step to block the project by nominating the Mather-Douglas House for listing on

Before

After

the National Register of Historic Places. Such recognition, the group felt, would strengthen its contention that the house was worth saving. As is routine, the Trust submitted its recommendation to the review board of the Connecticut Historical Commission, which advised that the entire South Green area was potentially eligible for listing. The national review board concurred, and in August 1975 the South Green Historic District gained National Register status.

Disagreement over the project continued. Spurred on by the National Register confirmation, preservationists maintained that the green and its environs were "a nonrenewable resource that many towns would cherish," and that the proposed substitution of a new piece of land would not compensate for the destruction of a historic district. A local engineer devised an alternative plan to shift and curve the realigned Church Street, thereby avoiding the swath of green, the Mather House, and several mature trees. Even regional HUD officials took notice of the protests and stated without ambiguity, "We have asked the local agency to reconsider and to reconsider, but apparently they don't want to reconsider."

Indeed, the redevelopment agency wanted to push ahead, stating that plans were too far along to be changed. In August 1976 the agency awarded the project contract to a local construction firm, the signal that bulldozers would not be far behind.

"Time is running out," declared William Howard, attorney for the G.M.P.T. and the newly formed Committee to Save South Green. Within a matter of days Howard brought the case before the U.S. District Court in Connecticut, seeking an injunction to halt the project on the grounds that HUD and the Middletown Redevelopment Agency had failed to undertake the required environmental reviews And impact statements. While a temporary restraining order prevented the work from proceeding, project backers prepared a defense to argue that the National Environmental Policy Act requiring such studies had not gone into effect until 1969, after the Metro South project had already received HUD approval. In November 1976, however, the judge ruled that the Middletown project had not received the final HUD sanction until 1970, when the loan and grant application had been passed. The environmental assessments were, therefore, required, and the project was called to a halt.

The ruling was not based merely on technicality. Under the National Environmental Protection Act, the federal government has a responsibility to ensure that "the Nation may . . . preserve important historic, cultural, and natural aspects of our national heritage, and maintain, wherever possible, an environment which supports diversity and variety of individual choice." This goal presumably would be better accomplished through the preservation of the historic South Green than through implementation of the Metro South project. Furthermore, the judge ruled that

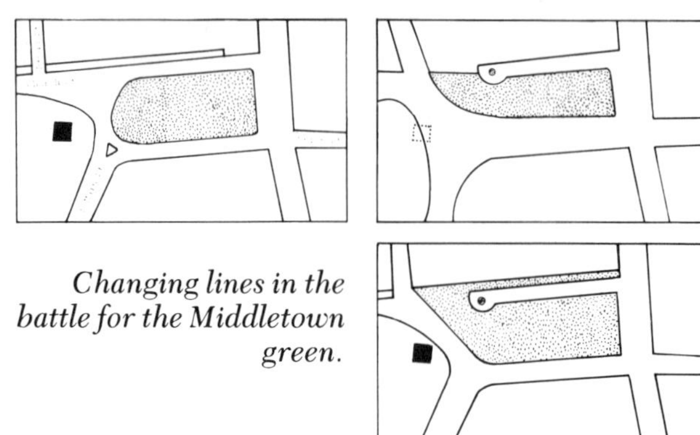

Changing lines in the battle for the Middletown green.

HUD should have contacted the federal Advisory Council on Historic Preservation regarding the proposed demolition of the Mather-Douglas house. Had HUD and the redevelopment agency conducted the required studies, they would have encountered opposition and the project might have been stopped considerably earlier.

After the ruling, there was still no clear-cut solution. A four-member Metro South review panel was established and both sides were willing to compromise, but once it was decided to save the Mather-Douglas House an eight-month deadlock ensued over whether or not to relocate it. It was not until 1980 that the project was finally completed. The solution: to create a cul-de-sac at the end of Main Street, leave the Mather-Douglas house in its original location, bypass the green with the highway—in fact adding a bit of land in the process—and transform the dejected patch of grass into an attractive park.

Under the terms of a memorandum of agreement, the G.M.P.T. oversaw the landscape restoration of the green, according to a plan approved by the state historical commission. The green had first been landscaped during the late nineteenth century; after research using old photographs and postcards, the rehabilitation featured appropriate landscaping and Victorian benches and other furnishings. A small plaza was installed near Main Street, and an old fountain was removed from its city hall location, restored, and placed on the green. Christmas 1980 was celebrated with the lighting of the Christmas tree on South Green for the first time in twenty years and a reception at the nearby historical society, where a new display presented the entire history of the South Green.

The same urban renewal funds that would have bisected the green with a highway were thus used to purchase new benches; and the Mather-Douglas house that was slated to be razed, today functions successfully as doctors' offices. Jan Cunningham, executive director of the G.M.P.T., says that the resolution of this controversy was "the turning point in historic preservation in the city," a claim supported by the Middletown Main Street restoration project, among others. The moral of the story? That you *can* fight city hall—and that it's worth the effort.

TRAFFIC

Introduction

This incised wooden traffic sign from near Williamsburg agrees with the character of greens.

The rise in popularity of the car after World War I brought a myriad of problems to downtown areas in general and greens in particular. Roads became wider and more numerous, stealing the edges of the green for pavement. The increased traffic made pedestrian access to the green more difficult, and the constant sight and sound of vehicles made being there less pleasant than before. Traffic and directional signs cluttered the edges of the green, and the ring of parked cars that hugged its perimeter made the green itself less visible. Many became little more than traffic islands, obstacles around which motorists sped with scarcely a passing glance.

These are problems that still plague greens today, and the realistic solutions are not entirely successful. As detailed in the "Landscape" section, one remedy is to solidly enclose the green with trees to block out the sight and noise of the street. Eliminating superfluous roads and narrowing others, discussed in the above "Encroachment" section, is a second possibility. The guidelines that follow also address the attendant traffic problems of parking, pedestrian access, and signage.

TRAFFIC GUIDELINE 1
Enforce low speed limits around the green.

Fast-moving traffic is one of the greatest deterrents to use of the green. Especially in the case of greens that have become circular in shape, automobile drivers tend to rush around with little regard for pedestrians and bicyclists. The ideal speed limit for encircling roads is fifteen miles per hour; and every effort should be made to see that it is strictly enforced.

TRAFFIC GUIDELINE 2
Provide adequate crosswalk access to the green.

The need for crosswalks depends upon the amount of traffic in the village, town, or city. In a small village, where the green is in a residential area, it is of little value to introduce yet another traffic-related feature. In a downtown shopping area or urban center, though, crosswalks are a necessity.

If there is enough traffic that pedestrians cannot easily cross to the green at any point, there should be at least one crosswalk leading to each of the green's corners. In the case of large greens, where one side exceeds four hundred feet in length, a crosswalk every two hundred feet is desirable.

The usual solution to crosswalk design is to paint stripes onto the road, but a more appealing alternative is to use a second paving material. Brick or granite slab is suitable; cobbles should be used only for edging, as they create a surface too bumpy for baby carriages and the elderly.

Since the time of horse and buggy, the circular common (now a city park) in Keene, New Hampshire has been isolated by wide streets. The town has made the best of a

bad situation by providing numerous crosswalks and intelligible signs.

The commons in Tallmadge, Ohio, before and after (opposite page)—an example of common land in a region settled by former New Englanders. Shown here is the circle before a project was implemented to reduce traffic congestion and confusion, and to add more green space to the fringe areas.

If the roads encircling the green are more than two lanes wide, consider creating islands at crosswalk midpoints for pedestrian use. These can also be helpful in intersections that lack signal lights.

**TRAFFIC GUIDELINE 3
Eliminate curbside parking along the perimeter of the green.**

As early as 1922, Robert Nathan Cram observed in his student thesis:

> The requirement of parking space for automobiles in populous areas causes an unusual tendency to encroach upon the common land to provide extra street width. Not only is this physical danger to the common considerable, but esthetically the appearance of a common bordered by a solid row of standing automobiles is most unhappy. (p. 153)

Today the problem is pervasive, and the results unhappy indeed. A stranglehold of parked cars deprives the town of the visual benefits of the green and also interrupts the view of the townscape from within the green's edges. The turf and trees are susceptible to abuse, especially if a curb is lacking; and the general activity of running motors and slamming doors is scarcely tranquil.

If at all possible, prohibit parking around the green and remove all parking meters.

In a residential area there is relatively little need for roadside parking, but in downtown centers merchants are often unwilling to eliminate parking spots—in fact, they are usually eager to create additional ones. Work with merchants and the local traffic authorities or planning commission to find less visible areas or to use existing lots more effectively. Most downtown areas have little available space, but there are sometimes open lots behind the main-street stores that can accommodate additional cars.

Occasionally the demolition of a building creates new downtown space;

but if this is to be used for parking, care must be taken to landscape the site, both to conceal the cars and to maintain the line of the street. The town may want to retain this valuable space for retail use, in which case it may wish also to consider the construction of a parking garage or a major lot outside of the central area as a more practical long-term solution to its parking problem.

In some cases it is advisable to allow parking at certain times or on certain days only. In Falmouth, Massachusetts, for example, churchgoers park their cars on one side of the green on Sunday mornings with little detrimental effect. On weekdays the "no parking" law is enforced and the green remains unobstructed.

TRAFFIC GUIDELINE 4
Restrict the number of signs on the green.

Stop signs, yield signs, one-way signs, route signs, street signs—these are more numerous than trees on some unfortunate greens. Highway departments do not seem to realize that drivers are confused rather than aided by such a barrage of instructions, and that in any case the green is not the place for this information. Signs on the green should be kept to a minimum, especially at the head of triangular greens where they can obscure the vista entirely.

Signs can often be removed to the opposite side of the street. If, however, the green is the only realistic location, consider placing signs lower than usual, perhaps attached to the fence. Signs should be of a design, material, and color compatible with the overall character of the green (see the "Furnishings" section of this chapter).

The type of sign that is welcome on the green, but is rarely found, is one that identifies the town or the green itself. If attractive and well sited, such a sign can be an asset by identifying and lending a sense of significance to the space.

Recycling a Road, Claiming a Common
North Andover, Massachusetts

Embellished by mature elms, oaks, and maples, and surrounded by impressive eighteenth- and nineteenth-century homes, the North Andover Common appears to be one of those traditional New England green spaces that time has passed by for the last century or two. In reality, this ten-acre common took on its current appearance scarcely twenty-five years ago, the product of a Village Improvement Association determined to remove buildings, assemble parcels of land, close a road, and provide the town with a spacious common of which it could be proud.

North Andover, like the nearby towns of Lawrence and Lowell, owed its nineteenth-century prosperity to the mills and factories of the industrial revolution. It was a community of contrasts: wealthy mill owners and immigrant workers, luxurious estates and worker housing, sweeping lawns and bare patches of dirt. It was a town with both attractive and unattractive sections, and by the 1880s some of the town's leading citizens began to think about beautifying those areas that offended their sensibilities. Accordingly, under the direction of the Boston merchant and gentleman gardener J. D. W. French, the Village Improvement Association was formed in 1885, "for the purposes of encouraging agriculture, horticulture, and for improving and ornamenting the streets and public squares . . . ." Its members were drawn from the upper echelon of North Andover society, and one of its earliest projects involved the common.

The town had acquired a small patch of land to serve as a common in 1825, located in the old center. Over the course of the next sixty years a firehouse and a bandstand, deemed "very objectionable" in one account, had been built on this common land, and the Village Improvement Association set out to clear these away. The firehouse was relocated to a nearby street and subsequently converted to a Masonic Hall; the bandstand was simply demolished.

The common was then improved, agreed association members, but still too small. They decided to acquire more land, both public and private—and, being the leaders of the town that they were, they knew this was a perfectly feasible approach.

The first step was the closing of a portion of Essex Street, an underused road immediately north of the common, and the annexing of property on the opposite side. Moses T. Stevens, the founder of Stevens Mills and a member of the association, bought the property known as the old Moody Bridges Homestead. The

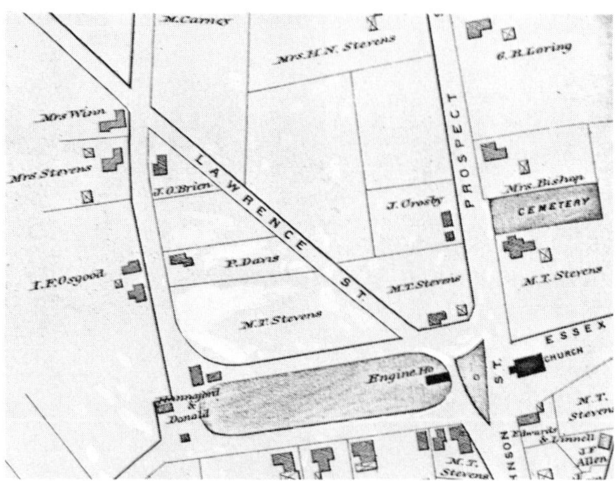

Once a road, this strip of land is now part of the North Andover Common.

association then raised the funds to purchase it from him, and late in 1897 tore down the house and barn that stood on the land. A duplex house on the west side of the common on Osgood Street was also purchased and razed by the group in that year. This accomplished, the association (now renamed the North Andover Improvement Society) went on to purchase additional parcels in 1902, 1903, and 1926. But it was not until 1959 that the project was completed. The group sold and moved one last house before granting the property as a whole to the town, nearly three-quarters of a century after it took up its cause.

While the society was piecing together, jigsaw puzzle fashion, numerous bits of land, it was also keeping a watchful eye on the character of the area and maintaining a strong defense against encroachment. In 1931, the society persuaded the state to refrain from making highway improvements along one side of the green, and their efforts prevented the development of a major through-traffic road. The area around the common today retains the village character that the society deemed desirable.

Thus, at a time when most communities were bisecting their commons with roads and trolley tracks and paring down the edges for street-widening projects, North Andover was doing just the opposite. The spacious and handsome common stands as a testament to just how much a concerned—and powerful—group of citizens can accomplish.

TOWNSCAPE

For better or worse, the green is an integral part of the surrounding town. The configuration of streets, buildings, and street furnishings that collectively form the "townscape" of an area plays a major role in determining the character and quality of the green. While a row of clapboard houses may create a charming nineteenth-century scene, a parking lot in front of a convenience food store can undermine the best traditional green. Any efforts to improve the green must, therefore, also include the overall context in which the green exists.

If the existing townscape is attractive, then it is important to ensure that its character is maintained. As discussed in the introduction to this chapter, the local historic district is the most effective tool for preserving extant buildings as well as establishing design review guidelines for new construction. However, there may be some townscape components that need improvement; thus this section addresses change as well as preservation.

TOWNSCAPE GUIDELINE 1
Preserve the townscape enclosure of the green.

While some greens adjoin open land, the usual situation is enclosure by a more or less continuous row of houses, stores, or public buildings. Although open space may separate these structures, as side yards do in residential areas, the line of the street is frequently reinforced by fences, shrubs, and trees. This sort of line, varied in texture yet unbroken, gives the street a continuity of its own and also defines the green.

At all cost, prevent the demolition of any structure that is structurally sound. A gap of open land, like a missing tooth, is unattractive, and a parking lot creates one of the worst settings for a green. In an area that is changing from residential to commercial use, an older house can almost always be adapted for new purposes through rehabilitation or addition. A concerned and vocal group of townspeople can often convince a homeowner or merchant to leave well enough alone.

If demolition is unavoidable, or if a gap already exists, insist on high-quality infill construction that is compatible in scale, mass, fenestration (placement of windows and doorways), roofline, materials, and decoration with what is already in place. It is not necessary—or even desirable—to copy earlier styles exactly, but any new building should complement its older neighbors. A new

A handsome sign on the common identifies the town of Haverhill, once a coachstop on the main road through the state.

Variations on a theme: white wooden fences and eighteenth and nineteenth-century houses form the perfect backdrop for the village green in Falmouth, Massachusetts.

A view of the Westford Police / Fire complex, showing the old Town Hall to the left.

Designing in Context
Westford, Massachusetts

When given the opportunity to design a new building, an architect often employs the same criteria as a pizza-parlor owner choosing a neon sign: the bigger, brighter, and more conspicuous, the better. The goal of most twentieth-century architecture has been not to blend in but to contrast, to look not to the past but to the future. As Brent C. Brolin wryly commented in *Architecture in Context*, "If a design does not stand out from its neighbors, most believers in modern architecture seem to feel it has failed: it is neither original nor creative."

Such thinking has created architectural sore thumbs in any number of New England towns, where designers simply could not resist introducing a facade of concrete into a brick-lined street or a ten-story tower into a row of triple-deckers. And such easily could have been the case in Westford, Massachusetts, when the police and fire departments outgrew the old town hall and decided in 1974 to erect a new structure at the head of the common.

No new buildings had been erected around the common in more than a hundred years. The result was a neighborhood consisting of a homogeneous group of structures, including houses, a church, and the 1870 town hall. All share certain features of the eighteenth- and nineteenth-century New England tradition: built of wood and sheathed in clapboards, they are essentially rectilinear in form, often with the triangular gable end turned toward the street. They feature small-paned windows, usually rectangular, that punctuate the wall surfaces at regular intervals; and most of the buildings are painted white or yellow with accents of black or green. All in all, this shared architectural vocabulary created a cohesive and quiet ambiance that might easily have been disrupted by a noisy newcomer.

A variety of styles was represented in the early proposals submitted for the new fire/police headquarters. One school of thought favored a brick structure with a mansard-style roof; although this design made some reference to its historic surroundings, it was not particularly well suited to Westford. Not until the Cambridge-based firm of Ecodesign became interested in the project was there any thoughtful attempt to design a building for this unique setting.

Ecodesign's first priority was to maintain the architectural integrity of the historic common. Accordingly, the firm conducted an historical analysis of the town and an investigation of the site, discussed future commercial building, for example, should not be of concrete if the rest of the street is brick; it should not be eight-stories tall if its neighbors are two and three stories; and it should not have an illuminated plastic sign if adjacent signs are made of wood.

A familiar landmark building embellishes the town in the same way a bandstand does the green. Both suffer from competition, though, and the view, or "sightline," of these landmarks from the green and major thoroughfares should remain unimpaired. Do not allow new construction to overshadow towers, steeples, or cupolas whose appearance, even in the distance, enhances the green's atmosphere.

building plans with town officials, and developed six different design schemes. The final choice of a plan was made, in an unusual and laudable manner, by the townspeople themselves. The six options were presented to the citizens of Westford at their annual town meeting, and their vote determined the winning design.

The old and new buildings now form a single unit. The long, low police building serves as a link between the town hall and the fire station, and similarities of both form and detail relate the new to the old. Like the town hall, the fire station stands with its gable end to the street, and its essentially rectilinear form is relieved of any starkness by a variety of smaller appendages. The large doors needed for the fire trucks could have been problematic, creating an appearance of gaping holes, but the articulation of these doors into small panes of glass is in keeping with the architectual vernacular. Also consistent with tradition is the white, two-inch-wide siding that covers the new construction. Chosen to match that of the town hall, the new siding is actually maintenance-free vinyl, as desired by town officials, rather than wooden clapboarding. The inclusion of wood detailing at the corners of the new construction, though, makes it all but impossible to distinguish between the old exterior finish and the new.

The cluster arrangement of the new complex is particularly successful in its relationship to the common. The new construction is contained in one area, rather than enveloping the common; and the resulting courtyard complements the adjacent green space. In addition, by paying such overt homage to the old town hall, the new complex has helped to ensure the careful preservation of its predecessor.

Brent Brolin, writing again in *Architecture in Context*, soundly endorses the perceptive approach adopted by Ecodesign. Brolin states:

> When a new building is to be fitted into a neighborhood with such a strong visual character the best solution is often . . . to design as though you were working in that period. This does not necessarily mean copying the . . . facade literally, but suggests working in the formal language of that era, with an eye towards relating the face to its immediate neighbors . . . . [T]here can be considerable leeway in such an approach, depending only on the skill and ingenuity of the designer. (p. 72)

One need only look at towns like Waltham, Massachusetts, where a new bank building on the common has done its best to disregard its older small-scale neighbors, to realize just how successful the Westford complex is. Admittedly, not every neighborhood is as cohesive architecturally as Westford; but many areas, residential and downtown alike, do have a unique scale and quality. Communities should follow Westford's lead in becoming aware of their distinctive architectural heritage and in taking an active role to see that it is sustained.

Architectural detail of the new addition.

Can a New Church Marry Old Ground?
Ipswich, Massachusetts

"If we had had an historic district then," bemoaned one resident of Ipswich, "things might have been different." What would now be different in Ipswich is the appearance of the new Congregational church on the town's North Green, built in 1971 after a fire damaged its predecessor. The siting and design of that new church were the source of considerable controversy, as a handful of townspeople waged—and lost—a battle to convince church directors that a contemporary white brick structure was not in keeping with the historic character of the green.

The North Green in Ipswich has actually seen a number of churches since the first was constructed there in 1634, but the one that remains fixed in the minds of most residents today dated to 1846. Known as the Old North Church, it was generally recognized as a fine example of mid-nineteenth-century Gothic Revival architecture, a style sometimes called "Carpenter Gothic" in reference to the wooden frame and sheathing used instead of the stone of the European tradition. The tall spire of the Old North Church was one of three that dominated the Ipswich skyline, and the church was distinguished by the conspicuous town clock in its facade.

In June 1965 a fire that started during a lightning storm damaged the church—or destroyed it, depending upon whose account one believes. One observer recalls that he drove past the church the following morning and could not tell that there had been a fire, but there was no talk of restoration. For either structural or economic reasons, the old structure was razed and church directors initiated plans for a new one.

Troubles began when the directors revealed that they intended to build a larger edifice than before and locate it somewhat differently on the 1.4-acre green. Since the church, in one form or another, had occupied the green for more than three hundred years, its directors and many townspeople alike assumed that the land was church property. In reality, the old common land had in 1926 been designated by the town as a park, with the exception of the precise spot then occupied by the Old North Church. Legally the organization could not build on a town park, and so church directors petitioned the town to purchase the land.

No one denied that the church should be able to erect a new structure on the green, but some residents such as Lovell Thompson of the Heritage Trust and Daniel B. Lunt of the Ipswich Historical Society had other objections. They felt that the proposed modified

The Old North Church, built in 1846 and demolished following a fire in 1965.

The new and controversial church on the Ipswich North Green.

A-frame structure was aesthetically ill suited to the green, particularly since the steeple would not be large enough to accommodate the old bell and town clock. They also objected to the church's plan to increase the size of the building and thereby decrease the area of open space, a popular children's play area. "Everyone wants a church on the green," declared resident Ray Sullivan, "but there should be a little room left for the rest of us." In an attempt to force the church to rework its design, a number of townspeople set out to oppose the sale of land to the church.

Acting on behalf of the trustees of the Heritage Trust, Lovell Thompson distributed flyers throughout the town that detailed not only the objections to the sale but also an alternative plan. Stating that "since the beginning the Green has been the jointly cherished possession of Church and Town," he proposed that the town should continue to benefit from the space as well as assume some financial responsibility for its use. Since church directors had earlier responded that it would be too costly to change the plans or build a larger steeple, Thompson developed a scheme whereby the Heritage Trust would donate $5,000 to cover the cost of relocating the church to leave more open space on

While townspeople and historical societies are usually aware of the significance of a colonial-period house or a Gothic Revival church, they may overlook smaller but equally noteworthy townscape features. Hitching posts, milestones, watering troughs, pumps, fences, stone walls, and century-old trees are all delightful survivors meriting preservation. Outbuildings such as barns should similarly be accorded a place in the community's esteem. These familiar features in the public domain, as well as those that are publicly visible but stand on private property, are themselves landmarks, and they also establish a context for the town's one or two architectural gems. Do not allow these features to disappear simply to accommodate parking or to ease maintenance—they are irreplaceable.

A project to improve the green should provide a good occasion for the owner of an adjacent house to invest in a new coat of paint or a nearby merchant to erect a more attractive sign. Involving the owners of these properties in improving the green is the first step toward a larger townscape project, which may be executed entirely by the private sector or may also include the town government.

First, solicit the support and advice of the green's neighbors concerning the work on the green and the surrounding area. Agree on what should be done and by whom, perhaps with the help of a local historical commission, preservationist, or architect. A homeowner or merchant who is reluctant to undertake any renovation can sometimes be persuaded by the enthusiasm of the major-

---

the green and rewriting the land-transfer legislation. Furthermore, the trust would match up to $25,000 of donations raised by the church, so that an additional $50,000 might be available for building a structure "designed to incorporate a clock tower and placed most effectively to embrace the interests of all."

Townspeople were given the opportunity to take a stance when the issue was brought before a special town meeting; the outcome was not happy for the architectural mavericks. Of the 771 townspeople who cast votes, 600 were in favor of granting the land—and carte blanche design capabilities—to the church. The final decision still lay with the Massachusetts state legislature, whose approval was necessary to redesignate the park land as church property; but with the support of the district state representative and the indication of public sentiment it was only a matter of time before the church had its way.

The new church on the green, described as "contemporary Gothic," does perhaps make some historical reference to its surrounding buildings with its pointed-arch window, and it does contain a clock; but its white brick construction material is purely twentieth century. The church lacks the massive quality of its predecessor, and few would say that it has any charm. Its siting is also unsatisfactory; as John Updike notes in this book's preface, the South Green is "overburdened by its sprawling modern meetinghouse."

There was some preconstruction talk of moving the building forward to preserve both the view across the green from side streets and some more open space in the rear, but this was never done. So the church now seems to occupy the entire space rather than to serve as its focal point.

The problem in Ipswich was that, despite the presence of preservation-oriented groups like the Heritage Trust, there were no legal means available to limit the design powers of the church. In Massachusetts the most effective means of ensuring a professional design review is the local historic district. But, as has occurred in other communities, Ipswich residents had earlier opposed the formation of such a district on the grounds that it permitted excessive interference with rights of property owners. The Heritage Trust made a valiant attempt to influence the building's design and siting; but with no legal footing it could only submit to a church that was more interested in building quickly and cheaply than working toward a design acceptable to the entire community.

When the South Parish House on the South Green was destroyed by fire in December 1977, the last of the three steeples defining the Ipswich skyline fell. There is, however, a somewhat hopeful outcome to this event. The town agreed to sell the green to the Heritage Trust for $16,000, and the group intends to hold the land until a suitable use for it can be determined.

ity, and if several neighbors are planning paint and carpentry work at the same time, the purchase of supplies in bulk and the sharing of tools can be an added financial incentive.

An organized plan by a group of citizens can then be used to encourage the town to play a role as well. Street trees, new sidewalks, benches, and trash receptacles are amenities that are often especially needed in commercial areas and that can be provided with public funds. A commitment of public funds can also help homeowners and merchants secure low-interest rehabilitation loans from a local bank.

Be sure that the rehabilitation work and new amenities are in keeping with the historic character of the green; the goal is *not* to "enliven" the townscape with revolving illuminated plastic signs! Your local or state historical commission can provide advice about color schemes and materials for building facades. New amenities such as benches or trash receptacles should match or be compatible with those on the green. (Their design is discussed in the "Furnishings" section of this chapter.)

Townscape rehabilitation has more than just visual rewards. Many New England towns derive considerable income from tourism, and the improvement of the green and its environs can have a positive monetary effect.

TOWNSCAPE GUIDELINE 5
Defend solar access to the green

In downtown urban areas, the land surrounding the green is often the most central—and hence the most valuable. The increasing price of land has encouraged developers to build taller and taller buildings, and while one shadow cast on the green is tolerable, the dark pall created by a dozen skyscrapers is not. Long shadows, especially in the winter, significantly reduce the usability of the green for sitting, and can also stunt plant growth.

As this trend toward tall buildings continues, communities must become more aggressive about reviewing plans *before* they are executed. Shade and shadow studies should be presented by the architect or developer, accurately detailing how much shadow will be created, where it will fall, and its duration over a twenty-four-hour cycle throughout the various seasons. Community groups should enlist the services of a knowledgeable architect to help review these studies. If the shadow is judged too extensive, the community should not be afraid to demand a reworking of the plans until they are satisfactory.

In his 1922 thesis on New England commons, Robert Nathan Cram bemoaned the recent blight of wires and poles that had settled upon some village centers; and he singled out the common in Hadley, Massachusetts, "whose open central panel is conspicuously enframed by two rows of mammoth telephone poles." Fifty years later little has changed in Hadley, where wires ideally should be undergrounded. At the least, some trees could be planted to hide them.

Oversized signs and brick infill disfigure these otherwise handsome storefronts.

Electricity and telephone wires not only detract from the visual quality of a townscape but also pose maintenance and safety problems. Although expensive, placing wires underground is by far the most desirable solution to the visual clutter they cause.

Some states such as California have ordered the power companies to bury wires underground as expeditiously as possible; but progress has been slow, in part because consumers are unwilling to pay the resulting increases in utility rates. The power company may also insist that the abutter pay for his own hookup, a requirement that can doom the project unless federal or private assistance is available. A few communities have negotiated the placement of wires underground in downtown areas by agreeing to grant other concessions to a power company, such as permission to expand an overhead transmission corridor on the outskirts of town. This strategy, however, merely creates another blighted area and is not recommended.

Before proceeding with the actual burial of utility lines, studies should be conducted so that damage to the green is minimized. Topography, paving, and tree roots may all be affected by such work. If underground wire installation is to be executed as part of a larger rehabilitation scheme, it should, of course, be completed before final touches such as planting new trees and laying turf.

A less desirable alternative—but better than nothing—is to plant trees to conceal the poles and wires. Even if you decide later to bury the wires, the trees are a good investment. Be sure, though, that you start with trees that are of a three- to five-inch diameter; saplings set amongst towering poles will only accentuate the problem.

Preservation Versus
the Parking Lot
Norwich, Connecticut

So far as anyone knows, George Washington never slept here.

In fact, there is no record that anyone of recognized historical importance ever set foot in the Eleazor Lord Tavern, built about 1760. And architecturally speaking, the two-story dwelling is respectable but undistinguished, its gable roof and clapboard exterior the rule rather than the exception in eighteenth-century design.

Communities across the country have come to realize, though, that even a perfectly ordinary building of 1760 is both noteworthy and deserving of protection. It is just such buildings that, in groups of twenty or fifty or a hundred, collectively create a historic setting and atmosphere that is greater than the sum of its parts. This is a notion with which the people of Norwich, Connecticut, concurred when in 1967 they established the Norwichtown Historic District to preserve the older section of town. Included within the boundaries of this district, whose focus is the Norwich-town Green, is the Eleazor Lord Tavern.

The district does not include the property immediately adjacent to the tavern, a McDonald's restaurant complete with an asphalt parking lot and golden-arches sign. The arrival of McDonald's, which also occurred in 1967, in this primarily residential neighborhood was a defeat for the chamber of commerce, city council, Norwich school board, Norwich *Bulletin*, Huntington Family Association, Southeastern Connecticut Regional Planning Agency, Norwich Founders Society, four labor unions, and eight hundred petition-signing residents who let it be known they did not want a hamburger stand in their midst. Townspeople cited a variety of reasons why McDonald's was ill suited to this location: traffic hazard at a nearby school crossing, public nuisance, depreciation of property values, and aesthetic incompatibility, among others. The McDonald's controversy inspired townspeople to "fight like crazy," according to Norwich realtor Norma Schnip, but to no avail. The area was commercially zoned, and the zoning board had no legal power to prevent the intrusion of the restaurant, despite public sentiment.

But five years later, when the owners of the Eleazor Lord Tavern wanted to tear that building down, the historic district commission could—and did—intervene. Owners Abraham and Irene Figarsky were required, by state and town ordinance, to apply

The Eleazor Lord Tavern, in a turn-of-the-century view.

to the commission for a certificate of appropriateness to make any changes to the exterior of the building, including demolition. The Figarskys' official reason for requesting permission to destroy the building was that it was in need of extensive repairs, the cost of which would amount to between $15,000 and $18,000. Townspeople soon discovered, though, that there was an additional motivation: McDonald's had offered the Figarskys' $50,000 for the land on which the tavern stood in order to expand the restaurant's parking lot.

The historic district committee unanimously voted to deny the Figarskys' demolition request. After a public hearing on the case and discussion with members of state and regional architectural organizations, the commission issued a written statement elaborating upon its ruling. Any change to the Norwichtown Historic District "must be seriously considered as being detrimental to its preservation," stated the commission, and "the building in question significantly contributes to the importance of the Norwichtown Green as an historic landmark." No claim was made that this one building was outstanding; instead the commission drew upon a letter from the state historical commission that defended the tavern as part of a unified whole, "no part of which can be removed without a definite and usually adverse effect on the character and appearance of the entire area." Furthermore, the state historical commission and Norwich Historic District Commission agreed that the tavern served as a sort of visual and physical buffer between the green and the less attractive commercial buildings nearby, including the McDonald's property. The attractiveness of the green itself depended upon the tavern, both for its architectural qualities and its role as a screening element.

Once again, the Norwich public let its sentiment be heard. More than one hundred people attended the public hearing, ten of whom spoke in favor of the commission's position to let the tavern stand and none of whom spoke against it. Townspeople also presented a petition signed by eighty-nine percent of the property owners within the historic district opposing approval of the demolition application. They had been

defeated by the plastic and asphalt of McDonald's once; they were not about to lose twice.

The Figarskys were equally determined, and they took the case to the court of common pleas. Failing there, they appealed to the supreme court of the state of Connecticut. At each step of the way the courts upheld the position of the historic district commission. The issues that the case comprised have implications for other historic district commissions throughout the country.

The Figarskys' principal claim was that the Norwich ordinance, as it was applied to them, was unconstitutional. Preventing them from demolishing their own building, they claimed, amounted to a taking of their property for public use without compensation. The Figarskys also contended that the ordinance was "vague aesthetic legislation," and that because of the denial of their application they would be forced to spend a considerable amount of money to maintain their property without being able to put it to any practical use.

The Connecticut supreme court replied with a general defense of the constitutionality of historic districts. All property, stated the court, is held subject to the right of government to regulate its use. This power is not unlimited, but rather "shall not be injurious to the rights of the community, or so that it may promote its health, morals, safety, and welfare." Does the historic district ordinance serve the admittedly amorphous concept of the "public welfare"? In a word, yes. The court looked to the legislation that enabled the establishment of such districts, and ruled that the general assembly had been aware not only of the intangible benefits to be derived from historic districts, such as an increase in the public's awareness of its New England heritage, but also of the economic benefits to be reaped by augmenting the value of properties and by encouraging tourism. The preservation of an area or a cluster of buildings with architectural or historical significance does indeed serve the public welfare, providing both aesthetic and economic benefit.

As to the Figarskys' remaining claims, the court ruled that the Norwich ordinance was not vague; the aesthetic considerations in the regulation were in fact set out in some detail, and the judges cited other cases that had recognized that "aesthetic considerations alone may warrant an exercise of the police power." Finally, the court rejected the Figarskys' argument of economic hardship. Legal rulings in other cases had established that police power could regulate the use of land such that the landowner might not obtain the maximum possible economic gain, from it and that some sort of relief must be granted only when such regulation practically destroys the value of a piece of property. The Figarskys had presented no evidence that the property was valueless, only that it was unoccupied and in need of repair. The court's conclusion was that the Norwich Historic District Commission had "lawfully, reasonably and honestly exercised its judgement."

This story, too, has a happy ending. The Connecticut Trust for Historic Preservation purchased the tavern from the Figarskys for $45,000, nearly the price that McDonald's was purported to have offered. The trust was assisted in the purchase by a grant obtained through the Connecticut Historical Commission, and the commission also awarded grants totalling $16,000 for restoration of the building. Exterior restoration was completed in the summer of 1978, and by 1980 the tavern had become a functioning office building. It does not seem likely that there will be any challenge to its well-being in the future.

The McDonald's sign looms ominously near, but the tavern is relatively unchanged and still standing, thanks to the Norwichtown Historic District.

USE

Introduction

How should a green be used, and by whom? Townspeople have wrestled with these questions since the seventeenth century, and no consensus has yet been reached. Specific questions have changed—today no one tries to establish his right to pasture cows on the common—but the general issues are surprisingly constant. How intensively should the green be used? Does everyone have an equal claim, or do some groups have priority? What types of activity are permissible? And who decides?

Each town has its own solutions, and these depend upon certain conditions and priorities that vary from one town to another. Typically, the major issue is use versus appearance. If the visual image of the green is a prime concern, town officials or the local department of public works may restrict use in order to keep the area pristine. With proper maintenance, though, most greens can—and should—withstand a reasonable amount of activity.

In *Village Greens of New England*, Louise Andrews Kent comments:

> The neatest and most picturesque commons do not always give the most pleasure. Sometimes they seem a little like those handsomely upholstered chairs with ropes across them in museums. Chippendale was a great cabinet maker and so was Sheraton, but no chair with a rope across it ever took the weight off weary feet. Velvety grass is an attractive feature of a common and so are white houses and arching elms but unless the place is used, it may become as prettily unreal as the backdrop of a village scene in a nineteenth-century play. (p. 223)

We agree. A green can be more than an ornament; it can be a space that brings people together, whether for a conversation, flea market, or holiday caroling. This social function is not to be underestimated and, as the numerous New Hampshire fairs, Connecticut art shows, and Vermont fiddle contests indicate, many towns have found that, year after year, the extra maintenance required for such functions is worth the effort.

Just as we feel that many practices and events should be encouraged, we would like to see others moved to more appropriate spaces. The following guidelines should help communities decide, for their particular greens, which uses are suitable and which are not.

Strolling, picnicking, playing frisbee, or just sitting and enjoying the scene—all are unstructured uses well suited to the green. Some greens are, admittedly, very small—perhaps too small for frisbee throwing—but if there is a patch of grass and a tree, townspeople should be encouraged to sit and chat. Benches encourage people to do so, especially benches in groups, and lights allow pedestrians to cross through the green at night.

The desirability of other more active uses, such as bicycling and informal games of catch and softball, depends upon the size of the green and the availability of athletic areas elsewhere. If ball playing interferes with sitting and strolling, it should be discouraged, especially if there is a sports field nearby.

Alternatively, if the green is large and such a use is long established, ball playing is acceptable if maintenance can keep pace with the stress of the turf.

There are many events, cultural and commercial, that can take place on the green: band concerts, square dances, fairs, puppet shows, flea markets, antique shows, art shows, rummage sales, bake sales, parades, group picnics, firemen's musters, Revolutionary War battle reenactments, songfests, and more. One other use should be singled out: gatherings and demonstrations of a political nature. Perhaps no other space is a better symbolic location for expressing our basic constitutional rights of free speech and assembly than these grounds, many of which were formerly training grounds for revolutionary militia. If the green is large enough to accommodate them, all of these events are well suited to that traditional gathering place, and they help to enrich community life.

Both private initiative and public authorization must come together for a successful event on the green. Too often the initiative is there, but the approval is not. Even when these events are controversial, as political gatherings often are, the town should permit them as long as the green and its environs will not be overburdened. Of course, organizations that want to use the green must be willing to do their part in preventing it from being damaged. They should, if necessary, hire policemen to direct traffic, and make arrangements for adequate parking facilities. Sometimes traffic problems can be ameliorated by closing surrounding roads or changing them to one-way streets for the day of the event, if public officials are willing.

If the event is an annual one, such as a fair, the sponsoring organization should be encouraged to be a "Friend of the Green" throughout the year, becoming involved in planning and maintenance responsibilities. In this way events are not burdens; they can help to develop a constituency that has a vested interest in the green and its well-being.

Annually, there are over twenty national holidays, but only a few of them—Memorial Day, Flag Day, Independence Day, Veterans' Day, and Christmas—are usually acknowledged on the green. Why not, for example, a May Day celebration that utilizes the flagpole as a Maypole, complete with streamers, flowers, music, and dancing schoolchildren? The New England climate limits the outdoor celebration of winter holidays, but the green could be used by church congregations for a brief prayer of Thanksgiving or by families for a snow sculpture contest on New Year's Eve. Festivals, pageants, and theatrical performances can also commemorate holidays.

These celebrations obviously benefit the participants, and they can help the green as well. At the least, they remind townspeople of the space's existence; and townspeople can become involved in its decoration, use, and maintenance for one day. Some of these improvements to the green can, however, be of a more permanent nature.

In this context we would like to rekindle an interest in Arbor Day, an almost-forgotten holiday with great potential benefit for the green and its environs. Arbor Day was originated in 1872 by Julius Sterling Morton, who urged states to set aside one day a year for the purpose of planting trees. The Arbor Day movement gained popularity with nineteenth-century Americans who desired to beautify their towns and who were also alarmed by the extent of deforestation in the country. Today, Arbor Day is officially observed in all fifty states, although the exact date of celebration varies regionally, according to the planting season. The traditional means of observance is the planting of trees by schoolchildren in order to impress them with the importance of conservation.

As most greens are in need of additional trees, townspeople would do well to begin their Arbor Day celebrations there. Work with the public works department and local conservation and garden groups to draw up a coordinated, long-range plan that identifies other areas in need of planting. The project could be as small as adding one tree to the green each year, or as large as a recent one in Iowa City in which residents planted 10,000 trees for a community Arbor Day centennial. Children and adults alike find that planting trees is fun; it is this type of activity that is needed to bring greens back to life.

<table>
<tr><td>USE GUIDELINE 4
Prohibit permanent facilities that benefit only special-interest groups.</td><td>

Townspeople of all ages, from children to senior citizens, should feel that the green has something to offer them—even if it is simply a patch of grass on which to play or converse. Facilities that serve only small groups and that interfere with casual enjoyment of the space are better located elsewhere. These are primarily permanent sports facilities, such as basketball courts, baseball diamonds, and soccer goals; yet even a stage or a bandstand, which is for the benefit of a broader audience, can be unwelcome if the green is so small that little open space remains.

Temporary facilities are often the solution. Tables and chairs can be brought out for a flea market, makeshift booths erected for a fair, and an
</td></tr>
</table>

Youngsters in Bristol, Rhode Island enjoy this basketball court, but it is to the detriment of the historic common.

Restaurant employees face off in a volleyball tournament, part of the festivities in a day-long food festival held on the New Haven Green.

Students and townspeople usher in the summer solstice on the New Haven Green with country dancing.

informal baseball diamond laid out for one day. For more extensive celebrations, such as town anniversary celebrations, additional temporary sculpture, potted plants, and platform construction are feasible. When the event is over these should be removed, so that the public ground can remain open for the enjoyment of all.

The Fate of the Fete
Falmouth, Massachusetts

It was in 1921 that the newly formed Falmouth Nursing Association, a nonprofit organization affiliated with the Red Cross, first held a summer fair on the town's village green. When it proved to be an enjoyable occasion for both adults and children as well as a successful means of fundraising for the association, the Nursing Fete, as it was called, was planned as an annual event.

Over the course of the next fifty years the Nursing Fete became a veritable "institution of Falmouth summer," as the biweekly Falmouth *Enterprise* proclaimed. Perennial favorites included the blue-and-white striped tents under which afternoon tea was served, table upon table of used books, ice cream and hot dogs, and Punch and Judy shows, all carried out under the direction of white-clad nurses with blue sashes. The *Enterprise* observed, "Although changes have been made, the festive atmosphere, the charm, the tradtional incorporated with innovations over succeeding generations have not changed . . . . [M]uch of the atmosphere seems eternal."

But eternal it was not. In 1979, upon receipt of the annual letter of request from the Nursing Association (now renamed the Community and Home Health Services, Inc.) to hold the fete on the Village Green, the Department of Public Works (D.P.W.) commissioners were suddenly hesitant to grant permission. The commissioners had discovered that Community and Home Health Services (C.H.H.S.) no longer served residents of Falmouth alone but also the neighboring communities of Bourne and Mashpee. "I thought this was just a Falmouth thing, and that the money went to help Falmouth people," stated D.P.W. chairman Manuel F. Rapoza. "Every year we have problems. The town is responsible for cleaning up the green, and all the other mess." Another commissioner proposed that each of the towns served by C.H.H.S. take its turn hosting the fete. A third, raising the issue of traffic problems, thought there should be input from the town selectmen. For the time, the issue was left unresolved.

The battle lines were soon drawn. The directors of the Falmouth Chamber of Commerce sided with the health services agency and sent a letter to the D.P.W. commissioners supporting the use of the green. The chamber of commerce based its argument on the value of tradition and nostalgia; one of the commissioners agreed with that view stating that consideration should be given to a fifty- or sixty-year practice. Furthermore, said Commissioner Richard Fish, the traffic problem created by the fete was only on one weekday a year, while the traffic attracted by the Steamship Authorities, whose ferries shuttle visitors to nearby Martha's Vineyard and Nantucket, created a chronic problem.

Commissioner Rapoza maintained, though, that the fete was "really a hazardous thing" that had outgrown the size of the village green and could be held instead at the town recreational field or the county fairground. Commissioner Richard Bennett was skeptical about the financial benefits of the event, claiming that the money made by C.H.H.S. was probably eaten up in repair work done to the green. He concluded,

"The point of tradition is fine, but at some point you have to move on."

The D.P.W. commissioners held their final meeting to decide the question in May 1979. A last-minute plea was heard from C.H.H.S. president Robert E. Wilson, Jr., who said that admittedly the $12,000 or $15,000 raised by the fete was not a lot of money. Since the organization was nonprofit, though, without the fete the money would have to be raised in other ways, and a great deal of planning had already gone into the upcoming event. His argument had only short-term appeal. The commissioners voted to approve the use of the green for the fete, but with the stipulation that 1979 would be the event's last year.

The 1979 fete on the village green raised more than $21,500 for C.H.H.S., a record amount. In 1980, the fete was not held. In order to raise funds, C.H.H.S. sold raffle tickets for an automobile. When asked late in 1980 about the future of the fete, Norma Holt of C.H.H.S. could only reply, "That's a good question. I'd like to know that too." Mrs. Holt said that it was always possible that the fete would be allowed to return to the green, but the decision rested with the D.P.W. commissioners.

Raffle tickets again replaced the fete in 1981, and it seems that the event is now gone for good. Falmouth Selectman Dr. William Jones says he does not foresee any future events similar to the fete being held on the green because of traffic problems and the number of people who crowd the downtown area. "It will just be the green," he concluded.

A week before the 1979 fete, the *Enterprise* published an article by Eleanor Conant Yeager, a Falmouth matriarch who grew up in one of the houses near the village green. Mrs. Yeager recalled how the fete had always been "one of the greatest days of the year" for her and her sister. She wrote, "Our remembrance of that day, the flags, the ladies in white smiling under their lovely hats, everyone attending dressed up in their best, knowing not only did they benefit from the fun, but that the wonderful nurses would also benefit, can we afford to give this up?"

Regrettably, in Falmouth the answer seems to have been "yes." But Falmouth is only one of many New England towns with such events on the green, and communities throughout the region must ask themselves what price they are willing to pay for tradition. Is it worth a day of traffic and crowds, and the extra maintenance needed to restore the green to good condition? If so—and we believe that in most cases it is—then townspeople should take steps to ensure the continued existence of such traditions *before* they meet with head-on opposition.

Form a Friends of the Green group that can assume some of the responsibilities for the green, both in terms of maintenance and policy decisions. Make sure that special events do not place an excessive strain on parks and maintenance workers by recruiting volunteer assistants or hiring private workers if necessary. Finally, should there be some talk of cancelling an event, organize a broad constituency of supporters who will be vocal in their backing. A Falmouth *Enterprise* editorial observed early in that town's struggle, "It will depend upon how much the fete is wanted. . . . Not many years ago, the fete would have rallied very quickly a strong support, persuasive, influential, demanding. . . . The D.P.W. will be watching and waiting. If there is not an impressive demonstration that the fete is important, it may decide that this is the year to make the change." The writer was baiting the community, but the townspeople did not rise to the challenge. The Falmouth Village Green now seems destined to be, in the words of Selectman Jones, "just the green"—nothing more.

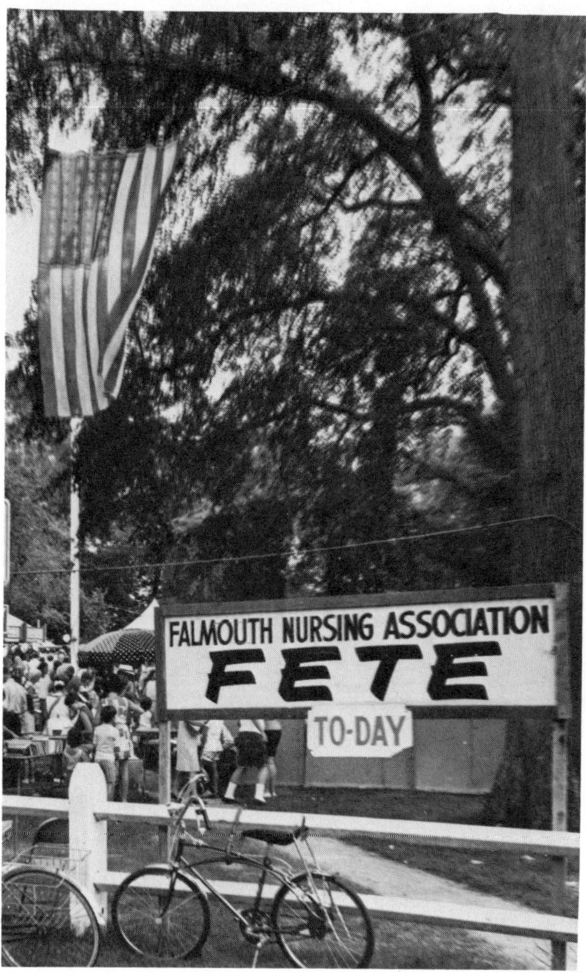

The Falmouth Nursing Association Fete, an annual event for more than fifty years, as it appeared in 1972.

Published bimonthly by the New Haven Downtown Council, "Downtown Headliners" is an eye-catching way of informing the public of events scheduled for the green and its environs.

<table>
<tr><td>USE
GUIDELINE 5
Establish a system
of management for
special events.</td><td>Town officials may be reluctant to intensify the use of the green if they know that the burden of scheduling and maintenance will fall upon them. A "Friends of the Green" organization can assist them in these capacities if necessary. Appoint a volunteer-coordinator for the green, and refer all requests for use and events to that person. Working with the town officials and parks maintenance department, the coordinator can help decide how many events the green can realistically support. The impact of each event, including its installation, duration, and the recovery period needed for the green, should be assessed. Sponsoring groups that offer assistance with maintenance of the green before and after their event deserve some priority.</td></tr>
</table>

MAINTENANCE

Introduction

As one planning director ruefully noted, "Our department is more construction oriented than maintenance oriented. We all are." True, most of us take greater pleasure in seeing a new bandstand than in knowing that fertilizer has been applied—until the grass dies. It is maintenance that makes the difference between a lush green carpet and a shabby patch of brown weeds; especially in light of recent parks budget cutbacks, it is critical to establish a thorough maintenance routine as a top priority.

As local and federal fiscal crises continue and CETA (Comprehensive Employment Training Act) maintenance workers become scarce, greens will need assistance from the private sector. Such aid can be either in the form of financial support, as it is in Lexington, Massachusetts, or actual labor. A "Friends of the Green" group can arrange with the parks department to assume responsibility for one or more components of the maintenance routine; especially if a number of townspeople rotate the jobs, it is not so difficult to mow the grass occasionally or to prune the shrubs.

Historically, greens and commons were land for which the townspeople shared a responsibility as well as benefits. Before it is too late, it is time for us to assume that proprietary interest once again.

<table>
<tr><td>MAINTENANCE GUIDELINE 1
Establish a system of routine maintenance.</td><td>

Maintenance is more than just emptying the litter bins and mowing the grass. Maintenance takes into account seasonal stresses on the green, existing and changing conditions of use, special problems, and annual needs. In order to have an attractive, healthy green, you should adopt a maintenance routine that is thorough, coordinated, and consistent.

</td></tr>
</table>

First, analyze your green for current problems. Does the grass always die in one corner? Are one or two trees sickly? Your maintenance program should correct these problems or deficiencies and then aim to sustain the green in a good condition.

Set down in writing a plan that can be followed year after year. This plan should be arranged in the form of a calendar, specifying the tasks to be completed during each month. Be on the watch, though, for changing circumstances. A new pattern of use will necessitate the adaptation of the plan.

Your routine should, broadly, encompass the following:

1. *Furnishings and structures:* cleaning, removal of graffiti, repair, replacement of damaged or lost parts, snow removal, installation and removal of temporary structures.
2. *Paving:* litter removal, edging, patching, snow removal.
3. *Electrical system:* repair or replacement of damaged or lost parts, replacement of burnt-out bulbs, hookup and removal of seasonal fixtures.
4. *Water system:* repair or replacement of damaged or lost parts, seasonal drainage.
5. *Turf:* litter removal including dog litter, mowing, liming, fertilizing, aerating, weeding, top-dressing, resodding, watering.
6. *Trees:* deadwood removal, spraying, fertilizing, replacement planting, special care of American elm.
7. *Shrubs:* as above, with the addition of pruning.
8. *Flowers and flower beds:* soil preparation, planting, weeding, watering, removal.
9. *Equipment:* regular service and repair of power and hand tools.

The method of maintenance for turf, trees, and shrubs will vary slightly according to local conditions and, to some extent, personal preference. As an example, we have included a grounds maintenance routine for the green in Litchfield, Connecticut (see Guidelines Appendix). This routine is adaptable to any green in the New England area.

MAINTENANCE GUIDELINE 2
Establish a hierarchy of maintenance priorities.

Realistically, you may not be able to afford all the items on your maintenance program the first year. Refer to the categories listed in the guideline above, and arrange them according to immediate need. Within each category, choose individual items that will receive primary attention and others that are of second priority; do not neglect entire categories.

Since turf is the most essential component of any green, it should never be neglected, nor should irreplaceable trees. You could, however, postpone replacing old benches until next year, or attend to a wooden flagpole or kiosk rather than a stone monument.

MAINTENANCE GUIDELINE 3
Supplement parks department staff with a private landscape maintenance firm if necessary.

Some cities and towns hire private firms to assist with services formerly carried out by the municipality, ranging from garbage collection to park maintenance. If the parks department is understaffed, assistance from a private landscape firm can ensure that the green will receive careful attention.

This contractual arrangement can be particularly valuable following a major rehabilitation of the green, when new grass and trees are vulnerable. The necessary additional funding for this more intensive maintenance is a good long-range investment, since no matter how much effort has been put into the green's appearance, it can all be undone in a matter of two or three years if poorly maintained. Private landscape maintenance can, of course, also benefit long-established greens if the parks department is unable to maintain its formerly high standards of upkeep.

If additional public funding is not available, this is a good opportunity for the private sector to step in. The Friends of the Green could organize a fundraising concert or fair and donate the proceeds, or the group could undertake a capital funds drive. For many greens, one or two thousand dollars can make a significant improvement.

MAINTENANCE GUIDELINE 4
Encourage owners of properties adjacent to the green to adopt similar maintenance programs.

Let the green stand as a good example to its neighbors. The municipality should assume responsibility for sidewalks, roads, and public-domain property such as cemeteries, and keep them in good condition. Similarly, merchants and homeowners should attend to their grounds, fences, and signs. The green is enhanced by well-kept surroundings—and vice versa.

Maintenance is a continual problem in most small towns with small-town budgets, and Norwich, Vermont is no exception.

A Caretaker's Commitment
Westford, Massachusetts

The Westford Common is so immaculate in appearance that one feels there must be some tricks of the trade or closely guarded secrets to account for its maintenance. But caretaker Clayton Dearth reveals that it is simply a routine maintenance program, carried out assiduously, that produces such an exceptionally elegant green.

Admittedly, Dearth can thank some of the earlier residents for providing the ingredients for success. While many New England communities are now setting out saplings to replace disease-ravaged elms, Westford's maples have never looked better. Double rows of mature trees, planted along two of the common's three sides, create a powerful sense of enclosure and spread a patchwork of dappled light on the central area of turf. It is a pleasure to enter such a space and, Clayton Dearth affirms, to care for it.

Yet as Dearth notes, the trees do not make his job any easier. Not only do they require continual trimming around the bases but they also compete with the turf for nourishment. "The trees take up so much goodness out of the ground; I've got to keep feeding it and feeding it," says Dearth. He supplies the turf with a fifty percent organic 10-6-4 fertilizer at least once every six weeks from spring to fall, which keeps both grass and trees healthy.

The turf also benefits from the frequent waterings and mowings it receives from Dearth and his two summer assistants, who spend at least one full day per week on the common. It is a generous amount of manpower, not excessive but one that many towns can no longer afford; the town's willingness to maintain this level of attention is a great boon to the common.

The town tree warden is responsible for setting out new trees in Westford, and he usually adds a few to the common every year primarily to fill in existing rows, but it is Dearth who selects secondary plant material. Both shrubs and flowers highlight certain areas of the common. The new flagpole at the center is surrounded by potted geraniums and low shrubs, which follow the shape of the curved granite benches there, and geraniums in wooden buckets punctuate two of the triangular common's three corners. Dearth tries to maintain this color in the fall with chrysanthemums, and in the spring with tulips. Flowers also surround the World War I monument and fill a cast-iron planter. "I'd love to have more flowers," Dearth professes, "but there isn't the time." His strategy of planting only as many as he can manage explains why they are all hearty.

Maintenance and use of any green go hand in hand, and Dearth has strong opinions about what activities should be banned: ball games, functions with tables, people with metal detectors, and any events that will attract too many people for the good of the turf. "I'm spoiled," he acknowledges. "I just like it for show." Dearth claims he is outnumbered by the selectmen and others who favor more intensive uses of the common, but in reality town policy is largely in his favor. The space is never used unless the selectmen approve the use, and the users "are usually associated at least indirectly with the common," according to the selectmen's office. Annual events include a strawberry festival sponsored by the church opposite the common and reenactments involving the Westford Minutemen, while one unusual event this past year was an outdoor wedding. In previous summers there were weekly band concerts featuring local school bands, but because of state tax cutbacks the school department in 1981 declined the invitation. Other than these few events, then, and an occasional frisbee thrower, the Westford Common is untrodden. Since the town does have ball fields and other park areas, few object to reserving the common as a space that is more ornamental than functional.

This relatively low level of use and the steady planting and maintenance program are the main reasons that the Westford Common looks as it does. Individual credit is also due, though, to Clayton Dearth, who has been known to spend his day off moving the sprinklers around every hour. The reason, Dearth explains, is simple: "I love my job." If every green had a caretaker like him, guidelines such as these would be superfluous.

Statuesque maples effectively screen out traffic from the enclosed common.

Guidelines Appendix
A sample maintenance calendar

A. Soil Test

It is desirable to test the soil once every 5 years. This test assures the best formula of fertilizer and best application rates of lime and fertilizer. Supply local agricultural experiment station with labeled samples (1 pint each) of soil taken from several representative areas.

B. Latest Recommended Herbicides and Pesticides

Consult local cooperative extension service.

C. Turf Areas—General Maintenance

Note: The following are one-time annual operations except as noted.

1a. *Overseed* thin areas at rate of 1 lb. per 1000 square feet.

b. Apply recommended *pre-emergent herbicide* to combat crabgrass. Follow manufacturer's instructions closely.

First Week in April

2. *Turf Dressing.* When sod is dry and firm enough to walk on without marking, rake thoroughly to remove dead grass and debris and loosen up matted areas. Cut out weed areas with small hoe. Cultivate bare spots with hoe (loosen soil), and smooth out surface. Fill any depressions with screened loam and rake thoroughly adjacent grades, maintaining slightly higher level to anticipate settling.

3. *Fertilizer Application.* In the absence of a soil test for specific N-P-K rates, a safe rule is to apply 20-5-10 fertilizer (with at least 50% of the nitrogen from slow release organic sources). Apply at a rate of 12½ lbs. per 1000 square feet (32′ × 32′ area). Use rotary spreader. Water fertilizer into turf thoroughly. This must be done twice yearly.

Mid-April

4. *Patching.* Seed all bare areas and rake very lightly. Use 4 to 6 lbs. of seed per 1000 square feet on bare areas and 2 lbs. per 1000 square feet wherever turf is thin. Use best quality seed of previous year's crop (Scott seed or equal), preferably of following mix: red fescue or Chewing's fescue, 50%; red top, 20%; Kentucky bluegrass, 20%; domestic rye, 10%. Water thoroughly but avoid surface runoff. The ground must never become dry or hot even if daily sprinklings are needed. Do not apply herbicides to these areas until fall.

5. *Lawn Rolling.* Roll all rough turf areas with half filled lawn roller when turf is dry.

Mid April through June—Weekly

6. *Mowing.* For spring mowing set mower blades at 1½″ cutting height. Do *not* collect and remove clippings during or after mowing, but mow often enough so that clippings do not mat upon the sod. About the end of June, set mower blades to cut at 2″. More lawns are damaged by close clipping than by any other cause. Do not use heavy highway maintenance mowing equipment. Mow 1 to 2 times per week maximum.

Mid April to Frost—Weekly

7. *Pesticide.* If soil insects are creating damage apply currently recommended pesticide, but in no case later than May 5.

8. *Watering.* This depends on the season. On established turfs in dry weather, water at least once weekly so that water penetrates 5″ or 6″, i.e., 4 or 5 hours, preferably in late afternoon or early evening (to avoid evaporation). Water at rate slow enough to avoid surface runoff. If soil has become compacted from overuse, preventing water absorption, aerify with coring type soil aerifier. Aerification can be provided by landscape services if necessary. To check effectiveness of watering rate, with augur dig for soil sample 8″ down. Squeeze. If it crumbles, water is insufficient. If it sticks together, water is sufficient.

9. *Edging.* Cut edge of walks as often as needed, but avoid close clipping of sod. Remove excess sod along walks.

10. *Litter Removal.* Rake or punch-stick and dispose of off premises. Remove litter year-round as needed.

Early May

11. *Weed Control.* Two operations as follows:
    a. If pre-emergent Tupersan used instead of others used in late March, apply now. Follow manufacturer's instructions closely.
    b. For weeds such as dandelion or chickweed, apply post-emergent herbicide such as Trimec (2, 4–D type). This comes in liquid form. Follow manufacturer's instructions.

July to Frost—Weekly or More Frequently

12. *Mowing.* Set mower blades to 2″. Close clipping to be avoided. Do *not* collect and remove clippings during or after mowing, but mow often enough so that clippings do not mat upon the sod. If mowing cannot occur this frequently, then cuttings must be removed and disposed of in a compost pile off the premises.

September

13. *Weed Control.* for weeds such as dandelion or chickweed, apply post-emergent herbicide such as Trimec (as in May). This comes in liquid form. Follow manufacturer's instructions closely. Use three-gallon sprayer.

14. *Fertilizer Application.* Apply 20-5-10 fertilizer (with at least 50% of the nitrogen from slow release organic sources). Apply at rate of 12½ lbs. per 1000 square feet (32′ x 32′). Water fertilizer into turf thoroughly.Use rotary spreader.

October-November

15. *Leaf Removal.* Remove fallen leaves once every 1 to 2 weeks.

Late November

16. *Lime Application.* Without the soil test a safe rule is to apply ground limestone at a rate of 50 lbs. per 1000 square feet, once every *other* year, late in the fall (in any case this should precede fertilizing by 2 to 3 months). Use rotary spreader.

Throughout the Year.

If turf disease occurs, consult local cooperative extension service.

Grounds Maintenance Calendar

<table>
<tr><th></th><th>specific operation</th><th>continuing maintenance</th></tr>
<tr><td>JAN</td><td rowspan="2"></td><td rowspan="2">tree litter removal as needed</td></tr>
<tr><td>FEB</td></tr>
<tr><td>MAR</td><td>(last week) spray elm, topseed lawn and apply pre-emergent herbicide</td><td rowspan="3">1½" turf mowing
watering, edging, pruning
litter removal as needed</td></tr>
<tr><td>APR</td><td>(first week) dress turf, renew mulch
Spring Fertilizing; patch & roll turf, pesticide</td></tr>
<tr><td>MAY</td><td>spring weed control</td></tr>
<tr><td>JUN</td><td rowspan="3">systemic elm treatment</td><td rowspan="3">2" turf mowing
watering, edging, pruning
litter removal as needed</td></tr>
<tr><td>JUL</td></tr>
<tr><td>AUG</td></tr>
<tr><td>SEP</td><td>fall fertilizing (turf) and weed control (turf, beds).</td><td rowspan="3">2" turf mowing
leaf and litter removal as needed</td></tr>
<tr><td>OCT</td><td></td></tr>
<tr><td>NOV</td><td>lime turf every other year</td></tr>
<tr><td>DEC</td><td></td><td>tree litter removal as needed</td></tr>
</table>

D. Trees—General Maintenance

First Week in April

1. *Fertilizer Application.* For new trees and most mature trees, apply 5-10-5 or 5-10-10 fertilizer (with at least 50% of the nitrogen from slow-release organic sources) around each tree, within an area between 2 circles on the ground, the first one on a radius of about 3 feet from the trunk, the second, 3 feet beyond the limits of the extended branches.

   Poke holes through turf with crowbar 10 inches deep, 2 feet apart, and apply fertilizer evenly (up to 6 oz. per hole) in per-tree rates given below. Water thoroughly. The holes allow the fertilizer to get below the grass.

   Apply the following rates:

   Deciduous trees: each, 2 to 4 lbs. per inch diameter of trunk measured breast-high.

   Evergreen trees: each, 2 lbs. per inch diameter of trunk measured breast-high.

A soil test may indicate specific fertilizer to use instead of 5-10-5 or 5-10-10.

Alternative time: October.

Throughout the Year

2. *Pest and Disease Control.* No general spraying recommended without expert advice. Even if tree looks healthy, an expert can detect harmful symptoms. Consult town tree warden, or certified tree expert on annual basis. Inspect for pests April to May.

3. *Watering.* In dry periods water beneath tree thoroughly once or twice a week, for 4 hours in late afternoon or early evening (to avoid evaporation) at a rate slow enough to avoid surface runoff. More frequent or faster watering are not desirable.

4. *Pruning.* Tree pruning should best occur under the supervision of the landscape architect to assure that proper tree form results. Removal of dead wood and thinning are desirable under such supervision. This should not be done after tree has dropped leaves. Do not prune August to frost.

E. American Elm Care

Mid to Late March

1. Spray with Methoxychlor.

June through August

2. Apply systemic injections of Dupont Lignasan BLP.

3. Pending E.P.A. approval, add, 40 feet away from each valuable elm, an elm-bark beetle trap (this has sex attractants for beetles and is matchbox-sized).

   Cost is aproximately $25.00 per tree per year. On a test plot of 5,000 specimens maintained by Elm Research Institute, Harrisville, N.H. 03450, this program has resulted in 99% survival rate.

F. Shrub and Vine Pruning

Shrubs and vines are not recommended for the Green except as softeners of monuments, as at proposed Beechers Monument sitting area. In pruning, it is desirable to avoid formal shaping of the shrubs. those with asterisk on recommended list should be pruned in spring before budding, that is by late March.

G. Expert Consultation

Consult qualified landscape consultant periodically to determine effectiveness of this program. Good health in plants, as in people, requires a check-up to determine any needed changes in health care. Disease symptoms occurring in grass, shrubs, and trees may go unnoticed without expert consultation.

H. Records

It is important to keep records of changes in the program and calendar of supplies and quantities used. This will help in proper scheduling of purchases, in upkeep of equipment, performance of operations, and implementation of replanting.

Revitalized Commons:
Three Case Studies

Time—and Money—Well Spent
Cambridge, Massachusetts

> [T]he physical condition of the Common today is no longer something that
> citizens of Cambridge can be proud of. The grass is worn bare in the southern
> portion so that it is dust in dry weather and mud when it rains. The benches have
> many broken or missing slats, the fences have missing rails, the shrubs and trees
> look starved and parched and much of the paving needs repair. The general
> impression of most citizens is that it is shabby and run down.

So begins a 1970 report on the Cambridge Common, an 8.6-acre triangle in the
center of the city. It was a depressing but accurate description of this once
elegant space. Intensive use, problematic landscaping, wind erosion, compacted soil, insufficient water in dry weather, and insufficient maintenance
throughout the year—all contributed to the common's sorry state. The parks
department, responsible for maintenance, was aware of the problems and
struggled to redress them. But by the close of the 1960s the common's
condition had outstripped the department's small staff and budget. Some
major action was in order.

The first step was taken in 1970, when the Cambridge City Council made
a $2,500 appropriation for a preliminary rehabilitation study. The ensuing
project spanned several years and involved numerous city agencies, designers,
special interest groups, and citizens. It was a major undertaking and not
without difficulties. Yet because the city was from the start solicitous of public
opinion, most of these difficulties were resolved in the planning stage. The
rehabilitated common measures up to the expectations of most of its users, and
this is, by and large, a success story.

Background

The common has been part of Cambridge since settlement of the town in 1630.
At that time the Proprietors reserved a large tract of land to be held in common
and used by the "first-comers" and others the Proprietors deemed eligible. It
served primarily as a cow pasture, occasionally also hosting military drills and
religious and political gatherings. As the settlement grew, though, so did the
demand for private land, and gradually the outlying common lands were given
over to other purposes and the central common also diminished. In 1724 the
northern portion of the "Cow Common" was subdivided as house lots, reducing its size from about eighty-six acres to sixteen. It ceased to be used for
pasture but still served its other functions and was still owned in common.

The relationship between the colonies and England worsened during the
mid-eighteenth century, and the military uses of the common accordingly
intensified. In 1769 the Proprietors conveyed the lot to the town to be used as a
training field, and it soon became the headquarters for the Continental Army
of the Revolution. George Washington reportedly took command of the army
troops there while standing beneath an elm; the Washington Elm, as the tree
came to be known, was revered as a witness to that noble event and immortal-
ized in poetry and prose until its demise.

Following the war, new houses defined the common in approximately its present configuration; but it was still merely a ragged field crisscrossed by dirt roads. It was not until 1828 that the Proprietors relinquished the last of their rights to the land, and not until 1830 that the Massachusetts General Court passed legislation allowing a group of citizens to improve it. Townspeople began to transform the space, enclosing it with a post and rail fence, diverting the intrusive roads, and planting trees—at their own expense. The project was received more enthusiastically by nearby residents than distant merchants and traders, some of whom argued that the fence would interfere with their livestock drives; in fact, the town meeting at which the fate of the proposal was decided was so well attended that townspeople were forced to adjourn from the courthouse to a larger meeting house. The final vote was 169 to 119 in favor of the enclosure. A year later there was further disagreement when some insisted that the enclosure act be repealed and one of the roads reopened. The case went to the state supreme judicial court, whose verdict was that, for public welfare, the enclosure should be maintained. The transformation from cow common to park was secure.

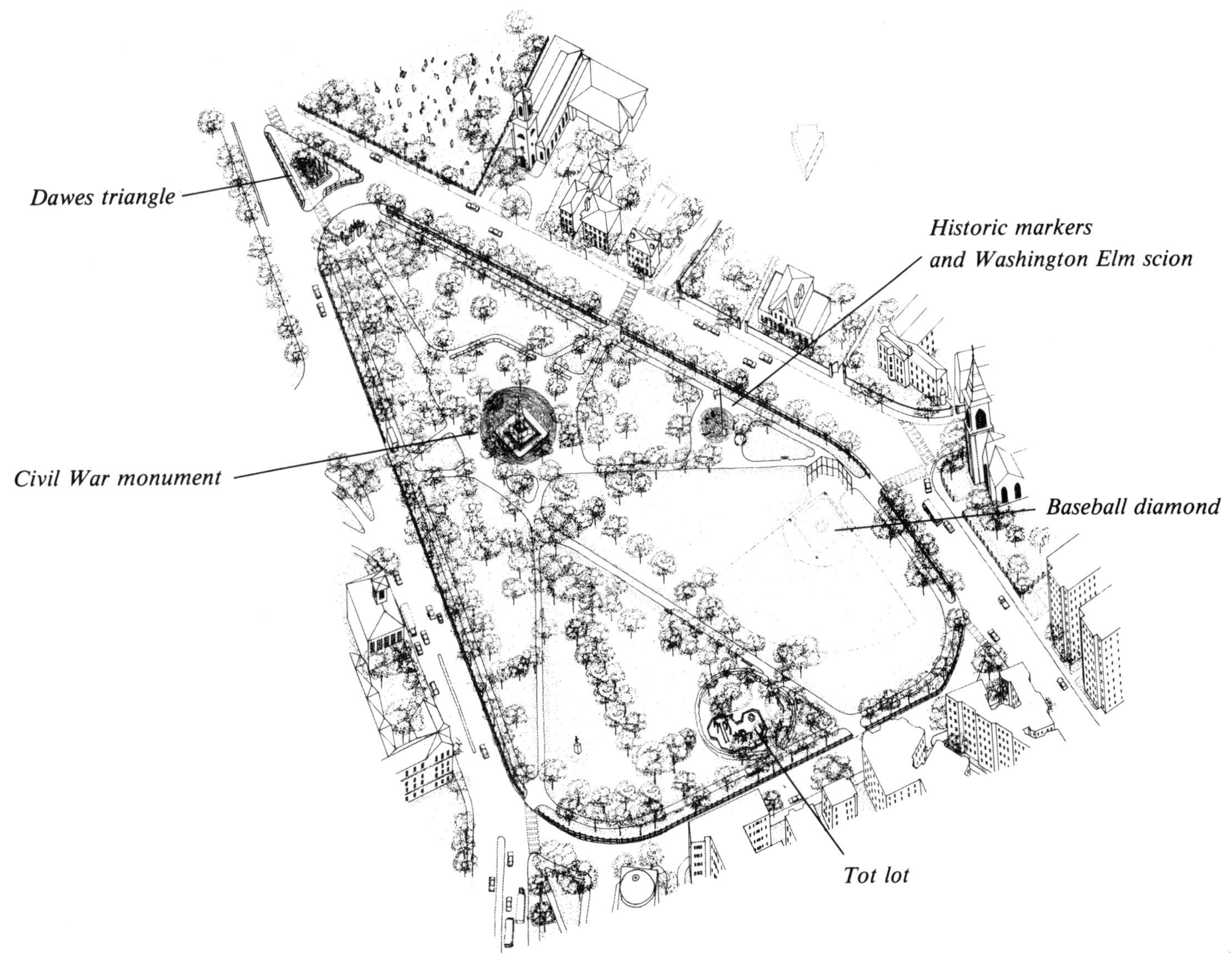

Cambridge Common

The remainder of the nineteenth century saw further parklike improvements: crosswalks, additional trees, monuments, statues, and granite markers.
It was a place for passive enjoyment and, after baseball was introduced in the
latter half of the century, active recreation. It was also a space with recognized
historical significance, as was evident by the celebration in 1875, the centennial of the Revolution. Crowds gathered in a huge tent on the common on July
3 to hear prominent men of the day such as Oliver Wendell Holmes pay tribute
to the former training ground and its role in the glorious war.

But while the common was gaining in glory it was beginning to experience
troubles. Enclosed by the increasingly commercial district of Harvard Square,
the campus of Harvard University, and a residential neighborhood, the small
triangle was subject to relatively high use; the 1893 report of the new park
board cited compacted topsoil and conflicting activities as the sources of the
common's generally poor condition. There was public concern over the aged
Washington Elm which, despite rescue attempts by horticulturists, finally had
to be removed in 1923. The park board attributed its death to the ring of
asphalt that had starved the tree's roots for several years, as the formerly dirt
roads had been paved to accommodate electric trolleys and the new automobiles. And there were the first signs of conflict over passive or active use of
the common, centering on the baseball field. Because of the common's central
location and proximity to schools, the field was much used and enjoyed by
some; but others argued that the danger to pedestrians, bad language of the ball
players, and unattractiveness of the field were grounds for its removal. The
conflict was summarized by one citizen who wrote in 1932, "It must be
admitted that the present treatment of the Cambridge Common is a decided
failure, from any artistic point of view, but it is certain that no radical change in
the ground plan would be tolerated by the People."

For the next thirty-odd years there were no radical changes. There was
occasional talk of improving the landscape or restricting use of the common,
but the reality was more intensive use. The 1960s were a time of frequent
political and antiwar gatherings on the common, and the regular Sunday
afternoon free rock concerts were even better attended. The concerts supplanted baseball as the new conflict of interests, and city council meetings
were attended by vociferous citizens arguing both for and against continuing
the weekly event. Meanwhile, the physical condition of the common declined
even more rapidly than before.

It was the Cambridge Conservation Commission, under the leadership of
longtime common guardian Alan Lefkowitz, which finally got the ball rolling.
In 1970 the city council gave the conservation commission $2,500 to conduct a
preliminary study for a rehabilitation project. The commission in turn interviewed ten firms and contracted with Mason and Frey, Cambridge landscape
architects. Although the city made no commitment beyond the preliminary
study, it was now possible to assess professionally the condition of the common
and to determine a scope of work.

The Planning Stage

In June 1970 the city in conjunction with Mason and Frey held a public hearing
concerning the common. Local newspapers carried an invitation to all residents of Cambridge, and special invitations were sent to organizations ranging
from the Harvard Square Businessmen's Association to the Jewish Community
Center and the Boy Scouts. The purpose of the hearing was to solicit opinions

about how the common should be designed and used; as Max Mason and John Frey explained at the outset of the meeting, "We want you to help write the program."

Many rose to the occasion, and their comments were summarized in a study report published in October of that year. The grass, trees, and shrubs needed help, observed some speakers, and the present open-space character of the common should be maintained. Others were more interested in how the space was used. Older people wanted some quiet areas maintained, while younger people advocated improved facilities for jogging, bicycle riding, softball, and ice skating. Some advocated a number of additions to the space: a bandstand, a new "tot lot," a decorative fountain, more benches, flower beds, and drinking fountains. Still others were concerned that the historical character of the common be a determining factor. It was, to be sure, a large order for an 8.6-acre park.

Mason and Frey did take popular opinion into account when proposing their preliminary scheme, but tempered their compliance with realism. They agreed to add trees and shrubs, encourage use of the path along the perimeter for jogging and bicycle riding, retain the softball field, and install several new drinking fountains. In agreement with some mothers and against the advice of some planners, they thought a tot lot should be retained and suggested remodeling the existing one. The designers agreed that the worn turf was unattractive, but they felt it was unrealistic to expect that grass could survive in some areas that were both tree-shaded and heavily used. Accordingly, they proposed the addition of a paved area around the central Civil War monument and an adjacent paved plaza. Constructed of brick, the plaza would have steps leading to a sunken area containing a platform, to serve as a stage, and an ornamental fountain. Benches, trees, and lights were incorporated into the plaza design. In addition, Mason and Frey planned for a smaller plaza at the northeast entrance, a new system of brick pathways to replace the older paved and footworn dirt paths, and an automatic irrigation system.

The total cost of the work was estimated at $965,067 if phased over five years, or $889,155 if completed within twelve months. These figures did not include improvements also suggested for the three smaller pieces of the common isolated by streets, nor the $100,000 fountain, nor the $92,000 for freezing coils to enable ice skating on the plaza. The project was now back in the hands of the city, which had to decide how much it was willing to spend and from what sources the money would come.

These decisions proved to be slow in coming, since a number of departments were involved. The planning and development department, the conservation commission, and the historical commission worked together to review the proposal and identify the most probable funding sources. Once the applications were prepared the approval of city council was needed to submit them, and that go-ahead was not given until 1972. The city received the first money for the project at the start of 1973, spent the year revising plans and drawing them up in greater detail, and commenced the first phase of construction in 1974.

The manner in which the project was funded created certain construction priorities. The city first applied for funding from the U.S. Department of Housing and Urban Development (HUD) Open Space Land Program, a federal source that provides fifty percent of the cost of a project or part of a project; the other fifty percent must come from local funds. The first federal money, $175,000, arrived in 1973, which when matched by the city provided an initial amount of $350,000. Additional federal funding was then sought from Land and Water Conservation Funds, administered by the U.S. Department of the Interior. This money must also be matched by local funds, and in Massachusetts it is targeted for urban recreational needs. Since the softball field and tot lot were the most recreational components of the project, they were relegated to this latter phase of funding and construction. This division was also practical since both the softball field and tot lot are in the northern part of the common, while the other major improvements proposed were primarily in the southern section. Landscaping and benches were divided between the two phases.

One additional seal of approval was needed during the planning stage. Since 1964 the common has been the heart of the Cambridge Common

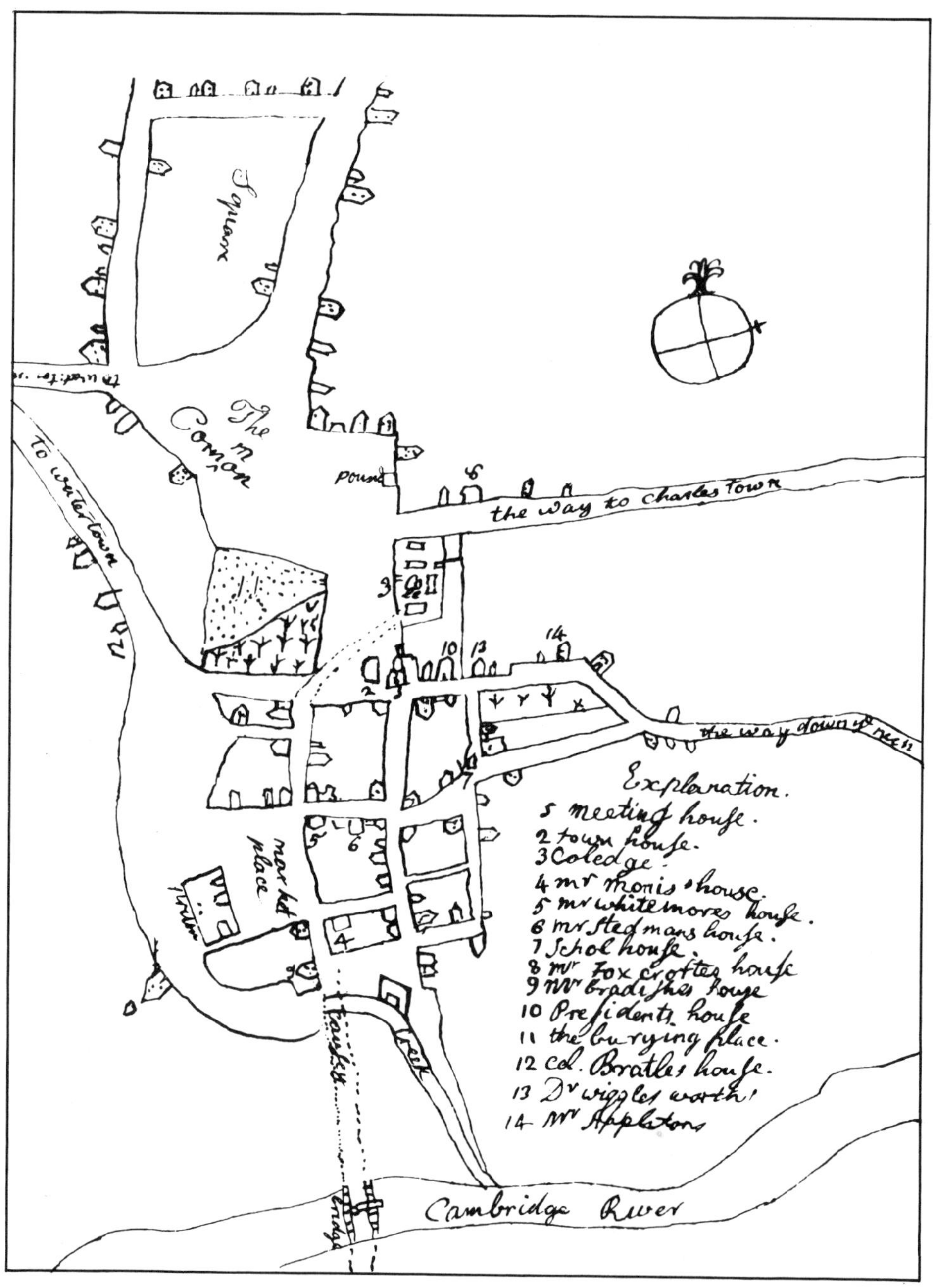

Historic District, listed on the National Register of Historic Places. In accordance with state and local ordinances, the Cambridge Historical Commission must rule on any changes proposed within the district, and Mason and Frey therefore submitted their plans. Since the commission had been closely involved in the planning process, approval was granted, in the form of a certificate of appropriateness, without further ado. By 1974 the project was put out for construction bids and work begun.

The Rehabilitation

Phase I construction lasted from the spring of 1974 until December and the final touches were added in the following spring. When $90,000 was secured from the Land and Water Conservation Fund and matched by the city later in 1975, Phase II proceeded as anticipated; plans were made final in spring 1976 and implemented in 1977. The last construction vehicle departed in fall 1977, more than three years after work had begun.

Excluding the $2,500 study grant, project funding totaled $530,000: $175,000 from HUD and $90,000 from the department of the Interior, both matched by the city. Since Mason and Frey's early master plan had estimated costs at more than $950,000, some items obviously had been cut.

Most noticeably missing was the sunken plaza with its attendant platform stage, fountain, benches, trees, and lights. It was perhaps the easiest omission, since the concerts for which it would be used were controversial and since the plaza alone was to cost nearly $150,000. It was also the only major omission from the original plan. The planners decided to cut back in other areas, but all of the planned improvements were implemented to some degree.

New brick paths replaced the old bituminous concrete, and their configuration was considerably simplified. Some paths were eliminated altogether, creating larger areas of green space, while others disappeared as a result of the extensive paved area surrounding the Civil War monument. The sixty-foot-high monument had long been an informal gathering area, and the turf had suffered accordingly—Mason and Frey described it as "alternately a mud hole or a dust bowl"—so the new design featured a circular base of granite cobbles surrounded by an irregularly shaped plaza of brick. Platform-style granite benches line two of the plaza's edges, and trees are interspersed throughout. All paths radiate from this plaza to the perimeter of the common.

One path leads to the southeast entrance, where a smaller brick plaza was laid. The flowers that the designers had intended for this area and two wood benches (for the central plaza as well as here) were omitted, but the Memorial Gate was retained and given a new setting. The gate faces the center of the common and serves as a sculptural entrance. A small plaza at the northeast entrance, "with seating to more graciously receive the visitor," was never realized. The other newly paved area is to the southwest, where the Revolutionary War cannons were relocated closer to a scion of the Washington Elm. Granite markers inform visitors about both embellishments, but the larger historic plaque program was not implemented; the concrete wall, onto which the plaques would have been mounted, would have cost $11,000, and ten bronze markers were estimated at $600 apiece. Four were installed.

The softball diamond was resodded and a semicircular backstop, finished in black instead of the usual metallic surface, was put into place. In the early planning stages there had been a proposal to erect high-intensity lights for night games, but these met with disapproval from some neighborhood residents and the historical commission, so the idea was dropped. One drinking fountain was installed next to the diamond and another in the tot lot.

The tot lot was entirely reworked, the design a result of collaboration between Mason and Frey and a group formed expressly for this purpose, the Association for Children's Environment (ACE). ACE was a coalition of parents, mostly mothers, from the neighborhood adjacent to the common, who wanted to become involved in the design process since it was their children who would most often use the facilities. Members met with Mason and Frey early in 1976, and the result was a scheme that satisfied all involved. The play area was moved closer to the northern end of the common, at the request of city officials who wanted it to be less obtrusive, and new equipment replaced the pieces garnered from the recreation department that had created, according to one planner, a "willy-nilly" appearance. It was not the result that Mason and Frey first envisioned, a below-grade area with "a paved tricycle run, water for play, rocks, wood, playhouse, steps, tunnels, planting, flowers, and sitting areas for older people." Instead, the construction material is primarily unfinished wood, used for a climbing pyramid, a frame for hanging rings, and climbing platforms with slides and a rope ladder, which are surrounded by a sand lot. A low wood frame encloses the lot, and another encloses a swing set; both can be used for seating. Benches and shrubs encircle the wider periphery, masking a low chain-link fence finished in black.

Trees and benches were added throughout the common. The trees are primarily red oak, scarlet oak, maple, magnolia, and crabapple. A species of Scholar tree was used in the plaza area to approximate the more statuesque but disease-susceptible elm. Metal tree grilles that would have cost $200 each were eliminated. Rectilinear wood benches line the paths; they were originally pressure-treated wood which needs no finish, but they have needlessly been painted green. Also located throughout the common are metal halide lights, black fixtures with cylindrical heads on eighteen-foot poles; and an underground irrigation system was installed. The granite-post and wood-rail fence was repaired by replacing missing rails, except at the southeast edge where pedestrians need access to the public buses. There the rails were omitted but the granite posts left standing.

Although construction work lasted from 1974 through 1977, the two-phase plan created a hiatus in 1976. It was fortuitous timing. Ruth Birkhoff of the conservation commission recalls the difficulties in convincing the city to rehabilitate the common until planners threatened it would otherwise "look like hell" for the bicentennial. The argument was convincing, and the city had agreed to the project with the bicentennial in mind—but not anticipating that construction would continue for the better part of the decade. The result of the two-phase plan: an undisturbed and already partially improved common for 1976.

<table>
<tr><td>Design Analysis</td><td>

The budget shortcomings of the rehabilitation could have been catastrophic had the planners cut back unwisely. For example, more dramatic results might have been achieved by pouring most of the funds into an embellishment such as the sunken plaza—certainly more of a showpiece than wooden benches and Scholar trees. Such a decision is entirely possible in cities and towns where the designer wants to make a name for himself and where the decision-making power rests in the hands of a few individuals. Fortunately, this was not the case in Cambridge.

Eliminating the sunken plaza was no tragedy—in fact, it may have been for the best. Although the city does need an outdoor performance arena, the

</td></tr>
</table>

The common as it appeared in the early twentieth century, a simple space of grass and trees enclosed by a post-and-rail fence.

common is probably not the best site since such a quantity of pavement would tip the balance from an open green space to an urban plaza. With a softball field and tot lot the common is already burdened with activity areas, and the paving around the Civil War memorial did create an area that can be used for performances, though it is less than ideal because of the central monument. But times have changed since the 1960s and there is no longer such a demand for performance space. It is more likely that, in the 1980s, a sunken plaza would have been underused and problematic to maintain.

As to the softball field and tot lot, they do not truly belong on a common. But the city of Cambridge is unusual: the stock of public open space in relation to population amounts to about three acres for every thousand residents, less than one-third the acreage desirable according to national standards. Kenneth Holway of the Cambridge Recreation Department reports that there is "never enough open field space" in Cambridge. There are 122 softball teams in the city and ten softball diamonds, and in the Harvard Square area the common has the only one. In warm weather the diamond is used by school groups in the afternoons and by adult leagues at night, while the adjacent open space is used by a Cambridge youth soccer league. The facilities are extremely popular, there is no park or open space to which they could be relocated, and some argued that ball games had been on the common for more than a century and were now part of tradition. Under the circumstances the planners made the best of the situation. The tot lot is of natural-color wood, and the wire mesh that serves as a fence and softball backstop is much less obtrusive in black than metallic silver—a design solution that would improve the appearance of many parks.

The treatment of the pathways is commendable. By reducing the number of paths, the designers created additional green space, and the reorganization improved the circulation flow. Some have complained that the alley of trees at the northern end seems lost without a path, but the problem is more apparent in aerial views than at ground level. Although the cobbled, off-path areas are somewhat troublesome underfoot, the brick areas are as smooth as concrete and pose no problems even for baby carriages or bicycles. The only mistake is that the Phase I paving material was laid on a stonedust base and has become choked with weeds; while creating somewhat attractive bands of greenery, this is a maintenance problem. Phase II bricks and cobbles were laid on a bituminous base, preventing the growth.

Other omissions are not serious. The tot lot functions well without running water and rocks, and the contemplated toilets could not have been maintained properly. Tree grilles would have been attractive if constructed of wrought iron but the trees were of sufficient diameter to survive without them; and the northeast entrance plaza was an unnecessary bit of paving. The peripheral path was never repaved and is still asphalt, and the bicycle lane below curbside was never created; these would have been good additions, but to ring the entire common periphery with bricks was enormously expensive. Simple concrete cylinders were designed and constructed to hold lightweight expanded-metal trash receptacles. Though it had approved these cylinders during the project's design stage, the city public works department eventually brought in orange-painted oil drums to serve as trash receptacles. The department now plants flowers in the concrete cylinders.

In one instance the private sector stepped in to give the city a hand. The descendents of William Dawes, a rider on horseback who warned revolutionary Cantibrigians of the approaching British, volunteered to donate interpretive material relating to Dawes in particular and the history of Cambridge as a whole. The site was an adjacent traffic island at the southern end, formerly part of the common and slated for basic landscape improvements as part of the rehabilitation. Instead, the triangle became the Dawes Memorial. Bronze horseshoes and an inscription were set into the pavement; a bronze marker

This stone gateway, set in a new plaza of brick as part of the rehabilitation, provides a well-defined entrance to the common. The Civil War monument and contemporary lighting fixtures are also visible in the background.

Designed primarily by an organization of local parents, the Association for Children's Environment, the tot lot at the northern end of the common has proved popular. Construction materials of wood and black-coated metal are more compatible with the common than the anodized metal of standard playground equipment.

shows the route of Dawes's ride; and large enamel panels, prepared by the Cambridge Historical Commission, present the city's history through text, maps, and illustrations. Unfortunately, the large panels contain such a barrage of information that passersby are discouraged from reading them, and the scale of their concrete footings is oppressive in so small a space. A better solution would have been to omit the footings and mount the panels on the northern walls of the Memorial Arch, facing into the common.

On the whole, though, the improvements on this triangle and the larger common are in the best interest of the space and the people who use it. Such results were essentially ensured by the collaborative design process. Had Mason and Frey proposed, for example, to eliminate the landscape and tot lot improvements, they would have encountered insurmountable opposition from one or more groups—the conservation commission, the historical commission, the office of community development, ACE, or citizens who attended the open meeting. It was an effective system of checks and balances that prevented the interests of any one group from gaining the upper hand. As will be seen in the Waltham case study which follows, such participation is necessary in the design process from start to finish. Attempts to ignore the common's users or to turn to them as a last resort are bound to be unsuccessful.

<table>
<tr><td>Maintenance</td><td>

It is only in the area of postrehabilitation maintenance that Cambridge gets low grades. The first problem concerns the sprinkler system. As early as the summer of 1975—when the system had just been installed as part of Phase I construction—common watchers noticed that the sprinklers operated only sporadically. Complaints were made to the office of community development (formerly planning and development) and the situation was investigated. The conclusion was that police cars, city maintenance vehicles, and construction vehicles, which occasionally drove on the common and were responsible for some damage to the turf and brick walkways, were also to blame for broken sprinkler heads. Over the next few years the city repeatedly invested in repairs to the system, spending up to three times Mason and Frey's projected annual maintenance cost of $1,200 to $1,500 and at one point dispatching parks department crews to work on the system for four consecutive weeks. The labor and cost proved prohibitive, and by summer of 1980 the sprinkler heads had been dry for a year.

Community development officials no longer place all of the blame on vehicle damage, claiming instead that the original design was flawed. They note that the irrigation channels in more recent Cambridge parks have flush systems and are buried lower so that the protruding heads are less vulnerable. They also claim that some of the sprinker heads were badly located—beneath benches, for example. But James Woods, superintendant of the parks department, says the design has nothing to do with it.

"There hasn't been a sprinkler system there for two hundred and fifty years," observes Woods, "and there shouldn't be one now." He cites problems stemming from groundwater, frost, and ice in the mains, but he says that vandalism is the most serious problem. "Some people sleep on the common, and when the water used to come on early in the morning they would get up and break off the sprinkler heads." When the parks department painted the heads orange so their trucks could avoid them, it was that much easier for the morning sleepers to find the source of their unexpected shower—and destroy it. As a result of the sprinkler failures the turf on the common is patchy and

</td></tr>
</table>

weed-covered in some areas, particularly the open field to the northwest. The heavy recreational use this area receives intensifies the problem.

Aging and vandalism account for other maintenance problems as well. Benches fall into disrepair, fence rails break, graffiti cover the Civil War monument, some young trees die before reaching maturity, and a number of light fixtures fail to function. This last problem is one of the gravest concerns, as insufficient lighting discourages casual evening strollers and invites vandals.

Basically the issues are manpower and money. James Woods estimates that the parks department spends at least $25,000 per year on the common, but it is simply not enough. Only one man is there year around to tend to the grass; at one point two men were assigned to the common, but in 1979 the department was forced to lay off forty percent of its staff of forty-nine. Furthermore, the parks department has money only for maintenance, not for capital improvements. If a tree dies, no amount of maintenance will bring it back.

With Proposition 2½ continuing to slash public funds in Massachusetts, there are no easy solutions. The best answer would be to retain a professional landscape architect, who could review the condition of the landscaping, and furnishings on an annual basis, and to contract with a private landscape firm to carry out maintenance. Of course, this requires money—and money is needed, too, for capital improvements. It is unlikely that this will come from the public sector. What is needed is a Friends of the Common organization which would undertake fundraising efforts and, as a nonprofit corporation, would be eligible to receive grants. With a reasonable operating budget, the Cambridge Common could look much healthier than it does now, nearly five years after rehabilitation.

All this is not to say that the rehabilitation was in vain. As a result of federal funds and public participation, the common has become a rejuvenated space that is used by all members of the community, from toddlers to the elderly. Now what is needed is enough money to help the common continue to be a place of which the people of Cambridge can be proud.

(The Road to Hell Is) Paved with Good Intentions
Waltham, Massachusetts

Plazas, plazas everywhere, but scarcely a single new tree. That, in essence, is the result of a $350,000 federally funded project intended to revitalize the Waltham Common, and many of the city's residents and merchants are not very happy about it. Voicing criticism about how the money was spent, how the common is used, and the appropriateness of the so-called improvements that were made, local observers have deemed the project anything from "excessive" to "a total waste."

How did it happen? How was it that a project with preliminary planning, stacks of blueprints, professional design, and personal review by the mayor could result in such a plague of concrete and dearth of greenery?

There is no single answer, no one person or agency at whom to point the accusatory finger. Townspeople, who were outside the planning process, blame the insiders—the city planning department, the landscape architects, the mayor. These officials in turn blame the budget, explaining they had to make cuts they are not happy about. They feel, however, that when some additional money is secured, the completed project will be a success.

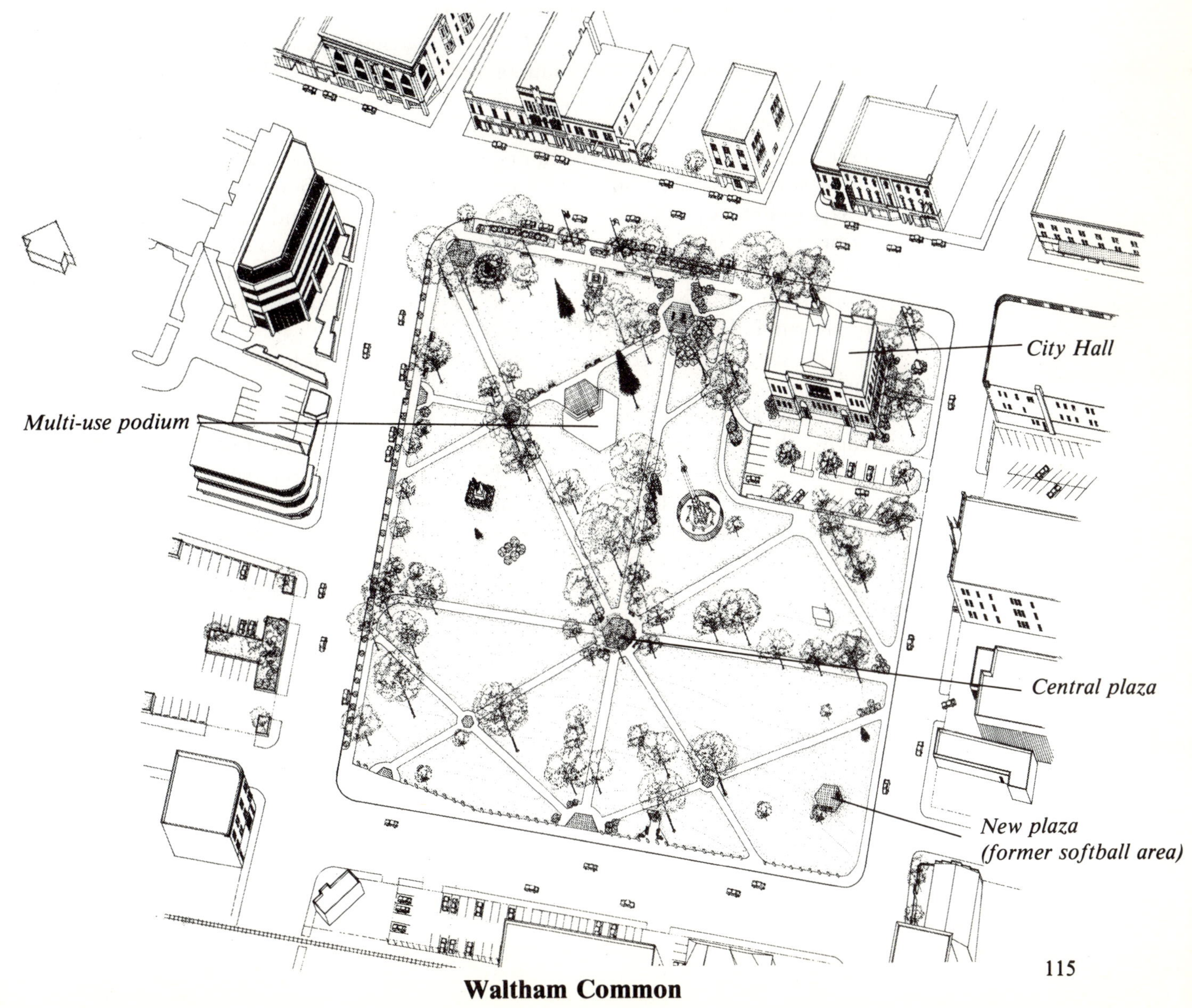

Waltham Common

To be sure, the project took a turn for the worse when the budget axe fell—although just how and why that happened is another question; and to be fair, some features of the rehabilitation are perfectly good. As becomes particularly evident, though, when one looks into the history of the common and this project, certain other aspects were questionable from the start.

As Alan McClennan, Director of the Waltham Planning Department, has correctly observed, the Waltham Common has a history that sets it apart from those of many surrounding towns. The centrally located square that is today the common is not the first or only piece of land townspeople have known by that name. Waltham in the seventeenth and early eighteenth centuries was an unincorporated part of Watertown, and Waltham-area residents shared the common lands of that sizeable township. After Waltham became independent in 1738, it built a meetinghouse more convenient to the population center and called that lot the "meeting-house common," although little is known about how it was used. It was not until 1854 that the town purchased from a local manufacturing company a lot of about five acres in size, and indicated in the deed that it should be "forever after kept open as and for a common for the use of the Inhabitants." Purchases of adjacent lots in 1859 and 1886 brought the common to its current size of about seven acres.

McClennan's point then is that in comparison with towns such as Cambridge, Waltham came by its common rather recently, and the appearance and use of the space has differed accordingly. Waltham in the mid-nineteenth century was developing into a busy manufacturing center. There was no need for common land to pasture cattle, no need to drill militia; but with a rapidly increasing population and a busier commercial center there was need—or at least a desire—to retain a bit of open space. This plot of land, bordered by two of the town's busiest roads, afforded the opportunity to beautify an area of mills, millworker housing, and shops, and to provide some park space for workers and residents. The town thus acquired the land for the purposes of ornament and recreation rather than utility.

As seen in photographs published in an 1882 local history, the early landscaping of the common was simple. A post and rail fence enclosed the square, and deciduous trees were set out in rows primarily along the common's edges, although saplings are visible in one photograph on either side of a central pathway. Owing to the size of the square and its recreational origins, there seem to have been pathways in greater quantity and of greater width than in the older utilitarian commons, where they eventually appeared through use rather than by plan. Next to one path there was a thirty- or forty-foot long low wooden bench of post and plank construction, which may have not been particularly elegant but undoubtedly was an inexpensive means of providing seating. The common boasted one monument to the Civil War, but otherwise the space was simply left open and unembellished. Its uses included active recreation—it is recorded that the local Mechanics Ball Club played a game there as early as 1858—and passive strolling and sitting.

When acquired by the town, the common had both a church and a semipublic hall on it. The church was subsequently moved across one of the adjacent streets, but proposals to move the hall met with opposition and it endured until it was replaced in 1925 by the current city hall. Incremental additions made during the twentieth century included war rosters, statues, a wooden gazebo-type bandstand that proved to be the popular site of evening concerts, benches, and streetlights—additions that did not necessarily enhance the common and eventually began to alter its idyllic character, especially as they grew shabbier over the years.

By the 1970s, insufficient maintenance and the lack of comprehensive planning had caught up with the common. Many furnishings had been vandalized or removed; those that remained, like the towering electric company standard streetlights, were inappropriate. As the condition worsened, the common was attractive only to gangs of youths and the city's homeless men, and townspeople who had formerly strolled through the square now skirted its edges.

The problems of the common were apparent to Waltham officials, who could witness its decay from their City Hall windows. But the solutions were clearly beyond the scope of the understaffed and short-budgeted parks department. Complaints were thus directed through this department to the office of Mayor Arthur J. Clark. When finally a number of city departments as well as townspeople pressured Mayor Clark to do something about the common's needs, he and the city council endorsed the idea of a large-scale rehabilitation program. Now what was needed was money.

Clark authorized the planning department to seek outside funding; through planning director Alan McClennan, the city applied for a grant from the Land and Water Conservation Fund, a funding source for the Heritage Conservation and Recreation Service (H.C.R.S.). (Under the Reagan administration this program may be somewhat restructured, although it is anticipated that some funding will still be available.) Under the auspices of the U.S. Department of the Interior, this federal program provides fifty percent matching grants for park and recreation projects; in other words, the program will supply one federal dollar to match every dollar the city can supply from another source, for a total of one-half the project cost.

Although the dollars are federal, the program is administered at the state level. In order to receive funds, each state is required to develop a comprehensive, statewide outdoor recreation plan that evaluates the supply and demand of existing outdoor resources and establishes priorities for funding. In Massachusetts, the 1978 plan that was to determine Waltham's eligibility was entitled *Massachusetts Outdoors*, and its emphasis was favorable for the city:

> The Commonwealth has over the past three years re-directed its programs to meet pressing needs of the urban core communities; the intent has been to revitalize the centers and improve their economic and social visibility.

The state recognized, though, that the rehabilitation of a park in an otherwise blighted area can be a wasted effort. Accordingly, parks projects that were part of larger urban renewal schemes were to be given high priority, and the state encouraged the use of Community Development Block Grants (C.D.B.G.) or Urban Development Action Grants (U.D.A.G.) as the matching funds for H.C.R.S. projects.

Waltham, with an ethnically-mixed population of about 55,000, fit the description of an "urban core community" and was already involved in a renewal project using C.D.B.G. funds. Its prospects for an H.C.R.S. grant thus seemed favorable, and in October 1978 the Massachusetts secretary of environmental affairs paid a personal visit to the Waltham Common, officially heralding the city's success in securing a $175,000 H.C.R.S. grant. "Densely populated communities like Waltham are prime examples of why preserving

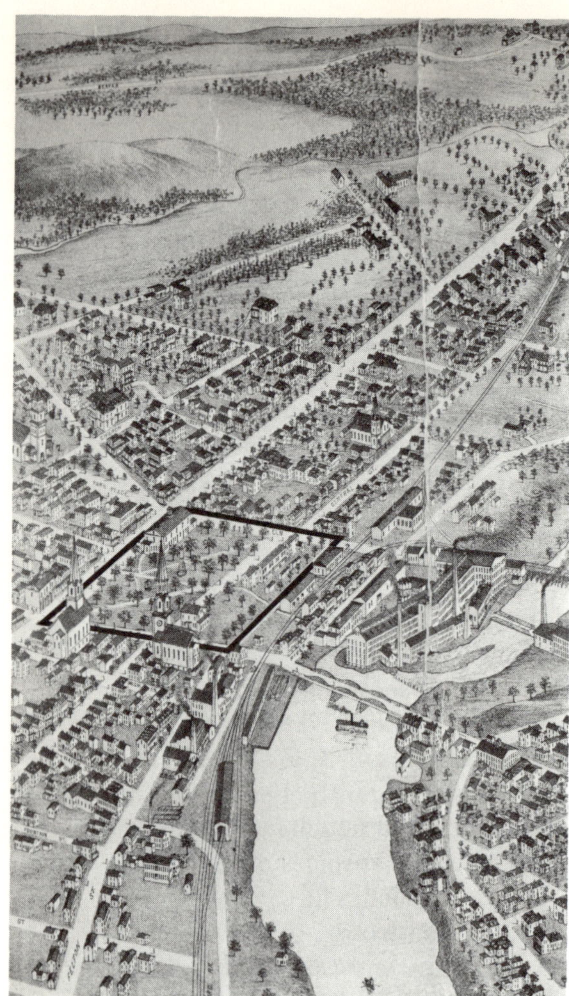

Waltham as it appeared in the late nineteenth century (at left), *with residences and a burgeoning downtown at the edge of the Charles River. The common* (outlined in black) *boasts the Civil War monument and a bandstand as well as the 1827 Rumford Hall, located where City Hall now stands. Other public and private buildings, later cleared, occupy the southern portion which in this view is set off by a road.*

open space is so important," proclaimed Secretary Evelyn F. Murphy. "The Waltham Common is a special place where all residents, young and old, can enjoy nearby amenities."

With the transfer of an additional matching $175,000 of C.D.B.G. money into the Waltham Common Restoration and Improvement Program, the city had a total of $350,000 available for the project. The question then was, simply, how best to spend it.

The Planning Stage

The project's first step was the creation of a planning team, a task which the mayor personally undertook. He appointed to the team a landscape architecture firm, Keyes Associates; an official from the planning department; and himself. No citizen advisory board? "You have to understand," explained Alan McClennan, "that Waltham is not like Cambridge. There are only a limited number of people active in the community." Perceiving little interest on the part of residents and merchants, the planning team did not investigate further the possibilities for more public involvement. Plans were developed according to the ideas and interests of the planning team members—exclusively.

One of their planning considerations was the historic character of commons in general and the Waltham Common in particular. McClennan was concerned that a distinction be made between a common and a park or playground. A common in his opinion, should be a gathering place for conversation, walking, or minor recreational use, but not for active recreation. At that time the southeast corner of the common was used occasionally for informal softball, and the planning team decided to develop a physical plan to break up this area. The team also decided to emphasize the particular late-nineteenth-century character of the common by selecting furnishings that were traditional in design and made of appropriate materials—wood, cast iron, and contemporary materials that resembled these.

Another general consideration was to make the common, in McClennan's words "more attractive to more people." As Secretary Murphy had affirmed, the common should be a space for all to enjoy, but the men and teenagers who loitered there were deterring other users. The planning team felt that if they could encourage a greater variety of people to begin frequenting the common, their presence would drive away the loiterers; one way to create an atmosphere that would bring in more people was simply to improve the common's general appearance. In addition, the planners wanted to make the current loitering spots less accessible, increase the effective illumination, and perhaps provide for such events as concerts.

The prospect of concerts raised the question of a suitable location. The old wooden gazebo had long since been removed, and although the band concerts by the schools and the American Legion had been a continuing tradition, the only facilities in recent years had been temporary trailers. Clark thought it would be appropriate for the common to have a new bandstand, but he saw an opportunity to kill two birds with one stone. Parades that marched around the common were another Waltham tradition, and the mayor and other local dignitaries viewed these from a temporary trailer as well. The new bandstand, he decided, should actually be a "multi-use podium" that would display bands, elevate parade spectators, and accommodate choral groups on its steps.

Other specific considerations for the improvement plan related to landscaping and maintenance. Since the grass dried out severely every summer, it was decided to install a permanent sprinkler system and new turf. New trees, perhaps two dozen, were to replace those that had died, especially along the perimeter of the common. Additional enclosure would be provided by joining the existing granite posts on the Carter Street side with horizontal rails. The

Two benches marooned on one of the stark new plazas. Designers of Robbin's Park in Waltham (below) a century ago had found a more satisfactory solution: plant rather than pave.

walkways were deemed beyond repair; the planners decided to replace them with new material and to add plazas with flowers and trees where two or more pathways intersected.

Keyes Associates drew up plans that incorporated these considerations, and sketches and blueprints were reviewed "with a red pencil" by the planning department and Mayor Clark. Some features were revised several times until one or another member of the team was satisfied. When possible, samples of proposed furnishings were installed for a trial period. For example, a street-lamp modeled after a nineteenth-century gas lamp was chosen and erected on the common, where it stood for a month before a final decision was made to accept it, and the walkways were resurfaced in patches. The streetlamp met with public approval; the walkways, however did not. Keyes Associates had favored several textured surfaces, but the planners found that "virtually every-one"—ranging from mothers with baby carriages to city maintenance work-ers—disliked these rough surfaces and vetoed the samples in favor of smoother concrete. The planners decided, in this case, to yield to popular demand.

As the final plans began to take shape, the project included: new furnish-ings in the form of benches, lights, fence rails, and the multi-use podium; replacement pathways and new plazas; new trees, shrubs, flowers, and turf; a new sprinkler maintenance system; and the relocation and relandscaping of some existing embellishments. The total projected cost? Four hundred fifty thousand dollars—one hundred thousand over the budget.

No one was sure how this miscalculation of almost thirty percent had been made, but clearly something dramatic had to be done to correct it. The planning team believed—perhaps erroneously—that it would not be possible to raise the additional money at that time, and their strategy was instead to cut costs. Cancel the plans to relocate statuary. Cancel the roof for the multi-use podium. And, most significantly, cancel almost all the landscape plans: the trees, shrubs, flowers, sprinkler system, everything but the turf.

The team believed that it was not to forget about the landscape improve-ments but to postpone them, raising the money locally once the remainder of the rehabilitation was completed. With the project now within the realm of the original budget, work could proceed.

<table>
<tr><td>The Rehabilitation</td><td>

The most extensive—and expensive—features were the new pathways and plazas. Paths were not merely resurfaced but entirely replaced, and both the removal process and the installation of new concrete were costly. The existing pathway network was preserved, with only one path added where determined pedestrians had worn the grass bare, but the plazas were a new feature. Eight in number, they are located at or near three of the common's corners (city hall occupying the fourth) and at pathway intersections. The plazas are circular or hexagonal in shape and distinguished from the pathways by insets of brick trifoliate paving material. Two or more benches are located at each plaza. In early plans, the plazas were to have been planted with Kwanzan cherry trees and red crocuses in the area behind the benches; as executed, these areas are paved.

One plaza links a pathway to the multi-use podium. Echoing the shape of the plazas, the podium is semihexagonal and is set at the top of a small rise, facing the corner of Main and Moody Streets. It is constructed of concrete, its top surfaced with a stone aggregate.

The new benches and lights were the other major expenditures. The

</td></tr>
</table>

benches feature curvilinear, black cast-iron armrests and legs, with unpainted wood seats and backs. While some benches line the edge of the common and face the street, most are located on the interior plazas. McClennan says the benches were not "scattered along the walks" but rather "purposefully brought to the crossroads" in an effort to create conversation places. The new lights are of black Lexon, a contemporary but fitting material, and they are in the style of the gas lamps that once lined Waltham's streets. Underground wiring contributes to their traditional appearance, and new electrical outlets were also installed at ground level with underground wiring for the annual display of Christmas lights.

The finishing touch was the installation of new turf, marking completion of the project at the beginning of fall 1980.

Analysis It is difficult to imagine what the planning team envisioned the day it decided to pave rather than plant, but the result, predictably, is a lot of barren pavement. The paths are bad—concrete and too wide—and the plazas are worse, as the isolated benches and an occasional lone sapling strive to create a place for conversational gathering. Particularly egregious is the plaza near the corner of Elm and Carter Streets, intended by the planners to break up the old baseball area; there are no trees to screen the busy traffic and no path to the plaza. Is this really better than an occasional ball game? Rarely does anyone venture here, nor do sitters linger in the other, equally bleak areas.

McClennan's intentions were good when he advocated design for passive rather than active recreation, but the enthusiasm for passive gathering places has substituted one problem for another. First, the amount of park activity does not warrant so much paved area. Narrowing the paths, even if they had been as wide in years past, would have improved the common's appearance and also saved money. The plazas are entirely unnecessary; they are unjustified in terms of use and there is no historical precedent for them. Perhaps the planners felt they would emphasize the late-nineteenth-century urban character of the common, and indeed an 1882 photograph of Robbins Park in Waltham reveals that there were large intersections where several paths met. These circles were planted, however, not paved. Finally, even if more people used the common, these plazas would still not serve their purpose, since the benches are considerably too far apart for conversation. The one exception is

The new paved plazas under construction: a major expenditure that is not warranted by the results.

The common's new multi-use podium is no substitute for a traditional bandstand.

the central four-bench plaza, which in fact has succeeded in attracting users—
the derelicts, who continue to deter others.

The benches that are "scattered" along the walkways seem to be more
popular than those on the plazas, and the benches near the bus shelter are in
constant use by people waiting for public transportation. The benches are well
suited to the common in appearance and sturdy enough to resist vandalism,
but there have been comments from residents that this new seating is not as
comfortable as the old. One passerby pronounced them "love seats" and
professed a desire for some "real" benches that were deeper and longer. An
inexpensive platform-type bench modeled after the one in the 1880s photograph would probably be a welcome addition and would be indisputably
authentic.

The lighting, while attractive, has also been somewhat problematic. The
intent was to increase the effective illumination of the common by increasing
the number of lamps and by selecting lampposts that were comparatively short
so that the light would not be diffused in the trees. However, the new lamps
were fitted with 150-watt bulbs and are too dim; all of the bulbs must be
replaced. A problem less easily corrected is that the center four-bench plaza
has too few lamps, creating a dark spot that encourages loitering. Additional
lamps—requiring additional funds—are needed.

The benches and lamps are appropriately traditional in design, but the
multi-use podium is blatantly modern. Dale Plante, a landscape architect with
Keyes Associates, said that his firm had studied period bandstands; it had
originally proposed a gazebo design, but this plan was rejected by other
planning team members in favor of the platform style. Once the budget
cutbacks precluded the roof from being constructed the design became even
less traditional, although the podium does have a virtue of being inconspicuous. The siting is poor; the podium faces the street rather than the common,
so that any large gathering must view performers from the rear. The platform
was sited to take into account its intended use for parade watching, but because
it is actually too low to afford a good view it may never serve that purpose.

Finally, much of the real improvement, like the new turf, may prove to be
ephemeral, since the project plans and funds did not provide for sufficient
maintenance. For a time the city received some help from Comprehensive
Employment Training Act (CETA) workers, who were able to perform routine
maintenance and carry out a limited amount of planting, but they left when
their CETA contracts expired. The planners' decision to drop the sprinkler
system is surprising given that both Dale Plante and Alan McClennan are
aware of what is likely to happen without it. McClennan commented that
people unfortunately are more enthusiastic about construction than maintenance—"We all are"—and although he hopes to get a mobile watering system he
is worried. Plante believes that "without that sprinkler system, it's going to
revert back, going to be sparse. It will invite back the people you don't want."

The maintenance and use of the common are sensitive issues with residents and merchants. Even those who praised the project often qualified their
approval with comments like "if they keep it up" and "so long as they don't do it
every year." Many were skeptical that the new furnishings would escape
vandalism—"Come back in a year and look at it," one cynic encouraged—and
they have not seen evidence that a wide variety of people will benefit from the

project. Observers are critical of the city for spending $350,000 to benefit what they consider to be a few vagrants and gangs of teenage boys. "To be honest with you, I'm afraid to walk through the center where those men hang out; I go around the edge," a female city employee admitted. "It seems a shame that they spent all that money and you look at the people who enjoy it."

The last chapter of this story has yet to unfold. The city hopes to secure additional funding for the planting and remaining miscellaneous aspects of the project, but it has not yet found a source for this money.

One possibility is that the community will donate the funds; in fact, the mayor appointed a special committee to solicit $50,000 from local businesses specifically for the planting. But having had no opportunities for participation in the planning, design, or execution of the project, most residents and merchants were not inclined to contribute. Several, in fact, laughed at the suggestion that they finance a project they already saw as a waste of money; McClennan reported that the amount raised was "not much."

The obvious problem in Waltham was that the planners turned their backs on the residents, merchants, and employees whom the project was supposed to benefit. Perhaps McClennan was right when he claimed that there are but few people active in the Waltham community. If so, the common rehabilitation project could have served to stir up some activity and create a group of "proprietors" who had never stepped forward before. Merchants whose shops face the common, and some of whom have looked out over that space daily for more than ten years all have something to say about the space, as do many residents; judging from their comments the project would have benefited from their involvement:

"I don't think it looks as nice as it did thirty, forty years ago. There were a lot more trees then."

"I think we could have lived without all of the grandeur."

"They could have put up a real bandstand; for $350,000 you can buy a lot of roofs."

"They were a little fancy in places where they didn't need to be."

"I remember twenty-five, thirty-five years ago when it . . . had a real bandstand; then they tore down the bandstand to 'beautify' the common."

"The nostalgia part of it is really lovely, but I just can't see spending all of that money when we had lovely sidewalks and green grass before."

If the rehabilitation of the common is to be complete, city officials will have to find ways to involve the community that go beyond asking for money. The city should conduct open meetings on future plans for the common and aggressively solicit advice from residents and the business community. Since, for better or worse, the common now has a multi-use podium, it should be put to good and frequent use—as defined by community wants and needs. One of Waltham's large corporations might be persuaded, in exchange for some good local publicity, to "adopt" the common and donate trees; school groups and civic organizations might be willing to help with the actual planting. Such participation would help the city financially and would also begin to give the community a sense that this space is really theirs.

There have been some design mistakes on the common that cannot be undone, but carrying out the original landscape plan will at least minimize their effect. And, if city officials can help to create a group of concerned and active "proprietors," there may be fewer mistakes in the future.

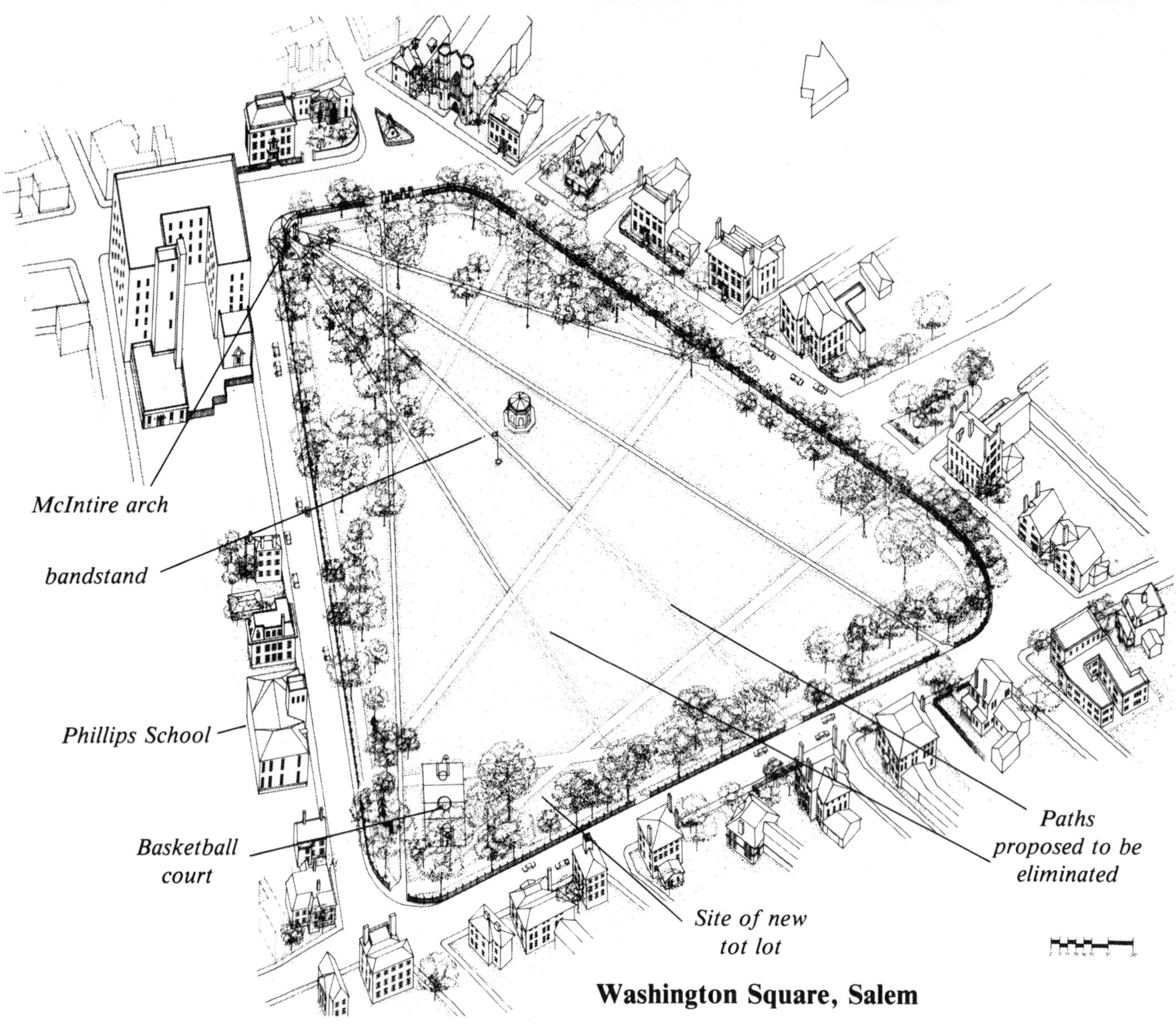

Washington Square, Salem

A Problem of Priorities
Salem, Massachusetts

Architecturally speaking, the common—known as Washington Square—in Salem, Massachusetts is one of the most noteworthy in New England. It was to Salem that Henry James returned when seeking to renew his impression of "the New England homogeneous," and had he not been so intrigued with Hawthorne's Seven Gables elsewhere in town he surely would have waxed eloquent about Washington Square. Standing shoulder to shoulder the houses bear an almost familial resemblance, each the same height and coloration, each with its taut skin of brick and rather stern facade. It is an assemblage that dates to Salem's heyday, between the Revolution and the War of 1812, yet it is as outstanding today as it was when the country was new.

All the more reason, it would seem, to rehabilitate the tired common which the houses embrace. Lacking the endurance of brick, the grass and trees have not fared so well over the past century and a half. The turf is patchy, worn to bare dirt in places; there are gaps in the periphery of trees where those that have died have not been replaced, and the swing sets are spindly and ill sited.

None of these problems is unusual—but what is unusual is that the Salem Planning Department has had a remedial plan for several years. Only one thing stands in the way: money, or rather a lack of it.

It is risky business to evaluate a rehabilitation project before it has been implemented; planning is one thing, but implementation according to a final budget is quite another. Yet so far as plans go, that of Salem is instructive, both in terms of the planning process and the end it seeks to achieve.

Background Located on Boston's North Shore, Salem was settled only sparsely during the first half of the seventeenth century because of the marshiness of much of the land. The town was established in 1668 and began to flourish in the eighteenth century, when its seaside location proved valuable for shipping. Although its maritime activities were curtailed by the British prior to and during the Revolution, Salem then enjoyed a brief period of grandeur between the two wars, when the shipping business brought considerable prosperity to families such as the Derbys and Crowninshields. The town was fortunate to play host to a rivalry between these two dynasties, as the resulting architectural legacy is the product of each trying to outdo the other.

As Susan Geib reveals in "Landscape and Faction," the spirit of one-up-manship extended beyond brick and mortar. Salem had a centrally located, nine-acre common, set aside in 1714 to be kept open as a training field. It was used as such throughout the century and served other purposes as well; the town almshouse was built there in 1772, and ropewalks and tanneries hugged the edges. Horses, cattle, ducks, chickens, and pigs roamed at will, circumnavigating the five ponds that lay within the common's boundaries. It was a functional but unattractive piece of land, and in a town that had begun to take appearances seriously it simply wouldn't do. Enter Elias Hasket Derby, Jr., who took it upon himself in 1802 to beautify the space—a task for which he could hardly be faulted but which had somewhat less than sterling motivations. Civic improvement entered into it, but it is significant that this was a Federalist-inspired project in an area of town that was primarily Republican. Renaming the common "Washington Square," as a tribute to the late Federalist leader George Washington, and erecting arched gates bearing his profile were merely the twists of the political knife for the Derbys. Yet the project was well received by townspeople of both camps, probably because each saw some advantage. For the Crowninshields the beautification created a more attractive setting in which to build, and increased property values of land they could sell. The Derbys, and Hasket Derby in particular, could take credit for the work and derive satisfaction from slipping in a Federalist memorial where it least belonged. Furthermore, the health and aesthetic improvements were undeniable. Acceptance of the project is indicated by the number of townspeople who pledged financial support—one hundred fifty-seven—and the equal representation of Republicans and Federalists.

The scope of work is indicated by the text of the subscription:

> For the purpose of Levelling the Common and laying it down to Grass, ornamenting it with a double row of Lombardy Poplar Trees, encircling it with a handsome railing of Oak joist and red Cedar posts, and painting it, laying out a handsome gravel walk, filling up the ponds, and decorating it in such a manner as will make it both elegant and convenient, and highly conducive to the health of the Inhabitants.

George Ropes's 1808 painting of training day on the common reveals, with some artistic license, that these intentions were largely realized. Gateways designed by Samuel McIntire and funded by a separate subscription were erected shortly after completion of the improvement. (For further discussion, see "A Resurrected Arch" in the "Guidelines for Greens" chapter of this book.)

The poplars, a brittle species that breaks easily in storms, blew down in 1818 and were replaced by elms and other hardwoods. Next to be replaced was the fence. By 1850 most of the houses that line Washington Square today had been completed, and residents undoubtedly felt that a wood rail fence was not up to par. In its place was installed an ornate cast-iron encirclement, the perfect backdrop for events such as the first ladies tricycle tour of the North Shore in 1885. The photograph of that occurrence reveals that the elms had taken hold with more success than the poplars and that the square was illuminated, at least in part, by gas lamps. Other late-nineteenth-century views depict handsome wood-and-iron benches around the periphery, while the center of the space was left open and embellished by only a flagpole and wooden gazebo.

The prosperity that Salem knew in 1800 was not in evidence a century later. Gone were the shipping trade and concomitant fortunes, and gone too were Hasket Derby and his willing subscribers to the common. In 1928 Washington Square was acquired by the park department as a playground, serving the adjacent Phillips School, and the space lost some of its former horse-and-buggy elegance. In 1976 the district was listed on the National Register of Historic Places, but the accolade was on behalf of the architectural surroundings more than the square. The 9.3-acre space was, according to Michael Moniz of the Salem Planning Department, "in pretty bad shape" by the late 1970s—bad enough so that comments on its appearance were forthcoming from a variety of sources. Townspeople complained that the square was shabby, with the fence particularly in poor repair. The mayor thought some immediate action was warranted. And members of the planning department learned that for the past several years the city had invested about $10,000 annually on spot repairs to the fence, a goodly sum hardly reflected in the square's appearance. When planners discovered that some funding potentially was available through the state historic commission, the result was a decision to formulate a rehabilitation scheme.

Planning and Implementation

The fence was the most glaring problem. Cast iron is durable but still susceptible to wear and tear and vandalism, and after a hundred and twenty-five years the fence was showing its age. Some pieces were damaged and in need of repair; others were missing entirely.

Over a two-year period starting in 1979, the planning department secured funding and repaired the damaged areas of the fence, completing what was termed the first phase of rehabilitation. It was labor-intensive work—each piece had to be blasted, scraped, primed, and painted in addition to the welding work—and it was expensive: $118,500. However, only $23,388 of this came directly from the city. The balance was secured from the Massachusetts Historic Commission, which provided $25,000 and a share of the city's federal Community Development Block Grant (C.D.B.G.).

The second phase involves construction of missing sections of the fence. About eighty sections, each roughly nine-and-a-half feet in length, are absent and must be recast using a fiberglass mold method. The planning department

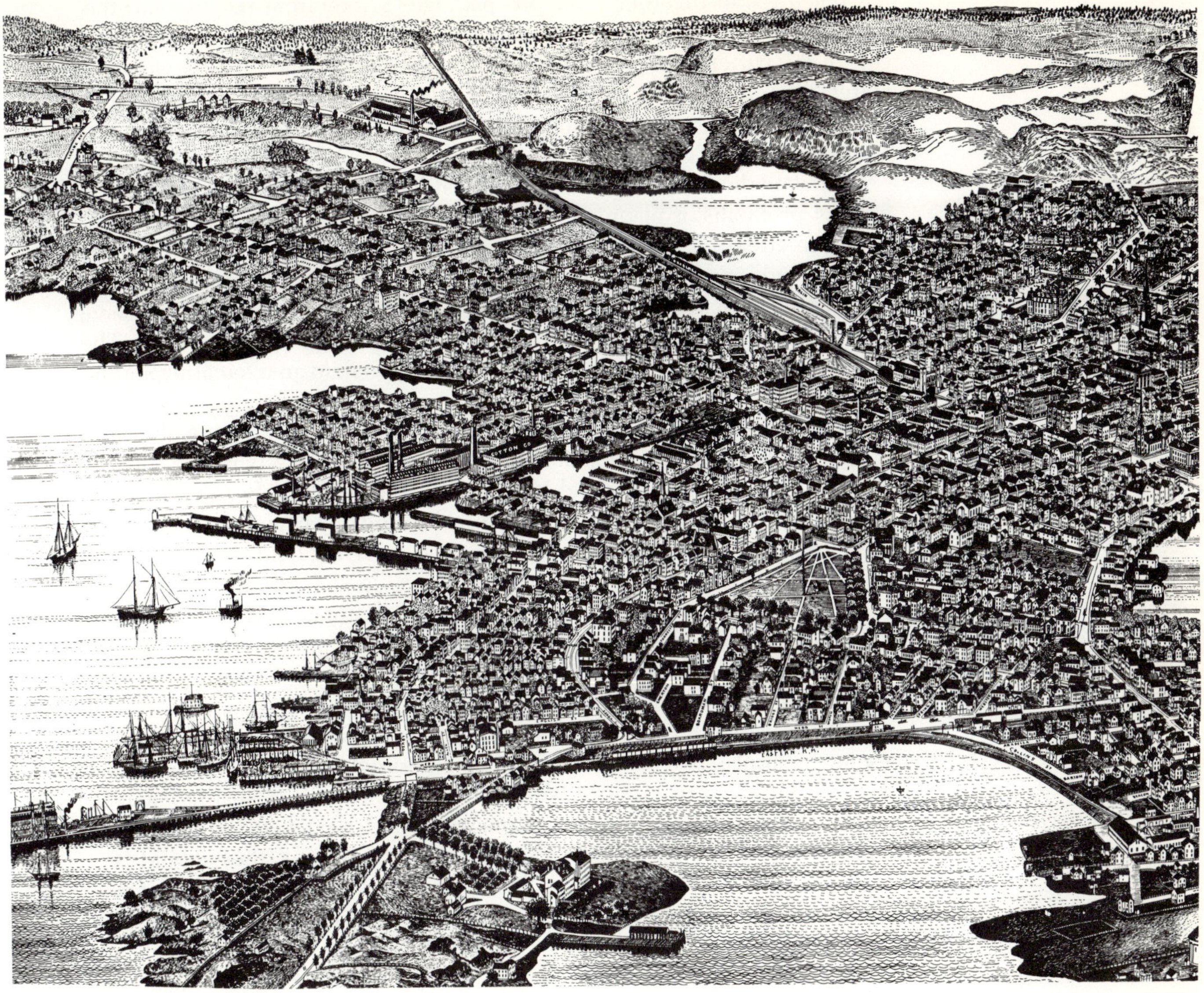

The port of Salem in 1883 (above) with tightly packed houses
surrounding the common. Close inspection reveals the radial
paths and cast iron fence that are still in existence; the flagpole and
bandstand have since been replaced. Trees on the southern side of
the common have been omitted in this view in order to show the
houses. A ground-level view (at right) from this same period
features the First Ladies Tricycle Tour of the North Shore.
(Courtesy Essex Institute, Salem, Mass.)

has recently put together a $42,500 package ($7,500 from the city and the balance from C.D.B.G. funds) to initiate the process. This sum will cover the cost of the pattern design, manufacture of the molds, and foundry work and materials for five finished sections. Other sections will not be so costly but will be $2,500 to $3,000 apiece, and the total cost for this second phase could run as high as $240,000.

To date the fence restoration is all that has been realized, but it is not for want of problems or planning. The turf, for example, also needs attention. Children attending the Phillips School have used the square as their playground, and swing sets and a basketball court were installed for them. These areas received particularly hard use, and although the recent school closing will ease that stress the turf is too damaged to recover spontaneously. The Salem Youth Soccer League practices on the open field area, creating another source of wear and tear.

Accordingly, the Planning Department would like to devote about $50,000 to aerating, loaming, and reseeding the soil—"It's what the common needs most of all," says Michael Moniz. Although there has been some opposition, from the city council and within the planning department, to allowing the soccer league to continue using the square as a playing field, the most recent thinking is that the activity should continue so long as the turf receives necessary attention. In fact, planners intend to eliminate portions of two of the radial paths in order to create an even larger area of uninterrupted green for active recreation. However, no permanent facilities such as soccer goals will be allowed.

Planners would also like to replace some of the trees that formerly created a solid enclosure, two rows deep, along the perimeter. About one hundred are missing, but even twenty-five would be sufficient to fill the gaps. The other major area of attention is the walkways, which are so cracked and uneven that James Foley of the parks and recreation department says they should be replaced before "someone gets killed" trying to walk a straight line. The planning department would like to remove the existing asphalt and use stone-dust instead, set on a concrete base to permit snowplowing of the radial paths; the perimeter and cross paths will be stonedust alone. Two paths will perhaps be added to compensate for those being removed to create the large playing field.

Neighborhood parents have expressed an interest in a tot lot to accommodate young children, and Polly Erdman of the planning department is currently working with several groups to develop a satisfactory design. The historic district commission must be consulted, since that group has jurisdiction over any alterations or additions made within the district, and the parks and recreation department has certain preferences in regard to maintenance. Erdman has met with a core group of parents from twelve to fifteen families several times and is now preparing a slide show to illustrate the materials and design of other tot lots. There have been no final decisions yet, since each group favors something different: the historic district commission prefers black metal or granite construction materials, the parents want wood, the parks and recreation department wants basic metal with no wood. Michael Moniz is optimistic that a compromise can be worked out, probably by employing a variety of materials. The tot lot will be located to the northeast of the basketball court.

It is likely that the tot lot, which will cost about $25,000, will be funded with C.D.B.G. money. As to the turf, trees, and paths, the project is at a standstill. The reason is money.

The planning department has tried to secure funding for Washington Square, primarily through an application to the Urban Park and Recreation Recovery Program (UPARR), a federal program that is part of the Heritage Conservation and Recreation Service (H.C.R.S.) and administered through the Department of the Interior. The application was turned down, probably, says Polly Erdman, because it was a conventional rather than a glamorous project and UPARR did not find it of merit. The city did receive some UPARR money as well as a Land and Water Conservation Fund grant, also through H.C.R.S., but in each case the money was for projects elsewhere in town. The UPARR funds are being used to rehabilitate a Y.M.C.A. building, improving its facade and converting part of the interior to elderly housing; and the Land and Water funding has been devoted to Nathaniel Bowditch Park and to assembling the 125-acre Forest River Conservation Area. No application was made to the Land and Water Conservation Fund on behalf of Washington Square, since the city had already received substantial grants for these other areas.

"The common is just not a high priority," explains Moniz, noting its location in the relatively well-to-do historic district. It is admittedly an inner-city park, but Salem is not so needy as Cambridge or Waltham. "Salem probably has more parks per capita than any other town or city in the state," Moniz notes almost apologetically. "We're fortunate that a number of parks were laid out in the nineteenth century, as they also were in Boston, and retained. And for open space, there's always the ocean waterfront."

The open field area of the common (above), *is a natural place for games of catch, soccer, and other recreational activities. Planners have deemed such uses acceptable but fear for the turf unless it is rehabilitated soon.*

Work on Washington Square (at left), *to date has centered on the fence, as funding for other improvements has been elusive.*

Undaunted, the planning department cast about for alternative funding sources. The state historical commission was not the answer. Its rehabilitation projects are oriented to the renovation of structures, and while it was willing to contribute to the work on the fence it was not eager to take up a landscape. Looking closer to home still, the planners developed a scheme using city money. When the city decided to close the Phillips School that faces the square, it was determined that the property would be sold and the building converted, possibly to condominiums. Since the parks and recreation budget is particularly tight in light of the state's tax-cutting Proposition 2½, it was agreed that part or all of the revenue from the sale would be funneled into that department. The planners hoped in turn to devote that money to Washington Square.

Their hopes were raised only to be dashed once more. Months went by and finally the sale was completed; the total revenue was one dollar. The city had decided to convert the school to housing for the handicapped rather than condominiums, and the property was simply transferred from one city department to another rather than sold to the private sector. The transaction took place in late 1981, and the planning department at this writing has no alternative schemes. The only other grant pending is a federal Urban Development Action Grant on behalf of the Hawthorne Hotel, the sizeable structure opposite the head of the square. Planners have hoped that a portion of the two hundred thousand dollars requested could be used for the common, probably to improve the fence near the hotel. Although there is no official word about whether or not the grant will be awarded, the planners have heard that the prospect is not good. Most recently the city has contemplated forming a not-for-profit corporation which could sponsor fundraising events and use the revenue for the square (a corporation perhaps similar to one of those discussed in the "Beyond the Village Green" chapter of this book and which have been successful elsewhere), but there are no definite plans.

Some improvements are being made: the fence is undergoing reconstruction, the tot lot was completed, and, as part of another city-wide program, an interpretive porcelain enamel panel will be erected soon at one corner of the square. Larger rehabilitation plans—turf rehabilitation, tree planting, and pathway reconstruction—are on ice until the necessary $102,000 can be found. It is a small sum, perhaps too small. Washington Square also needs new benches to replace the old concrete and wood ones, pedestrian-scale lights instead of the towering cobra-head fixtures, and trash receptacles. These later furnishings, though, are out of the question as far as the planning department is concerned; Moniz feels that if the city can't raise $102,000 for the essential work there is no point in trying to locate, for example, five hundred dollars for each new bench. He is probably right, except that if the project were a bit more glamorous it might attract some latter-day proprietors. Clearly what is needed is a twentieth-century Hasket Derby and his group of willing subscribers, who would—for whatever motives—invest their interests and money in the space. Until they appear, though, the future of Washington Square is uncertain.

Beyond the Village Green

The traditional town common has served as an enduring metaphor for a sense of community. The shared space of the green, dominated by the spires of churches and anchored by great trees, has a comforting sense of wholeness, of order engendered by shared authority and participation. Yet as the vignettes and case studies of the preceding chapters reveal, a close inspection of these hallowed spaces sometimes belies that idealistic image. One objective of this book, then, is to demonstrate that there is a need for increased care and conservation of these New England greens, lest that image of community care prove illusory.

But it is not enough for this generation simply to preserve these historic spaces. There is a constituency of people across the nation who have never cherished the lush green of Deerfield on a spring morning but who yearn to care about new common spaces. An equally important aim of our book is to encourage the creation of such new spaces—and at the same time to encourage the development of the sort of community values from which the original commons were derived.

We have identified that quality of care with the term "proprietorship," a word that indicates to us a special relationship between people and place. As John Stilgoe explained, the Proprietors, in the early years of many New England towns, were the formally organized group of settlers who served as the legal owners of common or undivided lands. Over the years, these groups often surrendered their authority to local governments or slowly sold off the lands under their care. The more than three hundred greens and commons still existing in New England, however, have survived because of the interest of some group or groups who have assumed what could be called a "proprietary relationship" to these patches of greenery. The deterioration of some greens has come about because neither public officials nor private citizens were willing to assume the responsibility of ownership or stewardship—"proprietorship," as we define it—that the existence of greens and commons entails. But other greens have been ushered into the present intact, precisely because some group of modern-day proprietors has felt an affectionate responsibility toward the land and has been willing to devote time and resources toward its care, regardless of legal entitlement.

As we delved into this concept of proprietorship, we realized that it was far from extinct, although it has taken on some hitherto unknown forms and characteristics. We heard the stories of community leaders, land management specialists, real estate developers, and corporate officials. We identified a whole spectrum of new proprietors, ranging from owners of brownstones in Brooklyn to a multinational corporation in California, and new types of common land that included condominium greens and urban public parks. And we were encouraged by what we found.

The examples that follow are divided into three broad categories that highlight differences in proprietary relationships. The first section explores the open spaces that embrace or are embraced by a residential community and are tended by individuals. The second investigates the new support relationships that have evolved as elements of the private and public sectors join to form effective partnerships and rescue or sustain public parks. The third section discusses one of the newest phenomena, parks that are privately owned but publicly used. Our intent is to make available to proprietors and proprietors-to-be the experiences of others with similar responsibilities, and to provide guidance based on these studies to assist those who wrestle with the problems and promise of common ground.

THE INDIVIDUAL AS PROPRIETOR

The Village Green

The Village Green, built in 1942 as a residential development in Los Angeles, California, is the result of an attempt to cope with the intrusions and indignities of the automobile age. With housing units arranged in a ring reminiscent of a besieged wagon train, the automobile is consigned to the fringes of the sixty-eight-acre "superblock," while the central portion is reserved for pedestrian use.

Like the numerous developments that sprang up after World War II, the Village Green—originally called Baldwin Hills Village—was constructed in order to provide moderate cost housing, in this case rental units, for an overflowing urban population. Most of these suburban estates of the forties and fifties set the stage for the full-blown Levittown, with its thousands of mass-produced single-family houses and individual postage-stamp-size lawns. The Village Green, however, was designed to maximize common open space; twenty of the sixty-eight acres are devoted to greens and garden courts, and most of the remaining acreage is occupied by the buildings. The work of the noted planner Clarence Stein, the project emulated a traditional closely knit village. Fourteen percent of the original budget was allocated for landscaping.

The development reached one hundred percent occupancy soon after it was completed, an indication of its popularity, and one long-time resident

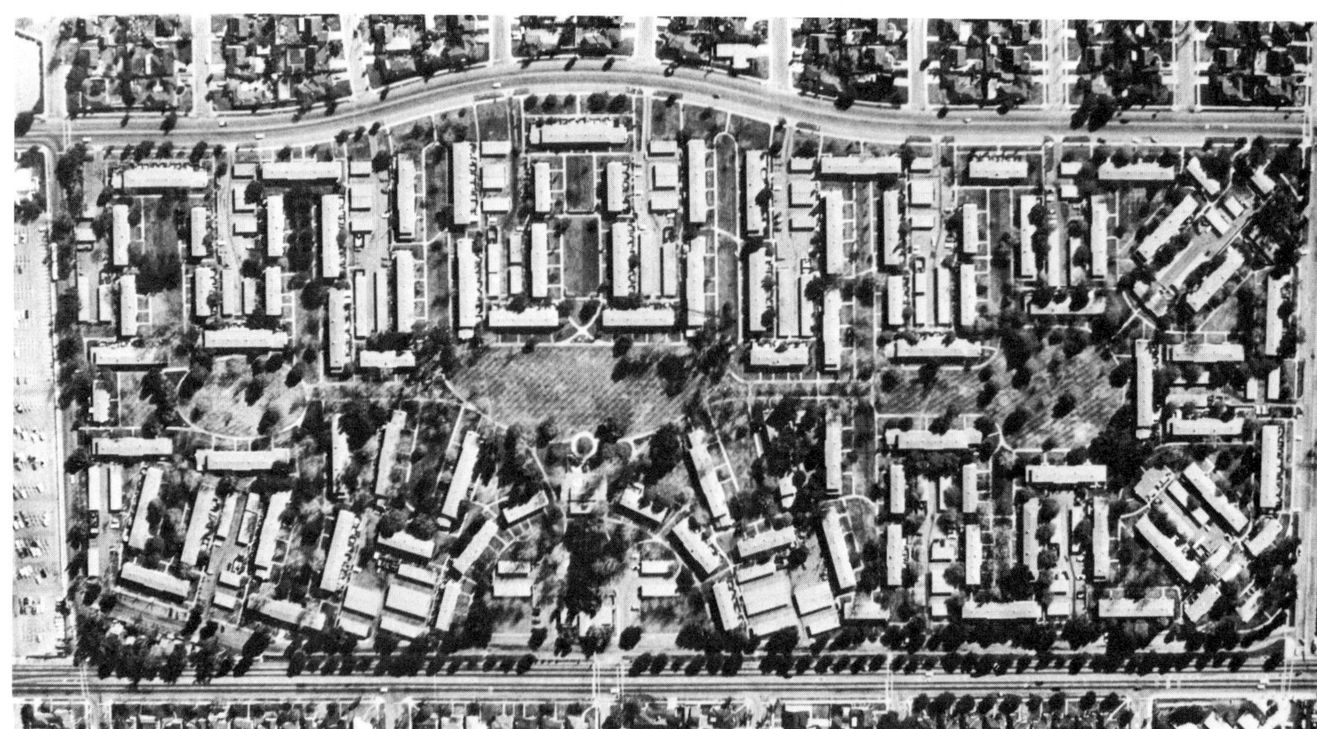

Aerial view of the Village Green development (formerly Baldwin Hills Village).

recalls that there was much camaraderie among tenants. Social events took place both indoors and out, in the common areas. Conversion of the development to condominiums in 1972 caused a large turnover in population, but neighbors are still friendly with one another and enthusiastic about their common space. Daniel Abeyta, treasurer of the Village Green Owners Association, comments that residents lavish attention on the common area; California's periodic water shortages, he says, cause residents to "get up in arms because they want it to be beautiful." "Everybody loves it!" is the report from Frank Dolan, a landscape architect.

Design. Within the boundaries of the rectangular estate are three major open spaces, linked by pedestrian walks and known collectively as "the green." Exotic species of trees and shrubs create a variety of colors, shapes, and textures, and the grass is carefully tended, creating a pristine appearance. The central location of the green makes it eminently accessible to every unit, and the paved walks allow residents to stroll around the open space on their way from one dwelling to another. The green thus becomes part of the context of everyday life in the community.

Although the green is large, it is enclosed and secluded by the surrounding clusters of buildings. Residents can watch over the green from their windows, and feel so safe there that they occasionally sunbathe in the nude. The green could be called "defensible space," defined by Oscar Newman as an environment under the control of its residents. Newman writes:

> [B]y grouping dwelling units to reinforce associations of mutual benefit; by delineating paths of movement; by defining areas of activity for particular users through their juxtaposition with internal living areas; and by providing for natural opportunities for visual surveillance, architects can create a clear understanding of the function of a space, and who its users are and ought to be. This, in turn, can lead residents of all income levels to adopt extremely potent territorial attitudes.

Residents of the Village Green do feel territorial about their open space, not so much in the sense of criminal defense as in responsibility. This attitude is evident in the system of open space management.

Management. While the community cares for the open space through any number of small daily actions, the formal apparatus for administration is the owners association. Decisions about the open space are made by the five-member board of directors, which serves a two-year unpaid term, and advisory committees made up of owners who have volunteered. The landscape committee is most closely involved with the care of the greenery.

Usually there are seventeen owners, one from each of the residential courts, on the landscape committee; they meet once or more a month to discuss maintenance and improvement of the open space. Officially the committee can only make recommendations to the board of directors, but the directors tend to approve all proposals. The landscape committee also undertakes certain projects on its own; in 1981 members rewrote the maintenance contract for the open space, solicited bids for it from private grounds maintenance firms, and carried out a tree replanting project with assistance from a landscape architect. The tree planting project was allotted $3,000; and the cost of maintaining the green in 1981 was $22,000. This amount was a sizable fraction of that year's $804,750 owners association budget, which is provided by the yearly lien on each unit in the development and paid by the owners.

Two views of common areas in the Village Green, linked by paths and lined by trees.

Conclusion. Owners treat the handsome green as if it were their own front yard, using it for private gatherings (including wedding parties and family reunions) as well as for community events such as picnics, the annual Fourth of July celebration, and a Christmas fair. It is a space well designed for owners' needs; it is not a park or playground, but since children are not allowed to live in the development, there is little need for recreational equipment of that nature. Village Green residents simply want the green to be neat and attractive, and they pay a private landscape maintenance firm to carry out their instructions. It is in their best interests to see that the grounds are in good shape, not only from an aesthetic standpoint but also from an economic one: Charles Brittin of the owners board notes that the resale value of the condominiums is accordingly increased.

This proprietary interest in the common area seems so straightforward and logical that one might assume it is typical of all such developments. As we see in our next case study, though, that optimism is not always borne out.

Laguna Village   Situated in Laguna Hills, California, on the outskirts of Los Angeles, Laguna Village is a housing development with roughly forty percent of its 159 acres given over to open space. It is a new project, inhabited but incomplete, and includes both rental and condominium units. Ultimately there will be 1,250 living units, nearly twice as many as the Village Green comprises.

Design. This is a countryside of hills and valleys; and Laguna Village is situated on the slopes that overlook the remaining fields of the Irvine Ranch. Dwellings are in rows, not clusters, with a street running in front of them and a strip of common land behind; and these strips are mostly forested, so that an observer from the valley will see only the roofs of the buildings. Visually, the device works, but the result is wooded hillsides that are discouragingly devoid of paths. Ardith Odous, who chaired the grounds committee in 1980, says that she walks through these wooded areas frequently but rarely meets other residents.

There is, however, other common land: a four-and-one-half acre plot called, once again, "the green". Originally planned as a bowling green to facilitate an increasingly popular southern California pastime, the green has few trees and is basically featureless, save for the clubhouse and swimming pool that occupy about half the area. This common space is no more popular than the hillsides, little used but for an occasional bowling match or volleyball game; and Bob Mariani, the on-site manager retained by the owners association, says that the community is not getting its money's worth from the annual $2,000 cost of maintaining the green.

The planners are to blame as much as the residents. The green, positioned at the edge of the development and a ten- or fifteen-minute walk from some residences, is too distant to invite spontaneous use. Furthermore, it is unclear why one would want to go there. With a road running along one side, and few trees to shield it from traffic or relieve the expanse of grass, it is just the opposite of defensible space. The best solution would be to relocate the green; barring that, some play equipment for children, more trees, and regularly scheduled activities could go a long way toward making the common area a true community resource.

Management. Management problems have been another impediment to the development among LagunaVillage inhabitants of a strong proprietary attitude toward their common land. As is customary for all condominium developments, the common property is managed by the homeowners association, which elects a board of directors for a one-year term. This term of office is simply too short; Mrs. Odous estimates that a new board takes at least four months to become effective in landscape management. Efforts to resolve the management problems brought about by the current system have exacerbated the situation, consuming so much time and energy that routine duties were neglected. For example, the homeowners association grounds committee, whose main task is to ensure that the grounds maintenance firm fulfills its contract, did not meet for several months during the summer of 1981, leaving the grounds uninspected during the critical, dry months of the southern California summer.

Conclusion. There is no guarantee that a piece of land designated as a common on a developer's plan will be cherished as such by the community. The

The four-and-a-half acre, featureless green at Laguna Village, a new development with some buildings still under construction.

proprietary spirit is brought out not by lofty ideals but rather by a place that affords some benefits, some pleasure, to its users. People will care for land only if they feel it is worthy of their efforts.

Nor can one assume that a single piece of common land will suffice. Village Green residents are a relatively homogeneous lot—all are of sufficient income to afford a condominium, all are childless—and the open space meets their similar desires. In contrast, Laguna Village is home to some who can pay the average purchase price of $135,000 and some who can afford only to rent. Some are families, some are couples. The community is ethnically diverse. Bob Mariani commented that the green in Laguna Village has not helped pull the community together to any appreciable degree, but perhaps such cohesion is a lot to expect—at least of four and a half acres. If the development had several smaller spaces or a large articulated green, with room for children to play and adults to relax; if it were an attractively landscaped space, and centrally located; then proprietorship at Laguna Village would have a good chance.

<table><tr><td>Columbia,
Maryland</td><td>

We turn now from these California developments to a considerably larger project on the East Coast. Columbia, Maryland is located midway between Baltimore and Washington, D.C., a planned unit development (P. U. D.) with 14,000 acres, a projected total population of 110,000 in 31,000 dwelling units, commercial districts, community centers, and a system of administration and management guided by elected officials. A brainchild of the Rouse Company, Columbia is functionally a town although not incorporated as such. Completion is expected, according to the Rouse master plan, in 1985.

</td></tr></table>

Design. Columbia is subdivided into eight villages, separated by common areas that are largely wooded, and open space in one form or another accounts for twenty percent of the total acreage. Mown fields, natural meadows, and woods wind through the development, penetrated by an extensive system of paths. It is, as some residents have commented happily, beautiful scenery; but the common land is also actively used, by children who play in the woods and fields and by adults who walk, jog, and ride bicycles along the paths. Other features vary from village to village; Oakland Mills, for example, has four ponds, an ice skating rink, three neighborhood centers with swimming pools, two tennis courts, sixteen tot lots, and six picnic areas.

The open space is as accessible as that of the superblock plan of the Village Green, as ruggedly handsome as the wooded hills at Laguna Village—but the woods here, with their surfaced pathways, are more than just a visual screen. Like Boston's Quincy Market, another project designed and built by the Rouse Company, Columbia is designed to please its particular audience.

Management. Residents are afforded an active role in planning for the common open space and caring for it. Open space committees, active in each of the eight villages, are staffed by volunteers who represent residents' interests and advise the Columbia Office of Land Management on relevant matters. In the villages that are just recently completed, the open space committees are forums for animated discussions on where to locate fields, tot lots, and walks— decisions that affect the property value of nearby homes as well as residents' activities. But committee members do more than just talk. Betty Miller, who chairs the Oakland Mills open space committee, relates that in 1980 her volunteers secured a $200 grant to fund activities that included a guided walk through the village's open space, attended by nearly one hundred residents,

Columbia, Maryland benefits from both common open space and wooded areas ribboned with paths.

and the production of an educational packet about local ecology for use in Columbia elementary schools. Committee members have also been known to roll up their sleeves and help plant thousands of seedling trees that the homeowners association obtains from the state forestry department.

Professionals in the office of land management attend to routine and technical matters that local committees are not equipped to handle. Pruning, mowing, and other maintenance chores are performed by crews from the office, while a full-time ecologist carries out studies to guide the efforts of the office staff and local committees. Funds provided by a lien of seventy-five cents per one hundred dollars of assessed valuation, levied on all housing units in the development, are allocated each year by the homeowners association to the office of land management; in 1981, the allocation was $757,000.

Conclusion. Columbia's residents have responded enthusiastically to a development in which open space is plentiful and professionally designed and maintained. What made Columbia planners include so much open space? Alton Scavo, vice-president of Howard Research and Development (a Rouse Company subsidiary), explains that it is good business. In 1975, Howard Research and Development proposed the construction of multi-unit housing in Columbia, for which it needed the approval of the local zoning board. With the support of the Columbia homeowners association, Howard approached the board with a plan to create an area with an open-space minimum of thirty percent—a substantial increase over the existing minimum requirement of twenty-three percent. The zoning board agreed that any potential problems caused by higher density multi-unit housing would be offset by the additional open space, and the proposal was approved. Ultimately the developer left thirty-six percent of the land unbuilt, since, as Scavo detailed, the potential financial gain from increasing the open space and reducing the number of units was greater than would be obtained by building more units; dwellings surrounded by copious open space sell faster and bring a better price than those in cramped quarters.

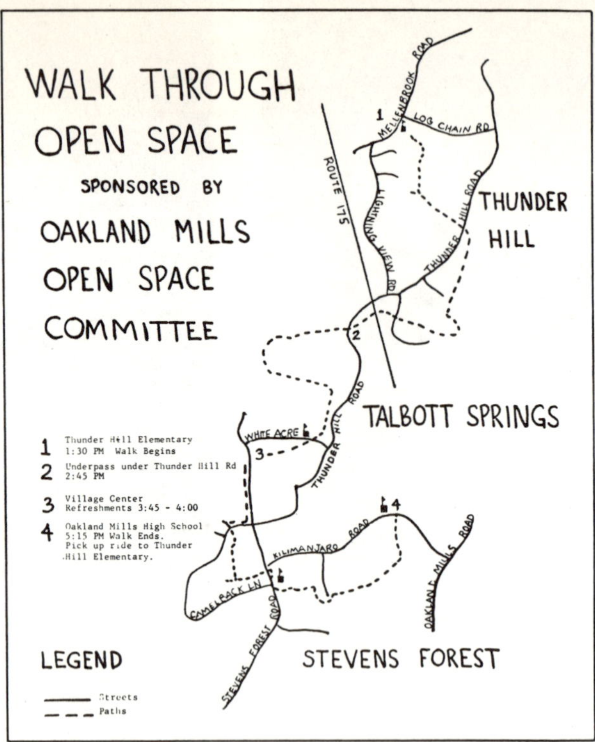

This simple flyer, distributed to the residents of the Oakland Mills village, encouraged residents to walk the open space together. Between eighty and one hundred participated in the four-hour hike, indicated by the dotted line.

Scavo hastens to add that profit was not the sole incentive for the developer. The Rouse Company is interested in producing, in his words, "a truly better environment in which to live," and inclusion of open space in such quantity and variety is in accordance with those ideals. It seems to be a successful formula. Residents are happy about the arrangment; as Charles Rhodehamel, ecologist at Columbia's office of land management, observes, "Most of the people like the idea of a contiguous park running through their neighborhood." And if open space is a marketable commodity, so much the better.

San Rafael Commons

The three preceding case studies have concerned open space that is owned by most of its users. Although a condominium or P.U.D. owner cannot point to boundaries of "mine" and "yours," he has bought a share of the common property and continues to pay for its upkeep. If he takes care to protect his investment, he can realize a profit when he sells his unit; and so we can expect that owners will have a proprietary interest in their common land at least in part for financial reasons. But what about users who are not owners, who have no monetary stake in the property?

San Rafael Commons is a federally subsidized apartment complex for the elderly and handicapped in San Rafael, California. Designed by the San Francisco firm of Kaplan McLaughlin Diaz, the eighty-three-unit project makes use of traditional cedar shingles and small-pane windows yet is contemporary in shape and plan, in accordance with the architects' intentions to create a "noninstitutional" look. Balconies and patios, and abundant plants and flowers give the complex a cheerful sense of detail. The series of three-story buildings that constitute the Commons enclose a central courtyard, a design intended to provide, according to architect Herb McLaughlin, "the security and feeling of a New England village."

Design. Architects often err by second-guessing the wants and needs of their clients, so Kaplan McLaughlin Diaz took an almost scientific approach. The firm conducted research on environmental design issues in elderly housing—including the need for individual security and privacy, community activity areas, meeting places, and circulation patterns—and also considered the results of a survey conducted by the Marin Area Agency on Aging, in which residents of three housing-for-the-elderly projects were questioned. It was found that those living in Martinelli House, which encloses an open courtyard, used the common space more often than those living in the more traditional interior courtyard buildings. The Martinelli plan was accorded high marks not only for beauty but also for outdoor protection; residents commented that they felt safer in a space that was enclosed than in grounds that were open to passersby. Their only complaint was that Martinelli House did not have the outdoor green spaces and private balconies found in the other two projects considered.

San Rafael Commons put this study into practice, incorporating both courtyard and balconies. Units are oriented toward the courtyard so that even those inside can keep an eye on the activities, and open air corridors also afford courtyard views and promote spontaneous gatherings.

Kereen Wendt of the Pacific Union Development Company, the developer of San Rafael Commons, spends time at several apartment complexes including this one. She says the difference in sociability of residents is marked. "There is much more camaraderie at the Commons. The courtyard is so enticing that it draws people out," Wendt explains. She believes the courtyard plan definitely enables residents to become more thoroughly acquainted.

The courtyard is a passive space, with several long benches in the center, and residents sit, socialize, sunbathe, and play cards. Those who are more active can play croquet in one portion, and some tend small four-foot by eight-foot individual gardens. Tenants also lend a hand with the courtyard's care and maintenance, undertaking minor watering and fertilizing chores and

Looking down on the courtyard at San Rafael Commons.

keeping the grounds litter free. The management employs a gardener who attends to the outdoor work, and residents are not required to assist—but they do, simply because they enjoy it.

Management. Tenants at the Commons have no formal power over how the open space is managed. There are no directors, no committees. But since the manager and developer personnel are sensitive to residents' needs and are available for conversation, there is informal influence; and requests residents have made for the croquet equipment and particular flowers and plants have been granted. Given that most residents, according to Wendt, rave about the courtyard's virtues, there is probably no need for a formal organizational structure to represent their interests.

Conclusion. A developer with a record of good performance, both in design and management, is likely to receive favorable attention from the Department of Housing and Urban Development (HUD) when the agency awards contracts. The San Francisco HUD office is noted for being especially sensitive architecturally—alert to creative designs that meet or exceed HUD's minimum standards, and that are responsive to the needs of the elderly tenants—and San Rafael Commons received federal assistance because the design met these criteria. Once again, a development that includes significant open space proved financially worthwhile to the developer.

As for the residents, their only complaint about the courtyard is that they cannot convert even more of it to gardens, preferably spaces that they could tend individually. As the courtyard is small and there is little ground not planted already, these requests have been denied. All indications are, though, that the tenants of San Rafael Commons would eagerly become more active proprietors, without ever realizing any profit other than pleasure.

Hoyt Street Garden

We have examined greens, woods, and courtyards that have become the object of attention and affection from their users. Some of these users are owners, and some are not; ownership does not seem to be the determining factor in whether or not people care for a space. Yet while all of these grounds have been common, they have also been quasi-private—used by only a limited number of people known to one another—and accordingly safe and defensible. Hoyt Street Garden, which is often open to whomever passes by, further tests the limits of the proprietary spirit.

Boerum Hill is a community of predominantly brownstone houses in Brooklyn, New York. Although residents previously warded off threats of large-scale demolition, they launched their first major counterattack when they undertook to develop a garden at the intersection of Hoyt Street and Atlantic Avenue. The garden has since become a focal point for community activity. And the organization that first served to create and maintain the garden has gone on to confront a wide range of other community issues and problems.

When a streetcorner building was razed in 1973, it left an empty lot that went the way of all such dead spaces: accumulating trash, it became an eyesore. In the following years, two plans were developed to transform the site into a source of community benefit. The first, proposed by the owner—Iglesia del Cristo Vivo, a Spanish Presbyterian church—was to pave the area and provide parking for four or five cars. The Hoyt Street Association had a greener solution, though, and the church gave its assent.

The transformation: from rubble-strewn lot to a floral retreat, complete with mural.

Design. Described as "better than the Brooklyn Botanic Gardens" by one admittedly biased observer, the garden measures only twenty by fifty feet. But this small space is densely planted with a bevy of polychromatic flowers, shrubs, and trees; and it is embellished with curving brick walks and several comfortable benches. A mural of a spreading "Tree of Life" enlivens the wall of a building at the garden's rear.

Funds for the creation of the garden were raised by holding a block fair, selling T-shirts in a nearby shop, and soliciting contributions from private foundations and individuals. These efforts netted an initial sum of about $4,000, most of which went for plants. The cost of garden construction was minimized by using salvaged materials and volunteer labor. Detritus from the former structure on the site, the walkway bricks were simply dug up from the lot; the benches were fashioned out of an old bunk-bed set, and the fence was rescued from abandonment in the Bronx. Set between brick piers, the wrought-iron fence contains the space but still allows people on the street to see within. It is worth a look; the design is a lively, creative response to the physical constraints imposed by the lot, providing a variegated collection of foliage in the nooks and crannies of the relatively small garden.

Management. The movement to obtain the empty lot and transform it into a garden had "the spirit of a crusade about it," according to Margaret Cusack, past president of the Hoyt Street Association. This process, as much as the garden itself, seems to have changed the lives of those in the neighborhood, transcending ethnic and social divisions. "It's been a way for all different types of people to get together," Cusack acknowledges. Even now that the novelty of the garden has worn off, neighborhood residents seem no less dedicated and effective in their care. Providing most of the needed organization and manpower are the members of the Hoyt Street Association.

The association's monthly meetings are the usual forum for discussion about the garden. Here, for example, the schedules for watering are made, and the people to do it are selected. The association plans and organizes the major landscaping efforts required each spring and fall and maintains an annual budget for the garden of $600 to $800, raised through community events such as the "Atlantic Antic" street fair. Also coordinated by association members in the Pooh and Company Sunday-afternoon free story hour, a spring and fall series of readings for children held in the garden. Volunteer readers bring their own books and fasten a banner to the wrought-iron fence to indicate that the story hour is underway. Some also bring refreshments and musicians to the sessions—all free of charge.

Shoza Nagano, the "master gardener" proprietor of the Hoyt Street Garden.

Conclusion. Early plans for the garden left it wide open to the street, but church directors, fearing that the park would become a hangout for undesirables, insisted upon a fence. The garden creators acquiesced and installed a locked gate as well, but they have taken every precaution to ensure that the garden remains a resource for the entire community. The key is given out freely to those who express an interest—about 250 keys are currently in circulation—and an unwritten rule is that the garden gate must remain open whenever a keyholder is inside. In this manner the garden is open to the public, and Margaret Cusack says the nicest thing is that one can meet people—like groups of teenagers waiting for their friends—one normally would not approach. And the policy has worked. Although Atlantic Avenue is described by Cusack as "not one of the most reputable areas around," there has been almost no vandalism. Area residents who do not use the garden nevertheless keep an eye on it, and even the hardcore drinkers have reportedly assumed a protective attitude. Some community gardens have sprouted in other Brooklyn neighborhoods, and at last count there were four similar endeavors in Boerum Hill, all directly inspired by the success of the garden at Hoyt Street.

The ornamental garden realized through the efforts of the Hoyt Street Association has brightened up this neighborhood considerably, perhaps increasing owners' property values. However, residents did not undertake the project with money in mind; Margaret Cusack replies that the garden was created "simply to enhance community and personal life in Boerum Hill." That spirit is echoed in the closing paragraph of mimeographed instructions to Pooh and Company story readers: "We hope you'll make use of Hoyt Street Garden key and visit the garden as often as you like. The only rules are that when you're in the garden, leave the gate wide open and encourage others to come in."

THE CORPORATION AS PROPRIETOR

The Brooklyn residents who are to be credited with the success of the Hoyt Street Garden are proprietors in the most direct sense of the word. They employ no maintenance crews, pay no annual fee to a homeowners association; instead, they get out their shovels and, one by one, devote their time and energy. The result—a green space in which they can relax, a park to which their children can go in safety—seems to them worth the work. It is for the good of the community, but for their personal pleasure as well.

There are some open spaces, though, most notably public parks, that are outside residential areas and have no immediate constituency upon which to draw. Furthermore, some are so large that it would take an army of shovel-wielding volunteers to keep them in shape. Over the course of the past century we, the public, have seen to the care of these spaces only indirectly, relinquishing our proprietary involvement to local and regional parks departments. We have supplied tax money, but not much else. And, although this system has not given us the sense of personal involvement that Hoyt Street residents feel, it has provided parks maintained at a professional level and ready for enjoyment.

At least, this is how the system has worked. More recently, voters have won passage of tax-cutting measures such as Proposition 13 in California and Proposition 2½ in Massachusetts, and the effects have been sorely felt by public departments that depend upon tax dollars. The East Bay Regional Park

District in Oakland, California, for example, lost forty-seven percent of its tax revenues during 1977–78, threatening efforts simply to maintain the district parks in their current condition as well as plans for the future. Our next case study looks at one solution: a new type of proprietor, the corporation.

Among the parks endangered by the Proposition 13 cutbacks was Roberts Regional Recreation Area, one hundred acres on the fringes of the residential district of Oakland, California. It is a diverse facility. Part of the Redwood Regional Park, it has several stands of those *Sequoia sempervirens* for which the state is famed, and a portion of the park is taken up by the East Bay Skyline National Trail. Other parts are intended for more specific recreation, and popular activities are accommodated by a swimming pool, an equestrian trail, a ball field, picnic areas, archery ranges, and play equipment. Roberts is used heavily, and its facilities require constant and thorough maintenance.

Adopt-a-park. Stifled by the lack of tax dollars, the East Bay Regional Park District decided to turn to other sources, developing a program to solicit contributions from corporations and businesses. Called "adopt-a-park," the program creates a partnership for park support between the district and the private sector. Essentially, the adopt-a-park program seeks a three-year or longer commitment to a single park from the interested corporation, with support taking the form of cash donations as well as "hands-on" or in-kind help from company personnel. The partnership projects are designed by the park district staff to answer the needs of the park, while at the same time taking into account the desires and financial commitments of particular businesses.

Park district staff set out to find corporations willing to participate. Businesses were approached on the basis of information gathered in a wide-ranging research effort by the park district fundraising department, surveying the

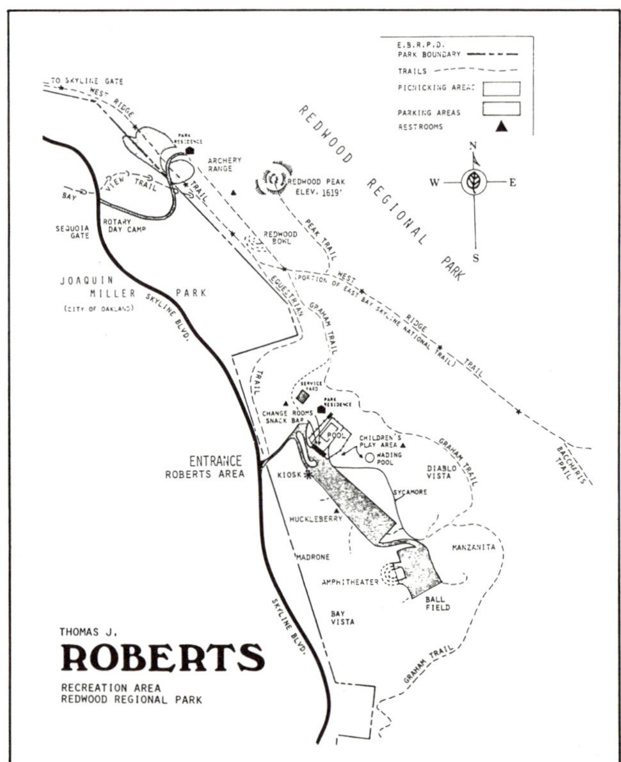

A plan of Roberts Recreation Area, indicating location of trails for hiking and horseback riding as well as the archery range, children's play area, wading pool, swimming pool, change rooms, snack bar, and kiosk.

A diverse one-hundred-acre tract, Roberts Recreation Area boasts redwood groves as well as playgrounds.

philosophy, interests, needs, and history of giving of various corporations. The findings persuaded park district personnel that the adopt-a-park program could be attractive to the Kaiser Aluminum & Chemical Corporation, the huge multinational headquartered in Oakland. An informal inquiry revealed that the company would be interested in Roberts Recreation Area, and the park staff soon compiled a "laundry list" of projects and repairs for Roberts that were top priority.

Kaiser Aluminum's response from 1979 to 1981 has resulted in the accomplishment of nearly all suggested projects. Some of these needed only the company's financial support—for example, the subsidizing of a bus route between a local Bay Area Rapid Transit station and the park—but others brought company employees out from behind their desks. About fifty volunteers from Kaiser Aluminum's Oakland headquarters helped assemble a wooden and steel play structure, a $10,000 gift from the company, while nearly one hundred and fifty turned out—admittedly enticed by the promise of grilled steaks at the end of the day—to install a newly purchased sprinkler system. The park district estimates that the value of in-kind and cash donations from Kaiser Aluminum have amounted to roughly $50,000 per year—a substantial addition to the district budget for Roberts, which stood at $174,200 for 1981.

It is an ideal arrangement from the standpoint of the park district staff. Corporations such as Kaiser Aluminum, which have made good on their promise to sustain their financial support for a period of years, provide a more stable source of funding than do taxpayers in these days of fiscal instability. It is, better still, support with no strings attached: the company merely chooses among projects that the park district proposes, and so the range of park expenditures is still determined by the professionals. The only constraints on use of the money are those that the park district itself establishes by the design of the specific proposals.

Incentives. What is in it for the corporation? Several things. Linda Chew of the park district's development and public information department, says that Kaiser Aluminum gains visibility and good publicity by "adopting" Roberts park. A description of the company's help is included in a pamphlet produced by the park district; the work has been the subject of a number of corporate public affairs press releases; and in 1979 the company was presented with the highest award for the promotion of parks and recreation from the U.S. Department of the Interior's Heritage Conservation and Recreation Service, as well as a "special citation" from the National Recreation and Parks Association. Such publicity is always good for a company's image.

Kaiser Aluminum officials point out, though, that the company already has high visibility in the Bay Area; it contributed in 1981 to more than 100 civic and charitable organizations. Company officials emphasize instead that Kaiser Aluminum was the first corporation to single-handedly adopt a public park; and that an important incentive was the opportunity to demonstrate how company involvement can provide support for a project that improves the quality of life for the community. Kaiser Aluminum has prepared a multimedia show depicting its participation in the adopt-a-park program, which was presented at a luncheon meeting attended by representatives from fifty other corporations. The firm has also offered to make its corporate staff available for discussions of the program with any interested business, in the hope that others will follow in its footsteps.

The federal government also provides some incentives for corporate contributions to projects such as adopt-a-park. Under the terms of a recent ruling, the Internal Revenue Service allows corporate charitable deductions of up to ten percent of a company's taxable income. Several other benefits follow from this tax provision. First, the corporation has the opportunity to direct money to the charitable goal of its choice; and second, it is able to observe closely the use of the money and ascertain whether it is well spent. Third, the contributor has the satisfaction of seeing the money produce local, visible results. As Mervin Morris, chairman of Mervyn's Stores and another contributor to the East Bay Regional Park District, quipped, "Why let the government do this kind of spending for you?"

Other corporations have agreed that it makes sense to lend a hand to public parks, although for different reasons and not always with such success—at least at first, as we discovered in the case of an urban park in downtown Manhattan.

Madison Square Park

Described as a "green rip in the city's brick and stone carpet," Madison Square Park was constructed in 1844 by the City of New York on land that had previously been a cemetery for the poor. The 6.2 acres of greenery and winding walks, shaded by mature trees, are today used primarily for sitting and relaxing, and a large open area sees daily use for frisbee games in warm weather. The park is frequented by occasional tourists, shoppers, and, during their lunch hour, corporate employees.

When the 1975 fiscal crisis hit New York hard, Madison Square Park began to suffer from neglect. The parks department found itself unable to maintain much of the property under its care; and as the park deteriorated, it was increasingly abandoned by genial and law-abiding citizens, who were replaced by drug peddlers, petty thieves, and homeless loiterers. By the late

1970s, the park had a menacing character, and its blighted condition cast a pall over the surrounding neighborhood.

The situation prompted some members of the business community around the park to take action. Rather than waiting like Kaiser Aluminum to be asked, three companies—Metropolitan Life Insurance, New York Life Insurance, and Helmsley-Spear—approached the city and entered into negotiations to arrange a contribution for maintenance of the park in their midst. But the companies encountered unforeseen problems. For one thing, the park department's accounting operations were not geared to handle such outside donations. Moreover, once the offer was finally accepted and the money spent, the businessmen discovered that the work for which they had contributed the funds had been done on the wrong part of the park; their efforts had a negligible impact on park problems.

Urban Park Plazas. It was an inauspicious beginning for these would-be rescuers, but all was not lost. In 1979, former city parks department official Donald E. Simon formed Urban Park Plazas, a nonprofit private corporation created "to promote long-term corporate involvement in the management and operation of local public parks," as the founder states. With initial funding from the Ford Foundation, Simon put together a proposal to solve the problems of Madison Square Park; with city approval, he approached the nearby corporations and sought their assistance.

Business executives were initially skeptical, but Simon's proposal was attractive. It provided that Urban Park Plazas would manage the corporate funds and contract for necessary services with private maintenance firms,

Madison Square Park, off Fifth Avenue between 23rd and 26th Streets in downtown Manhattan. To the rear is the familiar Flatiron Building.

thereby avoiding the bureaucracy of city government and giving contributors assurance that their money would be well spent. Four businesses—the three aforementioned together with the Rudin Management Company—chipped in a total of $32,500 for an operating period of four months. At the end of that time they renewed their commitment and were joined by thirteen other businesses and an individual, for a total of $61,725. Urban Park Plazas had nearly matched the city's allocation of $70,000 for the year 1980.

"We think this is the beginning of a trend," Simon told a *New York Times* reporter shortly after work began. "In the future, we believe, other companies will be paying to supplement city services, because the city just doesn't have the money anymore."

Lewis Rudin of Rudin Management indicated that business had little choice, commenting, "We're doing this because we can't wait for government to do the things that have to be done." But others emphasized more positive aspects. Gregory Batson of New York Life Insurance, indicating approval of the placards that have been placed around the park giving credit to the corporate proprietors, cited the importance of recognition for each company. People should be aware that some corporations are "responsible citizens," Batson noted, adding that the work was also good for morale within the company. About twenty-five New York Life employees showed up to take brush in hand for a Saturday morning painting project, at which food and music were provided, during the company's first year of involvement with the park. Richard R. Shinn, president of the Metropolitan Life Insurance Company, was pleased to see the improvements brought to the green space that his company's building has faced since 1893. "We have thought of Madison Square Park as our front yard," he observed, hailing the benefits for Metropolitan Life workers and the community at large.

Clearly, this is philanthropy with direct benefits. In fact, few of the companies have claimed their contributions as charitable tax deductions, considering them instead as part of their regular operating budgets. Corporate lawyers have advised that the I.R.S. would probably disallow such deductions of support for the park because of the immediate advantages these contributions provide.

Under Simon's direction, and with a period of intensive assistance from a unit of the city police, Madison Square Park has become a place that passersby and employees no longer fear. Will it remain so? If the high rate at which corporations have renewed their contribution contracts is an indication, then the answer is yes. The only uncertainty is this funding base, which must be maintained with contributions year after year and on which the condition of the park is now dependent. With this issue in mind, another New York park rescue team is trying to take the private sector involvement one step further.

Bryant Park The story of Bryant Park's decline and rehabilitation parallels that of Madison Square Park. This 9.5-acre square, which sits just behind the New York Public Library, at Forty-Second Street and Sixth Avenue, had actually experienced difficulties for years; a 1928 *New York Times* article deemed it "an eyesore," railing that "no other city in the world would have tolerated such a park in the heart of one of the most important districts." By 1976, muggers and marijuana dealers had found that the long corridors of trees made a good screen for their trades, and the next few years saw a series of efforts to clean up or save Bryant Park that had salutary but short-term effect.

Bryant Park (above, both pictures), *secluded by the New York Public Library and commercial buildings in midtown Manhattan. The plaza area is surrounded by a* *network of tree-lined walkways, and located at the periphery are two stalls for the Strand Bookshop and a new flower stall.*

In 1980 the Bryant Park Restoration Corporation was formed, and Daniel A. Biederman was appointed executive director. Like Donald Simon, Biederman put together a proposal and approached surrounding businesses, and he estimates that three out of four of the corporations and realty owners from which he solicited funds eventually contributed. The incentives were obvious: Edward Farrell, Jr., Vice President for Administration of the W. R. Grace & Co. (whose office building is adjacent to the park), related that the company simply hoped to improve the park's appearance, drive out vagrants, and create a more pleasant haven for employees. Noting that W. R. Grace pays "millions of dollars in taxes," he thought it would be nice to have a better environment.

Biederman succeeded in raising more than $138,000 in contributions and commitments that first year. His initial strategy was to retain the same landscape maintenance firm that took care of Madison Square Park and to attend to routine pruning; weed killing; cleaning up trash; and removing graffiti from the walls, monuments, and fountains. More recently, the city's nonprofit parks council has joined in, initiating efforts that have brought bookstalls, a seasonal open-air cafe, and a flower stand to the park in an attempt to interject more desirable activity. Merchants have received financial assistance to locate there; the $30,000 flower stand, for example, cost the owner only two-thirds that amount, with the remainder coming from parks council contributors.

Biederman's most innovative idea, however, is yet to be realized. His goal is to create a self-sufficient source of income for Bryant Park, and to that end he proposes to build a glass-enclosed, first-class restaurant on a currently weedy strip of park property along the back wall of the library. Pending submission of the final design, the parks department and landmarks preservation commission have nodded their approval; other relevant city departments have yet to reach a decision. Already, four restaurant operators have expressed an interest in the scheme, in which the restaurant would pay a "rental" fee directly to the organization responsible for care of the park. Too commercial, some say, likening the plan to recent federal schemes to introduce concession stands into national parks—a proposal many environmentalists were quick to label inappropriate. But the Bryant Park restaurant plan may prove a relatively inoffensive means of freeing that park and others from their dependency upon tax revenues or yearly contributions from private sources. Since the restaurant would have a vested interest in the well-being of the park, chances are it would be a proprietary asset.

Our last two examples are also New York City parks, publicly used but privately owned. Like the plaza in New York's Rockefeller Center and the Mellon Park owned by the adjoining Mellon Bank in Pittsburgh, these are an indication of how some private interests are beginning to create small but significant urban spaces, often designed and maintained at a standard considerably above that of traditional public parks.

THE PRIVATE FOUNDATION AS PROPRIETOR

Paley and Greenacre Parks

These two parks are strikingly similar in design, since one inspired the other. Opened to the public in May 1967, Paley Park was the result of William S. Paley's wish to honor the memory of his late father with a mini-park in the heart of the Manhattan business district on East 53rd Street. Mr. Paley established the Greenpark Foundation as legal owner and manager of the space, and he charged it with the task of encouraging the local business community to create other "vestpocket" parks in the densely built environment of New York. The late Abby Rockefeller Mauze stepped forward and established the Greenacre Foundation, which built, owns, and maintains Greenacre Park.

Design. Both parks are diminutive, with Paley measuring forty-two by one hundred feet, and Greenacre one and a half times larger at sixty by one hundred and twenty feet—about the size of a tennis court. Yet, as William H. Whyte discusses at length in *The Social Life of Small Urban Spaces*, they are spaces that are inviting in design. Each is elevated slightly above street level, producing a sense of transition when moving from street to park; but the change in elevation is not so great as to obstruct the view into the leafy green

*The urban oasis of Paley Park,
seen from above.
(Photo © Eugene Cook)*

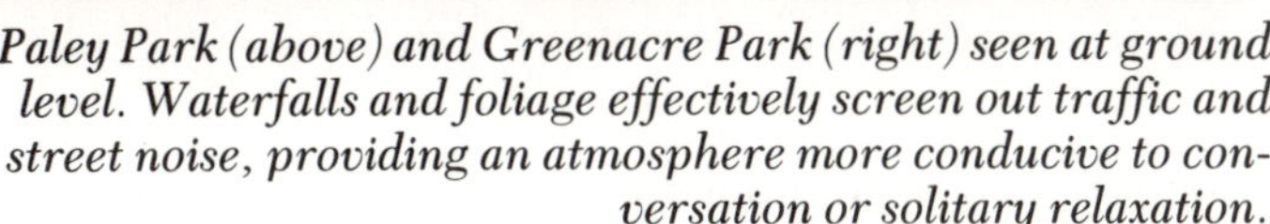

Paley Park (above) and Greenacre Park (right) seen at ground level. Waterfalls and foliage effectively screen out traffic and street noise, providing an atmosphere more conducive to conversation or solitary relaxation.

space. Locust trees provide a canopy that conceals the surrounding skyscrapers, and the central focus of each park is an ornamental display of falling water. In Paley, this takes the form of a twenty-foot-high waterwall extending across the rear wall of the park. With a cascade of water pouring down, the waterwall creates a continuously moving and sparkling facade; and the sound of the falling water replaces the cacophony of the street traffic. Greenacre's water display is similar, but designers sought to correct one problem they observed at Paley: when the water ceases to flow, nothing remains but a blank wall. The water at Paley therefore flows over a relief sculpture of multi-sized, rough rectangles of granite. The summer of 1971, when New York City experienced one of its periodic water shortages and all ornamental water displays fed by city water had to be shut off, revealed how valuable these water displays are. With the water silenced, Paley and Greenacre echoed with street and construction noises. "The entire atmosphere of the park was absolutely changed," reports Jean Branscombe of the Greenacre Foundation, and park use dropped dramatically until the foundation trucked in 25,000 gallons of water from outside the city and reactivated the waterfall.

Whyte has observed that the entrance steps separating park and street are "so low and easy that one is almost pulled to them," while movable chairs provide variety and flexibility. There are plenty of tables as well, and one can bring food in or purchase it from the snackbar at either park. No detail has been overlooked—the Greenpark Foundation has even conducted taste tests to choose what directors believe to be the best quality hot dog on the market. market.

These are popular spaces—so popular, says Philip Boschetti of the Greenpark Foundation, that he receives one or two calls a day from people requesting permission to use Paley Park for everything from weddings to film advertisements. He turns down these requests in the interest of the public, since the park is used by shoppers, office workers, and residents from morning to night. The users appreciate the space and act accordingly. Both parks have a constant staff, either snack bar attendants or security guards, but their work is made easy by parkgoers who tend to be self-policing; they pick up much of their own trash, occasionally admonish each other for picking flowers, and are apt to inform a newcomer about unposted rules—such as "no bicycles"—before the guard has a chance to speak. William Whyte notes that Greenacre guards also take a proprietary pleasure in the park and their role as hosts.

The only drawback to the creation of vest-pocket parks such as these may be the cost. Park foundations were reluctant to reveal the prices of Paley and Greenacre, as the initial investment—as high as three million dollars each—might discourage other businesses from exploring the idea. To be sure, the unique expense of real estate in midtown Manhattan inflates the cost of these parks, which one foundation member estimates could be reproduced for as little as a half or third the New York price—but even one million dollars is substantial. The finances may be a stumbling block, but these urban respites are an undeniable success, offering pleasure to those who enter in or simply pass by.

CONCLUSION

Our measured tread through these new commons strung across the country may not produce the "perfect exhilaration" that Emerson felt upon crossing a snow-covered New England common. Nor do these new recent spaces necessarily, in the words of John Updike, give evidence of a "manifest, workaday covenant with the Bestower of a new continent." We hope, though, that they have shown that there is a value to this modern-day common ground—value that depends not upon the accretion of memories or the symbolism of church spires, but rather upon a proprietory recognition of the intrinsic qualities of the spaces. And if there is no covenant with the Bestower, there is, we believe, a covenant between people and the land.

This covenant would probably not be overtly acknowledged by most of the groups that are exercising proprietorship—at least not in any formal or philosophical terms. But many understand that it is necessary to create conditions where the energy of caring can be nurtured. That sense of self-interest must be linked with the perceived value of conserved or enhanced space. As we have seen in this chapter, such worth is determined by the utility of a space as well as by its beauty, by an amalgam of practical design, and by sound management strategy.

We are hopeful about the future of some of these newer common grounds—but it must be recognized that we can no longer rely upon the passage of time and the onset of nostalgia to make us care about a place. John Updike spoke of how the old greens "permanently imprint the maps of these towns, and lengthen the perspectives of those who live within them." Today the challenge is to lengthen the perspectives of people regarding the worth of newer spaces, which may exist on the ground and on maps but which have yet to be imprinted in our mental landscape as something of value. We must accelerate the design and management strategies that nurture an ongoing sense of proprietorship.

As the vignettes in this book reveal, many traditional commons have been neglected. But we believe that the feeling of proprietorship for what Updike calls "the hearts of green" is a natural and quite visceral instinct—an attitude that can readily surface under the right set of circumstances and conditions.

We have seen how corporations, developers, foundations, and individual citizens can both create and respond to these conditions and circumstances, and by so doing affirm a covenant with common land.

Another tale from a town that we've already examined supports our contention. In Falmouth, Massachusetts, where the green is pristine but where its animating force of an annual fair faltered (see "The Fate of the Fete," pages 96–97), the incipient energy for caring about common ground is still at work, but on a new site.

Those who thought that the village green should remain a part of Falmouth community life, even if only for one day a year, were unhappy to hear the announcement by town officials in 1979 that the Nursing Fete could no longer be held in the town center. The town seemed to be experiencing more than its share of losses. The previous year had seen the demolition of the historic Oak Crest Inn in Falmouth Heights, a formidable nineteenth-century structure that had played host to returning summer families and older couples for many years. Recently dilapidated as the result of poor maintenance and overcrowding by college-age tourists, Oak Crest had been condemned and razed by the town. Many in town were distressed by its loss and by the condition of the Heights in general; filled to overflowing with rowdy summer youth, Falmouth Heights threatened to become, in the words of year-round resident Margaret Murphy, the "Atlantic City" of Cape Cod.

Someone hit upon the idea of using the empty lot as a park, and in 1979 the Falmouth Town Meeting accordingly voted $12,500 for the land's development. Creation of Oak Crest Park soon became the focus of public-spirited energy. A landscape designer donated his time and prepared a landscape plan; a local nursery donated labor; and trees were planted by crews from the department of public works. Funds for trees and shrubs came from individuals, businesses, a community yard sale, and civic groups. Even out-of-towners joined in; when the local newspaper included an article about the park in its annual mail-away edition, letters and contributions were sent by people from around the country who had fond memories of summers at the old inn. Particularly active was the son of the former owner of the inn, who had moved to California years earlier but still felt attached to his home town and hoped something could be done of which the town could be proud.

People are proud of the new park, which has done more than simply beautify the area. Margaret Murphy, a member of the Falmouth Council for Civic Beautification that spearheaded the effort, sees this act of proprietorship as an indication of a community renaissance. Families are now buying homes for year-round use and, says Mrs. Murphy, "a nucleus of stable people who are interested in the community is developing." Property values have already increased, and residents are currently talking about instituting a historic district to further conserve the character of the neighborhood.

The story of Falmouth is not a fairy-tale ending for a book on common ground. But it does illustrate that people do still care about spaces and that the spirit of proprietorship can be rekindled in a new place that meets new needs. The challenge remaining is to recognize and channel this energy, to achieve the necessary link between self-interest and community value, that can make such stories more frequent throughout America.

An Inventory of New England Commons and Greens

No book on greens and commons would be complete without some identification of those pieces of land that are the authors' concern. If we draw readers' attention to the handsome benches here and the exemplary stand of trees there, if we wax eloquent about the beauty of some greens and call for remedial care for others, then surely some list revealing the location of these revered spaces is in order.

Such a list is not, however, easily come by. New Englanders have tended to take the existence of greens and commons for granted, and it is emblematic of this attitude that no inventory has previously existed. Nor is it an easy task to pioneer one. Since there is no regional authority overseeing greens, or even a local source of information consistent from town to town, the compilation of an inventory has been slow, sometimes tedious, and undoubtedly fraught with error.

One need only look to England, a country one step ahead of us in such efforts, to gain a sense of the problems involved. England passed in 1965 the Commons Registrations Act, designed to establish conclusively which land is common land and what rights exist over it. The act provided for registration, for a period of three years ending in January 1970, of common land, rights of common, and town and village greens. Any local authority, local society, or private individual was entitled to file the registration application. Acknowledging that the status of some land might be unclear, the act made provisions for objection to be made to any registration; disputes were to be settled by specially appointed Commons Commissioners.

More than a decade later those disputes are still being heard, and one authority estimated recently that there were 2,000 to 3,000 disputes undecided. In many more instances than were probably anticipated, English townspeople have claimed that on various and assorted acres they have gathered berries, grazed livestock, and enjoyed games of football for a sufficient period of time to establish rights in common or rights of recreation—and the owners of the land have claimed otherwise. For each such case, applicants come before the Commons Commissioners and present evidence to attest to their use of the land. If the Commissioners decide in the applicant's favor, one more piece of common land is added to the register.

In New England, greens and commons have not—as yet—received such bureaucratic yet beneficial attention. These patches of grass may be dear to our hearts in some abstract sense, but few of us can identify with certainty a green other than that in our own town. In some places there is an equal confusion, if not apathy, within town boundaries; the authors' inquiries to local officials were met more than once with "You mean that strip near the school [or church or town hall or old watering trough]? Well, I suppose you could call in a green. . ."

Why is it that New Englanders are so vague about these hallowed grounds? Perhaps it is because there has been no reason to be definite. Common land, as we know it in these village and town centers, no longer serves any utilitarian purpose; we are quite willing to leave the quibbles over berries and firewood gathering to the English. Greens and commons are not protected by any unique body of legislation, nor are they eligible for particular funds. Whether an acre of grass is a green, a common, a park, or a traffic rotary has for many years now been a matter of little importance.

It may not always be so. With the increasing attention to preservation of our historic architecture should come, as it has in this book, an interest in our historic landscape as well. Some greens have indeed been included in local and national historic districts. Additionally, the parks of Frederick Law Olmsted have recently come into the spotlight, thanks to the work of the newly formed National Association for Olmsted Parks, and several of these are now the object of study and careful restoration. There is no reason why greens and commons should not be next—provided we can document their past and present existence.

And so we present an inventory, imperfect though it may be. Lacking a body of legislation or a group of Commons Commissioners to rule where these acres are and where they are not, we have solicited and usually accepted the judgment of countless town clerks, selectmen, librarians, or self-appointed historians. Where a green is called a green and a common a common, we have accepted the title as ample proof; we have also judged "once a green, always a green," and towns that now refer to their old common land or meetinghouse green as a park have been included as well. The authors welcome the inevitable additions or corrections to this list.

Connecticut Commons and Greens

Ashford	Naugatuck
Bethlehem	New Haven
Bolton	New Milford
Branford	New Canaan
Brooklyn	Norfolk
Canton	Norwich
Cheshire	Old Lyme
Colchester	Old Saybrook
Cornwall	Pomfret
Coventry	Salisbury
Durham	Scotland
East Haddam	Shelton
East Hartford	Sharon
Fairfield	South Woodstock
Falls Village	Southington
Glastonbury	Stratford
Greenfield Hill	Suffield
Guilford	Thompson
Kent	Vernon Center
Lebanon	Washington
Litchfield	Waterbury
Madison	Watertown
Meriden	Wethersfield
Middlebury	Windham
Middletown	Windsor
Milford	Winsted
Milton	Wolcott
Monroe	Woodbury
Mystic	Woodstock

Maine Commons and Greens

Alfred	Paris Hill
Bar Harbor	St. George
Bath	Thomaston
Bethel	Union
Brunswick	Wiscasset
Castine	York
Gardiner	

New Hampshire Commons and Greens

Acworth	Kingston
Amherst	Lebanon
Bath	Lyme
Bradford	Manchester
Chester	Mason
Canaan	Meriden
North Conway	Nashua
Deering	Nelson
Dunbarton	Newport
Fitzwilliam	Nottingham Square
Francestown	Oxford
Grafton	Plymouth
Greenfield	Rindge
Hampton Falls	Rochester
North Hampton Center	Rumney Village
Hancock	Temple
Hanover	Troy
Hebron	Walpole
Haverhill Corner	Warren
Hillsborough Center	Washington
Hollis	Wentworth
Jaffrey Center	Whitefield
Keene (Central Square)	Winchester
Kensington	

Rhode Island Commons and Greens

Bristol
Little Compton
Slatersville

Vermont Commons and Greens

Bakersfield	Newbury
Barre	Newfane
Bellows Falls	Norwich
Bennington	Rochester
Bethel	Royalton
Bristol	South Royalton
Checkerberry Village	Rutland
Chester	St. Albans
Chelsea	St. Johnsbury
Craftsbury Common	Shelburne
East Poultney	Swanton
Fairhaven	Thetford Hill
Grafton	Wentworth
Guildhall	Whitingham
Irasburg	Winchester
Manchester	Windsor
Middlebury	Woodstock
Montpelier	

Massachusetts Commons and Greens

Amherst
East Amherst
South Amherst
North Andover
Ashby
Auburn
Barnstable
Barre
Bedford
Belchertown
Berlin
Billerica
Bolton
Boston
Boylston
Boxford
Braintree
Brewster
Bridgewater
Brimfield
Brookfield
Brookline
Cambridge
Carlisle
Carver
North Carver
Charlestown
Chelmsford
Chelsea
Cohasset
Concord
Conway
Dedham (2)
Deerfield
Dennis
South Dennis
Dunstable
Duxbury

Easthampton
Edgartown
South Egremont
Essex
Falmouth
Framingham
Fitchburg
Foxboro.
Framingham
South Framingham
Grafton
Granby
Greenfield
Groton
Hadley
Hanover
Hardwick
Harvard
Haverhill
Hingham
Holden
Holliston
Hopkinton
Huntington
Ipswich
Lancaster
Lawrence (2)
Lee
Leominster
Lexington
Littleton
Longmeadow
Lowell
Ludlow
Lynn

Lynnfield
Mansfield
Marlboro Village
Marshfield
Middleton
Milton
Natick
Needham
Needham Heights
New Bedford
Newbury
New Marlborough
New Salem
Newton
Norfolk
Northampton
Northboro
North Carver
Northfield
North Reading
Norton
Norwell
Oakham
Pepperell
Petersham
Pittsfield
Plymouth
Prescott (Groton)
Princeton
Quincy
Reading
Rehobeth
Rochester
Rowley
Roxbury
Royalston
Rutland
Salem

Sandwich
Sheffield
Stow
Sturbridge
Sudbury
Sutton
Taunton
Templeton
Tewksbury
Tolland
Topsfield
Townsend
Tyngsboro
Wakefield
Waltham
Warwick
Wayland
Webster
Wendell
Wenham
Westborough
West Boylston
West Bridgewater
West Brookfield
Westfield
West Newbury
West Townsend
Westford
Westhampton
Weston
Westwood
Williamstown
Winchester
Woburn
Worcester
Wrentham

Bibliography

Adams, Andrew N. *History of the Town of Fair Haven, Vermont.* Fairhaven: Leonard & Phelps, 1870.

Anderson Notter Associates Inc. *The Salem Handbook: A Renovation Guide For Homeowners.* Salem, Massachusetts: Historic Salem Inc., 1977.

Anderson, Robert C. *Directions of a Town: A History of Harvard, Massachusetts.* Harvard: Harvard Common Press, 1976.

Barber, John Warner. *Historical Collections . . . of Every Town in Massachusetts.* Worcester, Massachusetts: Dorr, Howland, 1841.

————. *Connecticut Historical Collections . . . Relating to the History and Antiquities of Every Town in Connecticut.* New Haven, 1836.

Baker, Humphrey. *Commons: What They Are and How They Are Protected.* London, 1927.

Bearse, Ray, ed. *Vermont: A Guide to the Green Mountain State.* The New American Guide Series. 3rd ed. Boston: Houghton Mifflin, 1968.

Berry, Richard D. "Baldwin Hills Village: Design or Accident." *Arts and Architecture* 7, October 1964.

Bowles, Ella Shannon. *Let Me Show You New Hampshire.* New York: Knopf, 1938.

Brodeur, David D. "Geographic Consequences of the Location of Some New England Town Commons & Greens." Master's thesis, Clark University, 1963.

Brolin, Brent C. Sourcebook of Architectural Ornament: Designers, Craftsmen, Manufacturers, and Distributors of Custom and Ready Made Architectural Ornaments. New York: Van Nostrand, 1982.

Brown, Elizabeth Mills. *New Haven: A Guide to Architecture and Urban Design.* New Haven: Yale University, 1976.

Bryant Park Restoration Corporation. "A Plan for the Restoration of Bryant Park." Mimeographed. April 1980.

Bunting, Bainbridge and Nylander, Robert H. *Old Cambridge.* Survey of Architectural History in Cambridge, Vol. 4. Cambridge, Massachusetts: Cambridge Historical Commission, 1973.

Cambridge Historical Commission. "History of the Cambridge Common." Mimeographed, n.d.

Campbell, Ian. *Decisions of the Commons Commissioners.* London: Commons, Open Spaces and Footpaths Preservation Society, October 1972.

————. *A Guide to Commons Registration.* London: Commons, Open Spaces and Footpaths Preservation Society, October 1966.

Campbell, Ian and Clayden, Paul. *The Law of Commons and Village Greens.* 3rd rev. ed. Henley-on-Thames: Commons, Open Spaces and Footpaths Preservation Society, April 1980.

Center for Design Planning. *Streetscape Equipment Sourcebook 2.* Washington D.C.: Urban Land Institute, 1979.

Chamberlain, Samuel. *Six New England Villages.* New York: Hastings House, 1948.

Coleman, Emma Lewis. *A Historic Present Day Guide to Old Deerfield.* Boston, 1907.

Commons, Open Spaces and Footpaths Preservation Society. *Our Common Heritage.* London, 1978.

Coolidge, A.J. and Mansfield, J.B. *A History and Description of New England, General and Local.* Boston: Austin J. Coolidge, 1859.

"Counterattack in Bryant Park." *New York Times*, 13 November 1981.

Cowan, Peter. "A Park Made Just for Drunks." Boston *Globe*, 29 June 1980.

Cram, Robert Nathan. "New England Town Commons, Based on the Study of Certain Massachusetts Examples." With original photographs and blueprints. Master's thesis, School of Landscape Architecture, Harvard University, 1922.

Currier, John J. *History of Newburyport, Massachusetts, 1764–1905*. Newburyport, 1906.

Cushing, John D. "Town Commons of New England, 1640–1840." *Old Time New England* 50 (1961).

Cusack, Frank and Margaret. "A proposal for a park on the southwest corner of Hoyt Street and Atlantic Avenue." Mimeographed. 1974.

Department of Environmental Management, Commonwealth of Massachusetts. *Massachusetts Outdoors*. September 1978.

Department of Research, Old Sturbridge Village. "Report and Summary of a Study of New England Town Commons, 1790–1840." Mimeographed. Sturbridge, Massachusetts, 1959.

Drake, Samuel Adams. *Old Landmarks and Historic Personages of Boston*. Boston: Little, Brown, 1900.

Emerson, Ralph Waldo. *Selected Writings of Ralph Waldo Emerson*. William H. Gilman, ed. New York: New American Library, 1965.

Emmet, Alan. *Cambridge, Massachusetts: The Changing of a Landscape*. 2nd rev. ed. Cambridge, Massachusetts: President and Fellows of Harvard College, 1980.

Federal Writers' Project of the Works Progress Administration for the State of Maine. *Maine: A Guide 'Down East.'* American Guide Series. Boston: Houghton Mifflin, 1937.

Federal Writers' Project of the Works Progress Administration for the State of New Hampshire. *New Hampshire: A Guide to the Granite State*. American Guide Series. Boston: Houghton Mifflin, 1938.

Felt, Joseph B. *Annals of Salem*. 2nd ed. Salem, Massachusetts: W. & S.B. Ives, 1849.

Feiss, Carl. "Early American Public Squares." *Town and Square from Agora to the Village Green*. P. Zucker, ed. Cambridge, Massachusetts: M.I.T. Press, 1959.

Ferretti, Fred. "Private Funds Help Park To Get More Loving Care." *New York Times*, 1 November 1979.

Fleming, Ronald Lee. "Interpreting and Enhancing Townscape: Appealing to the Landscape of the Mind." *Small Town Design Resource Book for Small Communities*, November–December 1981.

———. "Recapturing History: A Plan for Gritty Cities." *Landscape*, January 1980.

Fowler, Glenn. "Some Success Seen in Effort to Reclaim Bryant Park." *New York Times*, 15 September 1980.

French, Jere Stuart. *Urban Green: City Parks of the Western World*. Dubuque, Iowa: Kendall/Hunt, 1973.

———. *Urban Space: A Brief History of the City Square*. Dubuque, Iowa: Kendall/Hunt, 1978.

Geib, Susan. "Landscape and Faction: Spatial Transformation in William Bentley's Salem." *Essex Institute Historical Collections* 113 (1977).

Gold, Seymour. "Urban Open Space in the Year 2000." *Ekistics* 273 (1978).

Hand, Douglas. "The Greening of the South Bronx." Blair & Ketchum's *Country Journal* 8 (April 1981).

Heckscher, August. *Open Spaces: The Life of American Cities*. New York: Harper and Row, 1977.

———. "The Public Realm." *Christian Science Monitor*, 5 June 1981.

Historic Concord and Lexington. Concord, Massachusetts, 1903.

Historic Guide to Cambridge. Cambridge, Massachusetts, 1907.

Howard, Rev. R.H. and Crocker, Henry. *A History of New England*. 2 vols. Boston: Crocker & Co., 1880.

Hoyt's History of Wentworth, New Hampshire. 1871. As transcribed from the original manuscript by Francis A. Muzzey. Littleton, N.H.: Courier Printing, 1976.

Hubbard, Charles D. *An Old New England Village*. Portland, Maine: Falmouth Publishing House, 1947.

Hudson, Charles. *History of the Town of Lexington*. Rev. ed. Boston: Houghton Mifflin, 1913.

Huntoon, Maxwell C., Jr. *PUD: A Better Way for the Suburbs*. Washington, D.C.: Urban Land Institute, 1971.

"In perspective: New England Tradition." *Progressive Architecture* 11 (1979).

James, Henry. *The American Scene*. 1907. Rev. ed. Bloomington, Indiana: Indiana University, 1968.

Johnston, Laurie. "A Flower Stand Enlists in Battle for Bryant Park." *New York Times*, 8 November 1981.

Kappel, Philip. *New England Gallery*. Boston: Little, Brown, 1966.

Kent, Louise Andrews. *Village Greens of New England*. New York: M. Barrows, 1948.

Lewis, C.A. "Sprouting of the Inner City: Neighborhood Gardens." *Psychology Today* 13 (June 1979).

Lewis, Paul J. "The Historical Development of Cambridge Common." Cambridge Historical Society *Proceedings for the Years 1973–1975* 43 (1980).

Lexington Historical Society. *Lexington*. Boston: W.B. Clarke, 1891.

Little, William. *Address delivered at the Centennial Celebration of the Town of Warren, New Hampshire*. Manchester, N.H., 1863.

———. *History of the Town of Warren . . . to the Year 1854*. Concord, N.H.: *McFarland & Jenks, 1854*.

———. *The History of Warren*. Manchester, N.H.: William E. Moore, 1870.

Livermore, Arthur. *Seventy Years Ago: Reminiscences of Haverhill Corner*. Woodsville, N.H.: News Print, 1902.

Lovejoy, Evelyn M. Wood. *History of Royalton, Vermont*. Burlington: Free Press, 1911.

Mackay, Duncan. "The Commons and Village Greens of England and Wales: Past Perspectives and Present Problems." Unpublished manuscript. August 1980.

Marinelli, Janet. "From Blight to Blossoms." *Environmental Action* (April 1979).

Mason and Frey, Landscape Architects. *A Preliminary Study for the Landscape and Development and Restoration of the Cambridge Common*. Cambridge, Massachusetts, October 1970.

Massachusetts Historical Commission. *Establishing Local Historic Districts*. 2nd rev. ed. Boston: Office of the Secretary of the Commonwealth, 1979.

Meyer, John Biddle. "The Village Ensemble in Northern Vermont." Master's thesis, University of Vermont, 1974.

Mussey, June Barrows. *Old New England*. New York: A.A. Wyn, 1946.

National Trust for Historic Preservation, Tony P. Wrenn and Elizabeth D. Mulloy. *America's Forgotten Architecture*. New York: Pantheon, 1976.

Nelson, Charles A. *Waltham, Past and Present*. Cambridge: Moses King, 1882.

"New Help for the Nation's Abused City Parks." *AIA Journal* (February 1979).

The New York State Urban Development Corporation. *Downtown Public Spaces: Business and Government Partnerships, Case Studies in New York State*. New York: New York State Urban Development Corporation, 1979.

Newman, Oscar. *Defensible Space: Crime Prevention Through Urban Design*. New York: Collier, 1972.

Osterweis, Rollin G. *The New Haven Green and the American Bicentennial*. Hamden, Conn.: Archon, 1976.

Paine, Nathaniel. "Worcester's Old Common, with some of its Neighbors and Incidents." *The Worcester Magazine* 1 (June 1901).

Perkins, Mary E. *Old Houses of the Ancient Town of Norwich, 1660–1800*. Norwich, Conn., 1895.

Perley, Sidney. *The History of Salem, Massachusetts*. Salem, 1926.

Phillips, James Duncan. *Salem in the Eighteenth Century*. Boston: Houghton Mifflin, 1937.

Pierce, Frederick Clifton. *History of Grafton*. Grafton, Mass., 1881.

Poole, Robert W., Jr. "Adopting City Parks." *Dollars and Sense* (July 1979).

Proceedings of the Sesqui-Centennial . . . of the Town of Waltham. Waltham, Mass., 1893.

Project for Public Spaces, Inc. *Bryant Park: Intimidation or Recreation?* New York, April 1981.

Quindlen, Anna. "Bright Note in a Seedy Park." *New York Times*, 31 July 1980.

Rand, Frank Prentice. *The Village of Amherst.* Amherst, Mass.: Amherst Historical Society, 1958.

Rimmer, Alfred. *Our Old Country Towns.* London: Chatto and Windus, 1881.

Records of the Salem Commoners, 1713–1739. George Francis Dow, ed. Salem, Mass., 1903.

Rutter, Josiah. *Historic Address . . . at Waltham.* Waltham, Mass., 1877.

Scranton, Hart Lee. "Our Beautiful Common." *Madison's Heritage.* Philip S. Platt, ed. Madison, Conn.: Madison Historical Society, 1964.

Seymour, Thom. "An experiment in city planning: Skip the planning." Boston *Globe*, 7 June 1981.

Simon, Donald E. "The Urban Park Services Project: A Proposal for Madison Square Park." Mimeographed. 14 November 1978.

————. "A Prospect for Parks." *The Public Interest* 44 (1976).

Smith, J.A.E. *History of Pittsfield.* Springfield, Mass., 1876.

Souvenir and Guide to Historic Concord and Lexington. Concord, Mass., 1903.

Staples, C.A. "A Sketch of the History of Lexington Common." Lexington Historical Society *Proceedings* 1 (1890).

Stein, Clarence S. *Toward New Towns for America*, 3rd ed. Cambridge, Mass.: M.I.T. Press, 1966.

Stein, Peter and Flores, Betsey. "Unused Urban Land Returned to Life: Livable Open Space." *Environmental Comment* (May 1979).

Stilgoe, John R. "The Puritan Townscape: Ideal and Reality." *Landscape* 20 (Spring 1976).

Sutton, S.B. *Cambridge Reconsidered: 3½ Centuries on the Charles.* Cambridge, Mass.: MIT Press, 1976.

Tree, Christina. *Massachusetts: An Explorer's Guide.* Taftsville, Vermont: The Countryman Press, 1979.

Tolles, Bryant F., Jr., with Tolles, Carolyn K. *New Hampshire Architecture: An Illustrated Guide.* Hanover, N.H.: University Press of New England, 1979.

U.S. Department of the Interior. "The Urban Park and Recreation Recovery Program: Fact Sheet." October 1979.

Urban Open Spaces. New York: Cooper-Hewitt Museum, 1979.

The Village Green Owners Association. "The Village Green: A Handbook for Owners and Residents." Mimeographed. Los Angeles, Cal., October 1980.

Walters, Jonathan. "The Ungreening of America." *Historic Preservation* 33 (May/June 1981).

Werbin, Stu. "The Common Freaks." Harvard *Crimson*, 23 May 1970.

Whyte, William H. *The Social Life of Small Urban Spaces.* Washington, D.C.: The Conservation Foundation, 1980.

Williams, W.H. *The Commons, Open Spaces and Footpaths Preservation Society 1865–1965: A Short History of the Society and Its Work.* London: The Commons, Open Spaces and Footpaths Society, 1965.

Willison, George F. *History of Pittsfield, Massachusetts, 1916–1955.* Pittsfield, 1957.

Wood, Joseph Sutherland. "The Origin of the New England Village." Ph.D. dissertation, Pennsylvania State University, 1978.

Yankee Magazine's Travel Guide to New England X (Summer/Fall 1981).

Contributors to Our Research

Our thanks to the following people for their contributions to our research:

Daniel Abeyta, Village Green Owners Association, Los Angeles, California
Michael S. Allen, Cambridge, Massachusetts
John Anderson, Historic District Commission, Concord, Massachusetts
Nancy W. Anderson, Massachusetts Association of Conservation Commissions, Medford, Massachusetts
Phyllis Anderson, Massachusetts Horticultural Society, Boston, Massachusetts
Kathryn H. Anthony, Kaplan/McLaughlin/Diaz, San Francisco, California
Thomas Arbuckle, Helmsley-Spear, Inc., New York, New York
Paul Barnhart, Kaplan/McLaughlin/Diaz, San Francisco, California
Gregory Batson, New York Life Insurance Company, New York, New York
Frank Beard, Maine Historic Preservation Commission, Augusta, Maine
Daniel A. Biederman, Bryant Park Restoration Corporation, New York, New York
Nanine Bilasky, America the Beautiful Fund
Ruth Birkhoff, Cambridge Conservation Commission, Cambridge, Massachusetts
Judith Bobker, National Conservation Recycling Corps, New York, New York
Paul Bockelman, Cambridge Historical Commission, Cambridge, Massachusetts
Robert Boles, Davis, California
Lesa Borg, Howard Research & Development Corporation, Columbia, Maryland
Philip J. Boschetti, The Greenpark Foundation, Inc., New York, New York
Frank Bracaglia, Federal Highway Commission, Boston, Massachusetts
Thomas B. Bracken, Cambridge Conservation Commission, Cambridge, Massachusetts
Jean M. Branscombe, Greenacre Foundation, New York, New York
Charles Brittin, Laguna Village Board of Directors, Los Angeles, California
Carlton C. Brownell, Little Compton Historical Society, Little Compton, Rhode Island
Steven Bucksot, Pointe Services Association, Indianapolis, Indiana
William Burbank, Scape Unlimited, Springfield, Massachusetts
Patricia A. Burke, Falmouth, Massachusetts
Michael Campbell, Town Council, Bristol, Rhode Island
Richard Candee, Kittery, Maine
Barbara Cassidy, Board of Directors for Laguna Village, California
George Y. Chalmers, The Newport Development Company, Los Angeles, California
Linda L. Chew, East Bay Regional Park District, Oakland, California
Ann P. Cleary, Falmouth, Massachusetts
Susan Coffey, South Royalton, Vermont
Cornelius P. Cronin, Battle Green Guides, Lexington, Massachusetts
Jan Cunningham, Greater Middletown Preservation Trust, Middletown, Connecticut
Margaret Cusack, Hoyt Street Association, Brooklyn, New York
Irene Cushing, Bethel Historical Society, Bethel, Vermont
Sherrie Stephens Cutler, Ecodesign/SPC International, Cambridge, Massachusetts
Clayton Dearth, Westford, Massachusetts
Edward F. Delaney, Department of Public Works, Waltham, Massachusetts
Patrick David Dillon, New York, New York
John P. Dumville, Agency of Development and Community Affairs, Division for Historic Preservation, Montpelier, Vermont
Jeremy David Eden, Cambridge, Massachusetts
F. Aldrich Edwards, New Haven Downtown Council, New Haven, Connecticut
Sara F. Ekholm, Historic Urban Plans, Ithaca, New York
Polly Erdman, Salem Planning Department, Salem, Massachusetts

Anne Farnam, Essex Institute, Salem, Massachusetts
Phillips Farrington, Woodstock Historical Society, Woodstock, Vermont
Barbara Fegan, League of Women Voters of Massachusetts, Boston, Massachusetts
Frederick E. Findlay, Keyes Associates, Waltham, Massachusetts
Gene Flaherty, Chamber of Commerce, Easthampton, Massachusetts
Nancy Fletcher, New Haven Downtown Council, New Haven, Connecticut
James Foley, Parks and Recreation Department, Salem, Massachusetts
John Frey, Mason and Frey, Belmont, Massachusetts
Susan Geib, New York, New York
Leonard Gill, Cambridge, Massachusetts
Harmon H. Goldstone, Goldstone and Hinz, New York, New York
Joan Friborg Gram, The Garden Club of Madison, Madison Connecticut
Cynthia Stuart Greene, Greater Middletown Preservation Trust Middletown, Connecticut
Elizabeth Griswold, Recreation Department, Santa Barbara, California
Robert Hamson, Board of Selectmen, Dedham, Massachusetts
Jay Hardiman, Waltham, Massachusetts
Robert Hardiman, Waltham, Massachusetts
Nan F. Heminway, Litchfield Garden Club, Litchfield, Connecticut
Bruce Hill, Terra Industries, San Diego, California
Jon Hill, Lexington, Massachusetts
Norma Holt, Community Home Health Services, Falmouth, Massachusetts
Suzanne Hopkins, Storch Associates, Boston Massachusetts
Robert Horne, Town Manager, Woodstock, Vermont
Deborah Howard, Massachusetts Conservation Council, Boston, Massachusetts
Richard S. Jackson, Jr., Pittsfield Historical Commission, Pittsfield, Massachusetts
Susan Jones, Village Green Owners Association, Los Angeles, California
Walter T. Joseph, Kaiser Aluminum & Chemical Corporation, Oakland, California
Gary Keating, Office of the Mayor, Lawrence, Massachusetts
Ernest E. Kirwan, Keyes Associates, Waltham, Massachusetts
Betty F. Kovacs, Town Clerk, Williamstown, Massachusetts
Bert Kubli, National Endowment for the Arts, Washington, D.C.
Jack Larkin, Old Sturbridge Village, Sturbridge, Massachusetts
Raymond G. Lughlin, Director Special Services, Roosevelt Island, New York
Thomas W. Leavitt, Merrimack Valley Textile Museum, North Andover, Massachusetts
Henry Lee, Friends of the Public Garden, Boston, Massachusetts
Jane M. Lendway, Agency of Development and Community Affairs, Division for
        Historic Preservation, Montpelier, Vermont
John Lerner, Conservation Services, Boston, Massachusetts
Richard Lockhart, Community Development Department, Cambridge, Massachusetts
Ancelin V. Lynch, Historical Preservation Commission, Providence, Rhode Island
Barbara B. MacDonald, The Litchfield Historical Society, Inc., Litchfield, Con-
        necticut
Wallace MacQuarrie, Selectmen's office, Westford, Massachusetts
Diane Maddex, The Preservation Press, Washington, D.C.
Steven Magliocco, Community Development Department, Cambridge, Massa-
        chusetts
Robert Mariani, On-Site Manager, Laguna Village, California
Paul Mazarrall, Parks Department, Lexington, Massachusetts
Robert McCarrell, Planning Department, Springfield, Massachusetts
Alan McClennan, Planning Department, Waltham, Massachusetts
Thomas McFarland, University Press of New England, Hanover, New Hampshire
Lee McGinley, Office of Community Development, Barnstable, Massachusetts
Gregor I. McGregor, The Massachusetts Conservation Council, Boston, Massachusetts

Nancy McKay, East Bay Regional Park District, Oakland, California
Joan McKenna, Right of Way Department, Boston, Massachusetts
Betty Miller, Oakland Mills Open Space Committee, Columbia, Maryland
John Mitchell, Littleton, Massachusetts
Bert Moffatt, former Town Manager, Bethel, Vermont
Michael Moniz, Salem Planning Department, Salem, Massachusetts
Michael Murphy, new Mark Commons Homes Association, Rockville, Maryland
Robert B. Murray, Aspen, Colorado
Francis Muzzey, Wentworth Historical Soceity, Wentworth, New Hampshire
Theodore M. Nelson, Town Manager, Bethel, Vermont
Laura F. Nichols, Lexington, Massachusetts
Wanda R. Nichols, Kaiser Aluminum & Chemical Corporation, Oakland, California
Toni Norton, Essex Institute, Salem, Massachusetts
Daniel O'Brien, Conservation Services, Boston, Massachusetts
Mary Lu Palan, The Newport Development Company, Los Angeles, California
Maureen Ferris Pepson, National Trust for Historic Preservation, Washington, D.C.
Barbara Perrault, Westford Public Library, Westford, Massachusetts
Dale Plante, Keyes Associates, Providence, Rhode Island
George Pratt, Farm Museum, Hadley, Massachusetts
Fred Pryor, Park and Recreation Association, Columbia, Maryland
Paul Racine, Easthampton, Massachusetts
Amy Rader, Falmouth *Enterprise*, Falmouth, Massachusetts
Ellie Reichlin, Society for the Preservation of New England Antiquities, Boston,
    Massachusetts
William K. Reilly, The Conservation Foundation, Washington D.C.
Charles Rhodehamel, Land Management Office, Columbia, Maryland
Patricia M. Rovegno, Kaiser Aluminum & Chemical Corporation, Oakland, California
William Rudin, Rudin Management, New York, New York
Gaynor Rutherford, Trustee of Lexington Public Trusts, Boston, Massachusetts
James Sander, Parks Council, New York, N.Y.
Edward Sanderson, Rhode Island Historical Commission, Providence, Rhode Island
Patricia Sanginetti, Planning Department of Pittsfield, Pittsfield, Massachusetts
Alton J. Scavo, Howard Research and Development Corporation, Columbia, Mary-
    land
Norma Schnip, A. Robert Schnip Realtors, Norwich, Connecticut
Greg Senko, Salem Planning Department, Salem, Massachusetts
Floyd Shaw, *Sunset* Magazine, Menlo Park, California
Kennedy Shaw, Massachusetts Municipal Association, Boston, Massachusetts
Geurson D. Silverberg, Silvergerg and Silverberg, Norwich, Connecticut
Donald Simon, Urban Park Plazas, New York, New York
Cathy A. Smith, Town Manager, Thomaston, Maine
Nancy Smith, First National Bank, Chicago, Illinois
Gilbert Stacey, Deerfield Academy, Deerfield, Massachusetts
Nancy Stack, Community Development Department, Lawrence, Massachusetts
Pauline Stiles, Wentworth, New Hampshire
Clark J. Strickland, Connecticut Historical Commission, Hartford, Connecticut
Robert C. Sudmyer, Town Common Committee, Grafton, Massachusetts
Charles D. Sullivan, Cambridge Historical Commission, Cambridge, Massachusetts
Frank H. Teagle, Jr., Chamber of Commerce, Woodstock, Vermont
Lovell Thompson, Heritage Trust, Ipswich, Massachusetts
David Tregilgas, Control Data Corporation, Minneapolis, Minnesota
Mario J. Tristany, Jr. Planning Department, Norwich, Connecticut
Phil Vaglica, Waltham, Massachusetts
W. Gerald Venable, Sasaki Associates, Watertown, Massachusetts
Jane D. Walburn, Executive Secretary to the Trustees of Grammercy Park, New York,
    New York

Herman Walker, Common Committee, West Brookfield, Massachusetts
Liz Warner, Greater Middletown Preservation Trust, Middletown, Connecticut
Elizabeth S. Warren, Historical Preservation Commission, Providence, Rhode Island
Susan O'Connor-Welch, Sasaki Associates, Inc., Watertown, Massachusetts
Koreen Wendt, Pacific Union Development Company, San Francisco, California
Patricia Weslowski, Massachusetts Historical Commission, Boston, Massachusetts
John S. White, Lions Club, Easthampton, Massachusetts
Vera F. Wingler, Assistant Town Clerk, Northborough, Massachusetts
Christopher T. Wise, Historic Preservation Commission, Falmouth, Massachusetts
Jeffrey Wold, Stockbridge, Massachusetts
James Woods, Parks Department, Cambridge, Massachusetts
Helena Wright, Merrimack Valley Textile Museum, North Andover, Massachusetts
Paula M. Wright, Deputy Clerk, Bethel, Maine
Bo Yerxa, Indian Township Tribal Government, Princeton, Maine
Kim Zarney, Townscape, Medina, Ohio
Lou Zehner, Treasurer, Town of Lexington, Massachusetts

Illustration Credits

Numbers indicate pages throughout

Looking at Common Ground

xviii. Courtesy of the Woodstock Historical Society   xx. (*bottom left*) Courtesy of the Woodstock Historical Society; (*bottom right*) Ronald Lee Fleming   xxii. (*top left*) Courtesy of the Greenacre Foundation; (*top right*) courtesy of the East Bay Regional Park District

A Tale of Two Commons

1. From William Little, *The History of Warren; A Mountain Hamlet located among the White Hills of New Hampshire.* Manchester, N.H.: William E. Moore, 1870 2, 5, 6. Lauri A. Halderman

Town Common and Village Green in New England: 1620 to 1981

11. (*top left*) Historic Urban Plans; (*top right*) J.D. Levine/Yale University, courtesy of Office of Public Information   12. Courtesy of the Essex Institute, Salem, Massachusetts   13. John Hill   14. Boston Globe photo   15. (*bottom left*) From Alfred Rimmer, *Our Old Country Towns,* London: Chatto and Windus, 1881; (*bottom right*) Anne D. Prescott   16. Courtesy of the Litchfield Historical Society   17. (*top left*) Courtesy of the Society for the Preservation of New England Antiquities; (*top right*) from R.H. Howard and Henry E. Crocker, editors. *A History of New England . . . Vol. 1,* Boston: Crocker & Co., 1880; (*bottom right*) David A. Riemer   18, 19. From John Warner Barber, *Connecticut Historical Collections . . . Relating to the History and Antiquities of Every Town in Connecticut.* New Haven, 1836   21. (*top left*) Courtesy of Litchfield Historical Society; (*top right*) courtesy of the Society for the Preservation of New England Antiquities   23. From John Warner Barber, *Historical Collections . . . of every town in Massachusetts*   24. From a drawing by Ben Johnson, 1774. Courtesy of the Essex Institute, Salem, Mass.   25. (*top left and right*) Courtesy of the Society for the Preservation of New England Antiquities; (*bottom left*) courtesy of the Essex Institute, Salem, Mass.; (*bottom right*) courtesy of the Litchfield Historical Society 26. (*top left*) David A. Riemer; (*top right*) courtesy of the Society for the Preservation of New England Antiquities   29. (*top left*) From *Harper's Weekly,* c. 1850; (*top right*) from Emma Lewis Coleman. *A Historic & Present Day Guide to Old Deerfield*   30. Courtesy of the Society for the Preservation of New England Antiquities   31. (*top left*) Collection of John R. Stilgoe; (*top right*) from Emma Lewis Coleman. *A Historic & Present Day Guide to Old Deerfield*   32. Courtesy of the Harvard Historical Society   34. (*top left*) Courtesy of the Merrimack Valley Textile Museum; (*top right*) David A. Riemer   35. (*bottom left*) David A. Riemer; (*bottom right*) Robert Burley Associates.

Guidelines for Greens

37. (*bottom left*) David A. Riemer; (*bottom right*) Lauri A. Halderman   39. (*top left*) Ronald Lee Fleming; (*top right*) David A. Riemer   40. (*bottom left*) Thomas M. Paine; (*bottom right*) David A. Riemer   41. Courtesy of the Essex Institute, Salem Mass.   42. David A. Riemer   45. From John Warner Barber, *Historical Collections . . . of every town in Massachusetts.*   46. Lauri A. Halderman   50. Alva D.B. Marsh, Garden Club of Madison, CT   52. Lauri A. Halderman   54. Renata von Tscharner   55. J.D. Levine/Yale University, courtesy of Office of Public Information   56. Courtesy of Merrimack Valley Textile Museum   57, 58. Lauri A. Halderman   61. (*bottom left*) Anne D. Prescott; (*bottom right*) Lauri A. Halderman   63, 64, 66. Ronald T. Reed   67, 68. Lauri A. Halderman   69. Ronald T. Reed   70. (*top left*) Renata von Tscharner; (*top right*) David A. Riemer; (*top lower left*) David A. Riemer; (*bottom lower left*) courtesy of Townscape, Medina, Ohio; (*bottom right*) Renata von Tscharner   72. (*top left*) Courtesy of Ann P. Cleary; (*top right*) Lauri A. Halderman; (*bottom right*) Anne D. Prescott   73, 74. Lauri A Halderman   76. From Evelyn M. Wood Lovejoy, *History of Royalton, Vermont.* Burlington: Free

Press, 1911.   77. (*left*) David A. Riemer; (*right*) CeCe Cunningham   78. (*top left*) Lauri A. Halderman; (*top right*) David A. Riemer   79. Courtesy of Greater Middletown Preservation Trust   80. Lauri A. Halderman   81. (*top*) Ronald Lee Fleming; (*bottom*) David A. Riemer   82, 83. Courtesy of Townscape, Medina, Ohio   84. From *Atlas of Essex County, Massachusetts* (1884). Courtesy of Merrimac'. Valley Textile Museum.   85. (*bottom left*) Lauri A. Halderman; (*bottom right*) David A. Riemer   86, 87. Courtesy of Ecodesign/SPC International   88. (*top*) Robert Nathan Cram; (*bottom*) David A. Riemer   90. (*bottom left*) Lauri A. Halderman; (*bottom right*) David A. Riemer   92. From Mary E. Perkins, *The Old Houses of the Ancient Town of Norwich, 1660–1800*. Norwich, Connecticut, 1895.   93,95. David A. Riemer   96. (*top left*) Peter R. Hvizdak; (*top right*) photo by Lee Robinson, courtesy of New Haven Downtown Council   97. Bradford B. Brayton, courtesy of the Falmouth *Enterprise*   98. "Downtown Headliners" published by the New Haven Downtown Council   100. Lauri A. Halderman   101. David A Riemer   103. Thomas M. Paine

Revitalized Commons: Three Case Studies

105. Ronald T. Reed   111. Courtesy of the Society for the Preservation of New England Antiquities   112. (*bottom left*) Ronald Lee Fleming; (*bottom right*) David A. Riemer   114. Ronald Lee Fleming   115. Ronald T. Reed   118. (*top left*) Courtesy of the Engineering Dept., City of Waltham; (*top right*) from Charles A. Nelson, *Waltham Past and Present*. Cambridge: Moses King, 1882.   119. (*bottom left*) Lauri A. Halderman; (*bottom right*) from Charles A. Nelson, *Waltham Past and Present*. Cambridge: Moses King, 1882.   121. (*bottom left*) David A. Riemer; (*bottom right*) Lauri A. Halderman   124. Ronald T. Reed   127. Courtesy of the Essex Institute, Salem, Mass.   129. (*bottom left*) Renata von Tscharner; (*bottom right*) David A. Riemer.

Beyond the Village Green

132. Courtesy of the Newport Development Company   134. Ree Overton Fleming   135. Renata von Tscharner   137. Courtesy of the Howard Research and Development Corporation   138. Courtesy of Betty Miller   139. Courtesy of Kaplan/Mclaughlin/Diaz   141, 142. Courtesy of Margaret Cusack   144, 145. Courtesy of the East Bay Regional Park District   147. Lauri A. Halderman   149. (*top left*) Lauri A. Halderman; (*top right*) Patrick David Dillon   150. Copyright Eugene Cook   151. (*top left*) Copyright Eugene Cook; (*top right*) courtesy of the Greenacre Foundation

Index

W

Walpole, Mass., 18
Waltham, Mass., xvii, 33, 87, 115–23
Warren, N.H., 1–6
Washington Elm (Cambridge, Mass.),
    27, *29,* 31, 104, 106
Washington Square (Salem, Mass.),
    27, 45–46, 124–30
Water systems, 99, 102–3
Watertown, Mass., 28
Waterwalls in urban parks, 151
Watson, Elkanah, 24, 27
Weed control, 102

Wellesley, Mass., 18
Wendt, Kereen, 139, 140
Wentworth, N.H., 1–6, *78*
Westfield, Mass., 28
Westford, Mass., 86, 101
Westwood, Mass., 18
Wheelock, Jerome (Grafton, Mass.),
    30
Whipple House (Wentworth, N.H.), 6
Whitfield Elm (Cambridge, Mass.),
    27, 31
Whitfield, George, 21
Whyte, William H., 59, 150, 152
Williams, Lucretia, 27
Wilson, Robert E., Jr., 97

Woburn, Mass., 28
Wolcott, Conn., 36
Woodstock, Conn., *19*
Woodstock, Vt., *xiv,* xvi–xvii, *70*
Wrentham, Mass., 18

Y

Yeager, Eleanor Conant, 97

Z

Zoning boards, 91–93, 137

About the Townscape Institute

The Townscape Institute is a nonprofit, public interest organization in Cambridge, Massachusetts concerned with increasing the livability of cities, towns, and neighborhoods through conservation and enhancement of the built environment. The institute acknowledges the human need for connection and identity with place, a relationship that enriches the spirit and heightens one's sense of aesthetic pleasure. The founders conceive of the organization as a vehicle for carrying out innovative projects—in environmental education, townscape design, cultural planning, advocacy, and environmental art—that synthesize their own experiences in these areas over the past ten years.

More recently Townscape has begun a publishing program. The group's first book was *Place Makers: Public Art That Tells You Where You Are* (New York: Hastings House, 1981), co-authored by Ronald Lee Fleming and Renata von Tscharner. Place makers are works of public art and design that capture or reinforce the unique character of a site or space. The book presents case studies from across the United States—of sculptures, murals, fountains, pavement inserts, and street furniture. In the often bleak urban landscape of concrete slabs and mirrored glass, in anonymous plazas, malls, and squares, place makers provide a human scale, restore a much needed sense of connection, and sometimes add a touch of humor.

As that book suggests, the authors are particularly concerned with a broader public accessibility to the meanings and uses of place. To that end, the Townscape Institute has developed techniques for compiling an "environmental profile" that assesses the changing physical condition of places over time—their folklore, history, artistic traditions, resources, and contextual design constraints. This profile, usually elicited out of intensive work sessions with local people, becomes a basis for developing design ideas and themes that respond to the special qualities of a particular place. Artists and artisans then creatively translate such a profile into environmental art and design. Working with arts commissions, preservation organizations, and planning and redevelopment groups around the country, Townscape seeks to initiate or renew the sense of connection to place that can be a source of *civitas*—a bonding between people and the environment that is ultimately the basis of a community ethic.

In Cambridge, this concern encouraged Townscape to initiate a project with the Peabody Museum's Institute of Conservation Archaeology to undertake jointly the development of subway exhibitions that celebrate place identity. Entitled "History on the Line" and funded by the National Endowment for the Humanities, the exhibitions will use archaeological artifacts, photographs, and text in the subway stations to interpret the changing condition of the places around them. It should complement the nationally recognized "Arts on the Line" project that Ronald Lee Fleming initiated as chairman of the Cambridge Arts Council.

In another project, the Bench and Bar Task Force commissioned Townscape to prepare a design strategy plan for Pemberton Square, a plaza in front of Boston's Suffolk County Courthouse, that will relate this space to the lives of five great Massachusetts jurists. The challenge there is to combine many different elements, such as bas reliefs, interpretive panels, pavement inserts, and sculpture, to transform the impact of what is now a bleak space. At Boston's Logan Airport, Townscape staff employed the "environmental profile" technique to define the context for a mural celebrating the changing character of the airport from Quonset hut to concrete colossus. In New Orleans, the mayor secured Townscape's assistance in interpreting the cultural significance of Treme, a largely black neighborhood that is the traditional stamping ground of many early jazz musicians. It is an intriguing project because the interpretive panels are slated for columns of the elevated freeway that now divides what used to be the oak-lined grand avenue through the district. Townscape's most recent concern is how to bring a stronger sense of play to Davie, Florida, a nascent commercial strip near Fort Lauderdale.

Townscape is in the process of preparing a third publication, *Facade Stories*. This book examines, again through case studies, the changing character of commercial building facades and the variety of current attitudes toward preservation.